THE ONE-PAGE FINANCIAL PLAN

EVERYTHING YOU NEED TO SUCCESSFULLY MANAGE YOUR MONEY AND INVEST FOR WEALTH CREATION

SAM HENDERSON

Wrightbooks

First published in 2013 by Wrightbooks
an imprint of John Wiley & Sons Australia, Ltd
42 McDougall St, Milton Qld 4064

Office also in Melbourne

Typeset in 11/13.5 pt ITC Giovanni Std

© Henderson Maxwell Pty Ltd

The moral rights of the author have been asserted

National Library of Australia Cataloguing-in-Publication data:

Author:	Henderson, Sam
Title:	The one-page financial plan : everything you need to successfully manage your money and invest for wealth creation / Sam Henderson.
ISBN:	9781118588499 (pbk.)
Notes:	Includes index.
Subjects:	Finance, Personal
	Saving and investment.
	Wealth.
Dewey Number:	332.02401

Cover design by saso content & design

Disclaimer: Text and tables in chapter 11 are correct at the time of publication and may be amended by the Australian Government Department of Human Services at any time. If seeking to rely and/or make a claim in relation to the text/tables, please consider the most recent version of the relevant text/tables available on the Department of Human Services website at www.humanservices.gov.au

BT Material © BT Financial Group 2013. BTFG makes no representation as to the accuracy of the facts or assumptions made in the Copyright Work, or to the currency of the information and no company in the BT Financial Group or Westpac Banking Corporation Group (BT Group) accepts responsibility for the accuracy or completeness of the Copyright Work. The BT Group and its officers, directors, employees, representatives and agents are not liable for and are released from any loss or claim suffered or incurred by the Licensee, Publisher or a third party in connection with the inclusion of the Copyright Work in the Licensee Work. The Copyright Work is provided by way of information only and is not, and must not be relied upon as, financial, tax, legal or other advice. Neither BTFG nor any of its related bodies corporate have any obligation to provide any updated information to the Licensee or Publisher regarding the Copyright Work.

Tables on pages 153 and 159 © Australian Taxation Office (ATO). The aforementioned and all ATO information included in this publication was current at the time of publishing. Readers should refer to the ATO website www.ato.gov.au for up-to-date ATO information.

Printed in Australia by Ligare Book Printer

10 9 8 7 6 5 4 3 2 1

Disclaimer
The material in this publication is of the nature of general comment only, and does not represent professional advice. It is not intended to provide specific guidance for particular circumstances and it should not be relied on as the basis for any decision to take action or not take action on any matter which it covers. Readers should obtain professional advice where appropriate, before making any such decision. To the maximum extent permitted by law, the author and publisher disclaim all responsibility and liability to any person, arising directly or indirectly from any person taking or not taking action based on the information in this publication.

CONTENTS

ABOUT THE AUTHOR

Sam Henderson is CEO and Senior Financial Adviser at Henderson Maxwell. Henderson Maxwell is a multi-award winning, independently owned financial advisory firm with clients across Australia.

Sam is the financial expert on Network Ten's *The Project*, and can be seen as the host of Foxtel's Sky News Business program *Your Money, Your Call* (the retirement segment) once a week. He is the author of the best-selling books; *Financial Planning DIY Guide* (2011) and *SMSF DIY Guide* (2012) published by John Wiley & Sons. Since publication, Sam's books have consistently been listed in the top 100 business book sales in the Nielsen Bookscan listings.

Sam regularly contributes to a host of print media including *Money* magazine, *Optus Insights*, *The Australian Financial Review*, *Independent Financial Adviser Magazine* and *Asset Magazine* and is a regular keynote speaker for the Australian Securities Exchange (ASX). Sam is also a regular presenter and an expert in financial planning practice management within the financial planning industry.

Sam has a Master of Commerce, a Commerce Degree (Accounting and Financial Planning), a Diploma and Advanced Diploma of Financial Services, an Advanced Diploma of Marketing Management and is an Accredited Mortgage Consultant, direct share specialist and an expert in Self Managed Superannuation Funds. He is also an SMSF Specialist Adviser accredited through SMSF Professional Association Australia.

Sam lives on Sydney's northern beaches with his wife and two children. He enjoys surfing, swimming, boating, snow skiing and reading about business and finance.

For more about Sam Henderson see www.samhenderson.com.au or www.hendersonmaxwell.com.au. You can follow Sam on Twitter: @henderson_sam.

INTRODUCTION: YOUR PERSONAL FINANCIAL REVOLUTION

The borrower is servant to the lender.

The Bible, Proverbs 22:7

Before take off, every airline gives a safety message and demonstration that instruct you on the procedures you need to follow and how to act in the event of an emergency. As I'm sure you know, there is also a safety card in your seat pocket that describes what to do in emergency situations in both illustrated and written format for ease of comprehension. Those instructions are clearly designed to save lives in an extreme situation that may arise from a multitude of different and complex scenarios when people would be in a highly anxious state of mind.

Both the written and illustrated nature of the safety cards, combined with the flight attendant's demonstration, acknowledge that people learn in different ways, which increases the effectiveness of the message and minimises harm to passengers. The distinct methods appeal to tactile, visual or auditory means of learning. Some people learn better by reading, some by seeing and many by hearing, but often it's a combination of these methods, with the added factor of personal experience, that completes the learning process. It's complex, but a universal approach works best.

My wish for you

My chief objective for *The One-Page Financial Plan* (a revamped and updated version of my book *Financial Planning DIY Guide*) is to allow you to create a written financial plan using whichever of the diverse ways of learning work for you, to ensure as many people as possible can discover the importance of good personal financial management. Creating a physical, easy-to-read and comprehensive document that is functional and adaptable is my primary aim for you.

To accommodate the style of the flight attendant's safety demonstration on a plane, I will also be providing educational videos on the website and I also offer a free subscription to a weekly newsletter to help keep you up to date with the latest news and views on all things financial. You will also find information on the website about seminars, webinars (web-based seminars), and my radio and television appearances, which may also offer additional ways of learning about the one-page financial plan. An educated client makes a good client. An educated investor makes a sound investor.

One of the commonalities among the list of instructions from the airlines is to apply your own oxygen mask before assisting others. Have you ever wondered why?

Hypoxia is a situation when your body is starved of oxygen, and at 11 887 metres, the average cruising altitude of today's airlines, there's very little oxygen. The first signs of hypoxia setting in are shortness of breath, confusion and dizziness, but at high altitudes this may lead quickly to unconsciousness, coma or death. So the reason they tell you to apply your own mask first is so that you can help others, particularly children, because if you're disoriented, unconscious or dead, you're not much help to anyone else around you.

The parallels between airline flight and personal finances are many. While poor financial management may not mean imminent death, as it could in an airline emergency, plenty of emergencies arise in our financial lives that can have a significant impact on our life and the lives of those around us.

The very same fight or flight situations that are experienced in an airline emergency can also arise in your personal financial life and, if you don't help yourself first, how can you possibly be expected to help others through altruistic pursuits such as philanthropy. So, too, if you don't help yourself, you will be reliant on others either in the form of welfare from the government or financial assistance from your family or friends. Education is the best way to avoid this.

For example, fight or flight situations arise financially every day in terms of extreme financial circumstances in personal relationships, such as couples fighting over money — a recent American Institute of Certified Practising Accountants (AICPA) survey stated that more than 50 per cent of couples fight over money — gambling problems, bankruptcies, theft and fraud. In the commercial realm financial threats arise in the form of companies going into administration, large-scale fraudulent activities or investments turning sour and taking valuable retirement dollars from needy retirees. You can take the concept to the extremes in criminal situations, such as fraud and extortion. Even on a national level, politics is concerned with managing the social and financial aspects of the population, with a financial focus on budgeting, welfare and good economic management, and there has been no shortage of wars fought over money.

While we would all like to live in a world that revolves around peace and love, many people continue to believe that money makes the world go around. The fear and greed created by the very existence of money and a desire to have more of it has changed the world we live in and changed the course of history many times over.

Avoiding these scenarios begins with better education to create a society that worries less about money and more about the health and wellbeing of its populace. Money may make the world go around for some, but it's the root of all evil to others.

In Australia, we have colossal financial issues, despite our wealth. We are still not yet taught about money in schools; we have a society that is heavily reliant on welfare; an ageing workforce that lacks sufficient retirement savings; and we have problems with crime. The changes we need begin with better education about money and finance, and that education needs to start in the home. Education needs to begin with children and showing them how to handle and respect money, educating them on the social effects of money and what it can do, and teaching them how to save it. Kids need to see the effects of having or not having money, and we need to get them involved in charity from an early age. Like all sides of education, including mathematics, English, geography and science, financial education needs to be a part of the school curriculum.

What we need in this country is a financial education revolution but before we get to that, let's have a look at what motivates us to act.

Take control of your finances

We all need to take it upon ourselves to better understand and manage our finances. It's not easy, not by a long shot. In fact, it's difficult. You've got family, work, friends and time constraints everywhere. You've got email, text messages, Facebook, Twitter, the internet, TV and many other sources of information all trying to distract you. You've got a lot going on in your life and that's why you'll probably need some help from a professional, but this book will give you a good grounding so you at least have the knowledge to create a structure to help develop a workable financial plan designed to help you attain your goals and objectives.

I believe that if you want to achieve consistent and long-lasting financial change, you need a process methodology to support that change. The methodology for flying a plane comes in the form of many hours of education and training, involving countless checklists, manuals and, of course, actual flying experience. This book aims to provide you with such a manual on all the financial topics you need, combined with a methodology and checklists to facilitate and record your goals, progress and financial wellbeing.

The money-go-round

The money-go-round affects much of middle Australia and creates a great deal of anxiety in our society. It's the circular life process of getting a job, a mortgage and a family, only to find yourself enslaved to a bank and a boss who care little about your progression or your family. Add a relentless flow of car repayments, credit card payments and interest, bill payments, expenses for the kids' education — these are financial obligations that just never seem to go away. It's simply not worth trying to keep up with the Joneses if you have to sign up for a life of debt.

When you get pay rises, are they quickly eaten up by a jump in your perceived standard of living as your rising income is closely matched by your rising expenses? It seems that the more you have, the more you need.

Many people get a job, buy a home and then spend much of their lives obliged to a bank to repay a mortgage in a seemingly endless procession of debt repayments marked by the major milestones of your ever-progressing age. Now it all sounds a little depressing, doesn't it? Sorry to be gloomy but this is the reality for many people. I may be a little sceptical since entering my forties—the acceptance of middle age can do that to a man—but I see many of my friends in this exact situation. Several have still not bought a home and are frustrated by their lack of financial progression.

If you're young and don't have a mortgage, then you may be under pressure from your parents to get a mortgage and buy a place of your own. If you're a few years into your investment cycle and paying off your mortgage, you may be under pressure to buy an investment property, a larger house or a share portfolio using debt with the aim of increasing your assets, which will simply further enslave you to the bank. Don't get me wrong, debt can be extremely useful, as I will cover in this book, but many people get it wrong and I'd like to help you get it right.

If you're in your 50s, 60s or 70s and considering retirement, or you have already retired, you may have seen property prices rise with less volatility than you have seen in the sharemarket or your super fund in recent years, and be tempted to become further indebted to expand your portfolio of assets to set yourself up for a better retirement. Debt may not be the answer if you want to exit the money-go-round.

Following the global financial crisis (GFC), it was common to see people parking their money in cash having seen sharemarkets plummet by up to 57 per cent and property markets by a similar level. It created an environment of fear. Over the long term, though, their cash returns are being eroded by inflation and their income depleted by falling interest rates so some exposure to growth-style assets will be necessary to maintain their purchasing power. The GFC made things just too confusing for many people, and they are unwilling to get advice because they don't trust anyone or are unwilling to pay for advice, having suffered losses. This book aims to help you consider your options, educate yourself and ensure you are on the best path to meet your needs.

You deserve more

No matter what your situation, you deserve the very best in life, but there are good ways and bad ways to go about investing. I want to reduce the risk factors throughout the entire investment process to increase your chances of financial success to allow you to meet your life and financial goals. My aim is to try to help you achieve your goals and objectives: this book isn't about whether Commonwealth Bank shares are a better investment than National Australia Bank shares.

Mistakes are inevitable and mistakes need to be treated as the cost of learning, but it's important you do not allow inertia to set in and stop you from doing anything. Doing something and making a small mistake is a great way to learn, so long as the mistake is not too large. Large mistakes can be costly, but you need to learn to be philosophical about things.

I want you to be able to get off the money-go-round and release the shackles of financial obligation. I want you to be empowered by your financial decisions so you can enrich your life through better decision making, motivated by progressive goals and objectives.

Even with the help of this book, the money-go-round may be necessary for a short time, while you get the bank working for you rather than the other way around. I want to help you get into a situation where you're working for an employer by choice because they are taking you to the place where you want to be in your career or financial life. There's nothing more frustrating than going sideways for a long time.

Your roadmap to financial success

The One-Page Financial Plan is designed to provide a roadmap to free yourself and your family from the slavery of the banks and major institutions that rule the lives of many Australians, essentially telling us what we can and can't do because of the financial handcuffs they have on our wallets and bank accounts. Financial freedom is the ultimate goal and *The One-Page Financial Plan* is the tool to help you achieve that goal. It will allow you to take the first steps in orchestrating a plan to financial freedom and help you construct a life that allows you to meet your needs, goals and objectives, and hopefully help others along your journey.

The concept of a graphically formatted financial plan in combination with a written format is designed to help people who respond to various types of learning, whether it be written, graphical, aural or verbal. It is also designed to make an easy reference point because it's your entire financial plan in a single A4 sheet of paper.

Start your financial revolution

What you need is a financial revolution. A revolution is not something that simply occurs without some discomfort and is usually accompanied by a strong sense of motivation and moral obligation to look after yourself, your loved ones and your community. It is a call to action for vast and swift change. A revolution often results from a sense of being dominated, mistreated or oppressed by a person or situation; it is closely accompanied by a feeling of deserving more and the right to a better quality of life.

A revolution requires significant, and often challenging, transformations or significant shifts of personal, cultural, social, technological, philosophical and political ways of thinking to achieve a state of emancipation and freedom. Highly successful people can be attuned to this way of operating and you may need to challenge yourself if you want to make big changes, learn new concepts and apply these concepts consistently over time.

Consider these words from one of my favourite books, Stephen Covey's *The 7 Habits of Highly Effective People*: 'Changing our habits to improve what we are can be a painful process. It must be motivated by a higher purpose, and by the willingness to subordinate what you think you want now for what you know you want later.'

Your personal financial revolution requires nothing less. It truly is a personal revolution. You may need to overhaul the way you think; create new, positive and possibly difficult habits to maintain; and learn new concepts and ideas that will assist you to maintain your path to financial freedom. *The One-Page Financial Plan* is designed to facilitate this process via an easy to understand and easy to use step-by-step methodology.

Many self-help books and financial improvement books tell you what to do, but not how to do it. You can quickly get side-tracked when a topic doesn't relate to you or your situation. *The One-Page Financial Plan* will provide you with a tactical process, as well as a number of strategic approaches, to help you meet your needs, goals and objectives. If some topics, such as Centrelink or aged care aren't relevant to you, then skip those chapters and come back to them later or point other people to them who may find this information helpful.

This is not a quick-fix or an instant gratification book, and you may still want to get some further education or assistance from a professional. However, *The One-Page Financial Plan* will provide you with a thorough overview of all the topics covered in a basic course of financial planning education. The text will give you a solid overview of all of the topics based on my many years of learning and experience.

There's no sure thing

Success is important, but so too is failure. It's in the face of failure that you learn some of your most valuable lessons, and if you don't make mistakes, you aren't challenging yourself enough. When you make a mistake, think of it as a cost of doing business, and part of the cost of your education in becoming a better investor and financial manager. I can't stress enough the importance of being prepared to make mistakes and learn from them. Never be too scared to make mistakes, and never be too hard on yourself for making them.

Five stages of your financial revolution

Your personal financial revolution begins and ends with these five 'shons' of success, which make up the basic tenets of sound financial management. I've added another two since I wrote my first book a couple of years ago. The five shons of success are motivation, education, organisation, application and emancipation.

Motivation

Clearly, if you want to improve your financial situation, you have to be motivated to do so. If you're not truly motivated, you will have no drive to succeed and will most likely keep tossing the whole issue of financial planning into the too-hard basket, as so many people do. The fact that you are reading this book, however, shows that you do have a genuine desire to understand and manage your financial affairs. On that basis alone, your chances of success are already looking pretty good.

Motivation is a psychological state that arouses action towards a particular goal that needs to be achieved to satisfy a desire. An important aspect of motivation is that you need to identify your goals and objectives clearly so you can set about achieving them. In order to achieve those goals you will need a set of strategies — broad descriptions of what needs to be done — and a set of tactics for each strategy. Tactics are specific and individual actions that need to be completed to achieve your goals — they are the detail.

In a detailed financial plan, you need to identify your goals, establish a set of strategies to achieve those goals and then outline the tactical responses and actions required for each strategy to achieve that goal. Motivation allows you to cast away the inertia that may stop you from taking that necessary action. Creating and maintaining motivation is therefore a fundamental requirement for success in managing your money better.

You are obviously seeking financial changes in your life and it's highly likely that you want to know a lot more in order to increase your chances of success in reaching your goals, whatever they are. You may be sick of going sideways in life: you may want to progress your financial knowledge further, but you will no doubt be seeking to make some sort of progress in your life. You may be sick of fighting with your partner over money or not having enough money. You may be tired of living from week to week without any savings or without any direction or reason for working so hard.

You may already be financially successful and be motivated by the desire to live from the fruits of your labour and not lose what you have acquired over the years. You may want to make sure that you have a reason for all the hard work, study and commitment you have given to your chosen field of expertise over the years of your working life. You may want to make sure you can retire in comfort and rely less on the government's Age Pension.

Perhaps your circumstances have changed via divorce, redundancy, moving country, death of a partner, disablement or illness, and your motivation is to simply do the best with what you have. Motivation in any of these situations can sometimes be challenging and difficult, but life must go on.

Your motivations will be contained in your desire for an outcome or a goal and objectives. We'll address your goals very shortly.

Education

Education is one of the greatest social equalisers and it provides the best opportunity for you to level the financial playing field. A good education, not necessarily of the scholarly type, is required to successfully manage your finances. Since personal finance isn't taught in schools yet, you will need to get your education from books, the press, media and finance specialists.

Educating yourself can be great fun and anyone can learn about managing their money. It's really not that difficult and this book is a great place to start!

Organisation

It's easy to get lost among the many areas involved in financial planning, or to be so focused on one area that you overlook or neglect others. For this reason it's important to organise your finances in a structured way that helps you keep sight of the big picture. Ideally, you need a document that sets out your goals and objectives and guides you, step-by-step, through the issues you need to consider when making any investment decision. In chapter 15 you will find my one-page financial plan template, which is designed for exactly this purpose. It will allow you to plan and monitor your finances using one simple, easy-to-read sheet of paper. You will need a good understanding of the financial concepts in this book to be able to use this plan effectively.

Figure 1 shows all the areas of money management covered in this book that you need to understand in order to construct your own one-page financial plan. They fall within three subject areas:

- identifying your goals and objectives
- managing and understanding your cash flow
- identifying your current assets (what you own) and liabilities (what you owe), including shares and funds, property, superannuation and retirement planning, debt, risk management and insurance, taxation and estate planning.

The book includes a chapter on aged care and how it can be financed, but this is a separate issue that can only be addressed effectively if and when the need arises. It doesn't form part of your financial plan.

Figure 1: the money-management wheel

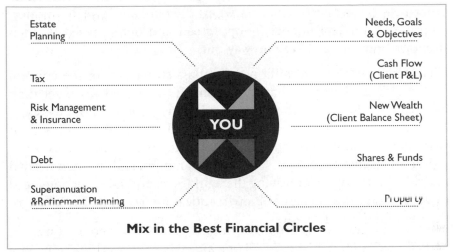

Source: Henderson Maxwell.

Some of these areas you will be able to manage easily yourself, and others will either need to be managed, or may be more effectively managed, by a professional. It's up to you to decide when you need professional help, but this book will help you to make the right decisions by giving you a deeper understanding of the issues.

Application

You can have all the motivation and structure in the world, but unless you apply what you learn, your efforts will be pointless. While the first step is always the hardest, many investors don't even get that far — they become frozen with inaction because they don't know what to do next. In other words, they learn the theory but never apply their knowledge. *The One-Page Financial Plan* will help you avoid this pitfall. It provides a step-by-step road map for the successful execution of your plan by identifying your goals, aligning your investment strategies to your individual goals and setting out the tactical steps you need to take to execute your strategies effectively.

Emancipation

My primary aim in writing this book is to help you achieve financial emancipation and freedom from the money-go-round. Emancipation is a very strong word, but plenty of people feel enslaved to their bank, other institutions and their boss when they are stuck in the money-go-round. They feel financially oppressed and demoralised by their situation and many can see no way out.

Even people who have millions of dollars struggle with the concept of retirement, worrying that they won't have enough to meet their expenses for the rest of their lives. And many people who have spent 40 years or more of their working life building and developing their work habits, ethics and sense of personal definition, find the idea of retirement is just so foreign. A personal paradigm shift is often needed to deal with thoughts of leaving the workforce, and many people need to achieve another personal growth milestone so they can let go of their working life and retire.

KEY POINTS

- My objective for you is to make financial planning easy.

- 80 per cent of couples fight over money, so put a plan in place and take control of your finances.

- Don't be held hostage by your finances or your debts; use *The One-Page Financial Plan* as your catalyst for exiting the money-go-round.

- The five 'shons' of success for your own financial revolution are motivation, education, organisation, application and emancipation.

CHAPTER 1

TAKING THE FIRST STEPS

Insanity: doing the same thing over
and over again and expecting different results.

Albert Einstein, physicist

By the end of this chapter you will have a thorough understanding of
the financial planning process and have completed a questionnaire
that will clearly outline your current financial situation. You will have
assessed your financial health, worked out your personal budget,
set your goals and be well on your way to completing some of the
most important elements of your one-page financial plan. This is an
important chapter in the book and an important chapter for setting
the scene and setting sail for a sound financial future.

Your financial planning process

The financial planning process is a journey of discovery. It not only
gives you insight into your own financial affairs, but it may also
give meaning to what you are doing with your time and your life. It
provides an opportunity for you to challenge your chosen direction
and quantify some of your decisions. You won't discover the meaning
of life, but the financial planning process will increase your awareness
in your decision making and give more meaning to your direction in
life for yourself and your family.

In the introduction I talked about the money-go-round — a frustrating
but very real scenario playing out in households around the country.
People feel enslaved to their job and the bank, and once the bank has

been paid, you need to start saving for a comfortable retirement. If you keep doing the same thing and expecting different results, then your path will remain unchanged.

Financial planning is like dieting. To maintain yourself at an ideal weight for the long term you will need to change your eating habits, gain an understanding of the principles of exercise and good diet, as well as an understanding of the food groups and their constituents and how your body processes those foods. Anyone can eat less fat or drink diet shakes for a few months, but your diet and weight won't be sustainable unless your eating and exercising habits are altered for life.

Any significant and lasting life change requires a mental paradigm shift. As Stephen Covey illustrates in his seminal book *The 7 Habits of Highly Effective People*, a paradigm shift doesn't require just a change in what you do but also a change to your lifelong habits and some of the underlying principles that rule your life — perhaps a change in perception is required. Money for money's sake is not the goal. The goal is to create a challenge for yourself, to provide opportunity for your family and to give your life meaning, and hopefully and ultimately, to help others in need. The aim is to create a better life for yourself and your family by taking control and having more choices.

Free financial health check

If you're interested in undertaking a free financial health check, go to my website (www.samhenderson.com.au) and complete one online to assess where you stand before you start the financial planning process. It may be interesting to look back on later.

Just seven steps

My process to help you work out your financial plan is shown in figure 1.1. It shows you the seven-step process to facilitate gathering and recording the data you need to populate your one-page financial plan. You can use the forms and software provided on my website (www.samhenderson.com.au) to complete all of these activities without cost — it's really easy. The seven steps are:

- discovery: (a) personal financial questionnaire, (b) budget, (c) risk profile and (d) tax returns.

- SMART goal setting

- gap analysis

- strategies and structure

- tactics

- your one-page financial plan

- ongoing review and active portfolio management.

Figure 1.1: the seven steps in developing your one-page financial plan

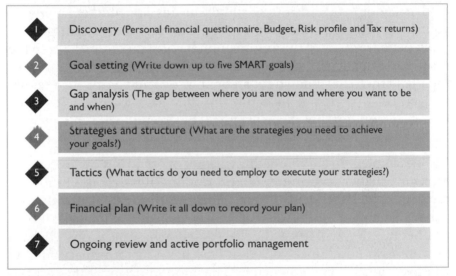

Source: Henderson Maxwell.

Step 1: discovery

The discovery step of the financial planning process is probably the most important and time consuming for your immediate future. You need to work through the topics included under step 1 in the list above to ensure you have a thorough understanding of your current situation. This will provide the impetus and platform for you to improve that situation. Until you know exactly where you are now, you cannot possibly imagine how you can progress.

Your financial questionnaire

Your personal financial questionnaire is simply a data-gathering document to record your personal details, goals and objectives, current income, expenses, assets, liabilities, super, insurance and estate planning details. To download your own blank copy of your personal financial questionnaire, or to complete your personal assessment online, go to www.samhenderson.com.au and go to the resources section to download your personal assessment pack.

Understanding your cash flow

Understanding your cash flow simply means knowing exactly what your income is and what your expenses are month by month over a given period. You need this information before you can make even the most basic financial decisions. Many people would rather chew off their left arm than sit down for an hour or two and work out a family budget. For true change to occur, you may have to cope with some level of discomfort, but the benefits will be exceptionally enlightening and extremely helpful. No pain, no gain!

If, for example, you are wondering whether or not to buy an investment asset or whether to borrow money, working through the following seven questions to calculate your budget will provide you with your answer. Finding these answers can be seen as a kind of financial litmus test, because they will reveal the effect that purchase decisions will have on your cash flow. Since your cash flow has a major impact on how you live your life, you are then in a position to decide if the sacrifice is worth the potential benefit. This is the risk–reward decision-making process — short-term pain for long-term gain.

What is your income?

Every taxpayer has to lodge an individual tax return, so be sure to include only your *own* income and expenses in this exercise. For example, if an asset, such as a property, is proportionately owned — you own 50 per cent and your partner owns 50 per cent — then list only the proportion of the income (or expense) that applies to you. In this case, you would include 50 per cent of the income from the property in your total income (and include 50 per cent of the expenses among your expenses). Fill in table 1.1 to calculate your income (A).

Table 1.1: your income

Income source	Partner 1	Partner 2 (if appropriate)
Salary		
Investment property 1		
Investment property 2		
Shares		
Franking credits from share dividends		
Term deposit interest		
Other income		
(A) Total		

What are your tax-deductible expenses?

Tax-deductible expenses are the expenses you incur in generating your income or in undertaking education relating to your work. The Australian Tax Office (ATO) website (www.ato.gov.au) has more information on allowable deductions. Some examples of tax-deductible expenses are work uniforms, education relevant to your work, motor-vehicle use to visit clients, and investment expenses, such as interest on investment loans. Table 1.2 provides a useful starting point for calculating tax-deductible expenses (B).

Table 1.2: your tax-deductible expenses

Expense	Partner 1	Partner 2 (if appropriate)
Motor vehicle expenses		
Work uniforms		
Depreciation on investment properties		
Interest on investment loans for property		
Interest on margin loan		
Other expenses		
(B) Total		

What is your taxable income?

Your taxable income (C) is your total income (A) minus any allowable deductions (B). Simply subtract your deductions from your total income.

Partner 1

(A) $_____ – (B) $_____ = (C) $_____

Partner 2 (if appropriate)

(A) $_____ – (B) $_____ = (C) $_____

What is your tax rate and amount?

Tax is calculated on a sliding scale: the more you earn, the higher proportion of tax you will pay. In the 2012–13 tax year, for example, if you earn $50 000 per annum, the first $18 200 is tax free; the next $18 800 (up to $37 000) will be taxed at 19 per cent; and income between $37 001 and $50 000 will be taxed at 32.5 per cent.

Using table 1.3 you can see your tax on $50 000 would be $7797 ($3572 + ($50 000 – $37 000 × 32.5% = $4225) = $7797). If you earn $80 000 per annum, you would pay $17 547 in tax ($3572 + $13 975). Tax on $100 000 of taxable income will be $24 947 ($3572 + 13 975 + (($100 000 – 80 000) × 37%)) = $24 947). See table 1.4 for a sliding scale of tax levels at given levels of annual taxable income.

Use the figures in table 1.3 and your taxable income from question 3 to calculate your tax payable (D) and fill it in below.

Partner 1

Tax payable on your taxable income is (D) $ _____

Partner 2 (if applicable)

Tax payable on your taxable income is (D) $ _____

Alternatively, you will find a simple tax calculator on www.samhenderson .com.au. This can be saved in Excel format for you to keep on your own computer, and the tax brackets can be changed as legislation changes. For an official ATO tax calculator, visit the ATO website (http://calculators .ato.gov.au/scripts/asp/simpletaxcalc/main.asp).

Table 1.3: tax rates

Tax bracket ($)	Tax rate (%)*	Amount of tax ($)
0–18200	0	0
18201–37000	19	3572
37001–80000	32.5	13975
80001–180000	37	37000
180001+	45	Not applicable

*These tax rates are applicable for the 2012–13, 2013–14, 2014–15 tax years, excluding Medicare levy of 1.5 per cent.

Table 1.4: easy slide scale for incomes and net tax

Your income ($)	Your tax ($)	Average percentage of tax (%)	Net income ($)
50000	7797	16	42203
80000	17547	22	62453
100000	24947	25	75053
150000	43446	29	106554
180000	54546	30	125454
200000	63546	32	136454
250000	86046	34	163954
300000	108546	36	191454
500000	198546	40	301454
1000000	423546	42	576454

*These tax rates are applicable for the 2012–13, 2013–14, 2014–15 tax years, excluding Medicare levy of 1.5 per cent.

What is your after-tax income?

Your after-tax income (E) is simply your taxable income (C) minus the amount of tax you have to pay (D).

Partner 1

(C) $_____ – (D) $_____ = (E) $_____

Partner 2

(C) $_____ – (D) $_____ = (E) $_____

What are your non-deductible expenses?

Your non-deductible expenses (F) are all of your living expenses apart from those for which you can claim a tax deduction. For most people, they include things such as food, rent or mortgage payments, council rates, entertainment, utilities (such as gas, electricity and telephone), and house and car insurance. A good guide to these expenses will be your bank statements over the past 12 months, credit card statements, receipts or any other source documents you have. Fill in table 1.5 with these details.

Table 1.5: your non-deductible expenses

Expense	Partner 1	Partner 2 (if appropriate)
Rent/mortgage on home		
Groceries		
Entertainment		
Council rates		
Electricity		
Water		
Gas		
Medical (doctor, dentist, specialist)		
Clothing		
Child care		
Transport		
Motor vehicle expenses		
Insurance		
Gifts		
Boat/caravan/trailer		
Holidays		
Other non-deductible expenses		
(F) Total		

What is your net income?

Your net income (G) (also known as your surplus or deficit income) is your after-tax income (E) minus your non-deductible expenses (F). In other words, your net income is your surplus income, the money that you have available for saving or investing (or it could be a deficit income, indicating that you are spending more than you are earning).

Partner 1

(E) \$_____ – (F) \$ _____ = (G) \$ _____

Partner 2

(E) \$_____ – (F) \$ _____ = (G) \$ _____

The importance of this process

Again, I'd like to stress the importance of undertaking this budgeting process each time you consider buying an investment asset or any major item. This is crucial, because the tax effect can be a real kicker when you find that the Australian government is contributing to your purchase via tax credits. Tax deductions are like having the government pay a large portion of your tax-deductible expenses, because those expenses are deducted from your gross income before you pay tax.

Once you have answered the seven budget questions and understand your own cash flow, you should monitor and review your cash flow as time progresses. Your cash flow will change for varying reasons, including job or career changes, having a child or more children, economic conditions and other challenges that may arise from time to time. While you should monitor your cash flow regularly, say every six months, it also needs to be updated each time something changes significantly. Changes will occur for better and for worse and so, too, your income will rise and fall throughout your life. But if you have a solid grasp of your financial position, you can make informed decisions in a timely fashion to cope with those changes.

Your risk profile

Assessing your attitude to risk has never been more important. If you are part of a couple, assessing your partner's attitude towards risk is also paramount, as people cope with different levels of risk-taking with their money differently.

Attitudes to money vary so vastly that skipping this step is both negligent and inconsiderate. The global financial crisis was a great reality check for some people who thought they may have a great tolerance for risk, because when they started to make actual financial losses, they found their capacity for risk dried up entirely.

I'll explore risk profiling in greater depth in the chapter on asset allocation and portfolio construction (see chapter 4) as the two are intrinsically linked. In the meantime, you will find the risk profile questionnaire both interesting and a good discussion point with your family and friends for assessing your own attitude towards risk. Go to www.samhenderson.com.au to download your risk profile questionnaire and assessment pack.

Get your tax returns up to date

It's important to get your house in order so that you know exactly where you stand right now. Start by ensuring that your tax returns are up to date and that you know where you stand with the tax office. You never want to be on the wrong side of the tax office, and if you are, it's important to rectify the situation and be proactive about the measures you need to take to bring yourself up to date. The tax office is far more understanding if you are proactive than if you wait for them to pursue you.

You need to know what your gross income, taxable income and after-tax income are in order to make informed decisions. Let's look at what these terms mean.

- *Gross income* is the sum of your income received from all sources, including your salary and bonuses, company or trust distributions, investment income (from an investment property or share dividends) or any other income you received in the tax year (from 1 July to 30 June).

- *Taxable income* is the amount of income you received *after* taking out your deductions and *before* tax has been taken out. Deductions are the expense items that you are legally entitled to claim and that reduce your taxable income. For example, interest on an investment property loan or a margin loan is tax deductible.

- *After-tax income*, as the name suggests, is your income after tax has been deducted.

It is possible to have an income of $150 000 and to pay tax only on $80 000 because you have deductions amounting to $70 000. For example, if you borrowed to buy an investment property and pay interest of $50 000 on your loan, and you have expenses of $10 000 per annum relating to the property (such as agent's fees and maintenance) and are also entitled to claim $10 000 for your motor vehicle usage for work, you can, perfectly legally, reduce your taxable income to $80 000.

In this example, the government is effectively paying for a large percentage of your expenses and you can bring your tax bracket down to the 32.5 per cent level from 37 per cent, or even 45 per cent under the current regime. This is the first principle of using someone else's money to pay for your investments. I have dedicated a whole chapter to this subject later in the book (see chapter 9).

Have a look at your last two tax returns or ask your tax agent to explain them to you so that you can identify your gross income, deductions, taxable income and after-tax income. This will give you a much better understanding of how your cash flow works and of how tax has affected the decisions you have made so far and, importantly, those you will make in the future.

Note to self (that's you!)

Look at your last two years' tax returns or call your tax agent and book an appointment to have your taxes brought up to date so that you know exactly where you stand.

Step 2: SMART goal setting

Your goals and objectives are the things that you would like to achieve in a given period of time. If you don't set goals and objectives, you have nothing to aim for and no reason to change.

Your goals will inevitably change over time as your income increases or your assets grow in value, and you will probably become more ambitious. So, too, your confidence will increase with each success you notch up, however small, and this will provide you with the impetus to push the boundaries of your goals a little further.

There's no sure thing

Success is important, but so too is failure. It's in the face of failure that you learn some of your most valuable lessons, and if you aren't making mistakes, you aren't challenging yourself enough. When you make a mistake, think of it as a cost of doing business and part of the cost of your education in becoming a better investor and financial manager. I can't stress enough the importance of being prepared to make mistakes and learn from them. Never be too scared to make mistakes, and never be too hard on yourself for making them.

Setting SMART goals

The word SMART is an acronym for specific, measurable, achievable, realistic and timely. Let's look more closely at these terms and why it's important to ensure your goals have these characteristics.

- *Specific.* These are answers to the important questions of who, what, when, where, why and which. An example of a general goal is 'to have more money'. A specific goal is 'to buy an investment property valued at $450 000 and to build a $100 000 share portfolio in the next three years'.

- *Measurable.* For a goal to be measurable, you need to establish a yardstick, and in financial matters that's very simple. The obvious measurement is in dollars or percentage terms. For example, 'After one year, I want to have equity in a property of $20 000 plus a share portfolio worth $25 000'. Or you may have the goal of 'achieving a 20 per cent return on a given investment within one year'.

  Don't be hard on yourself if you don't achieve the number you set. In time, you will learn what is realistic, but the important thing is to have a go and set a measurable target.

- *Achievable.* It's important for goals to be achievable, because it's easy to lose motivation if you don't attain your goals. And even when goals are achievable in theory, they won't always be so in practice. There will be times when the sharemarkets are volatile and property on Sydney's or Perth's waterfronts won't sell — that's a fact of life, and the earlier you acknowledge it, the better off you will be. My advice is to ensure that your goals are high enough to make you run, but low enough to keep you motivated. My favourite saying here is, 'Aim for the stars, and if you hit the moon, you've done really well.'

- *Realistic.* A goal must be something that you are willing and able to achieve. You can set your goals high, but try to be realistic as to how you are going to attain them. Remember, the higher your goals, the stronger your motivation needs to be. If you have a salary of $200 000 and $300 000 in cash, you can clearly afford to have higher goals than someone who is on $50 000 a year and has no assets to invest. Your goals need to be appropriate for you. It's also important to review them from time to time in the light of your progress. I recommend that you do this every six to 12 months. Don't worry if you have modest goals or a low salary to work from — we all have to start somewhere and everyone can benefit from better financial management.

- *Timely.* You need to allocate a time frame to your goals and set a date by which they are to be attained. If you don't set a time frame, it's all too easy to procrastinate or to allow an unproductive situation to continue for too long, and both these forms of delay can be very costly. Time-based objectives also increase your motivation and make you try harder. Procrastination stops many would-be investors in their tracks, preventing them from even getting to step one. Don't let it stop you. Nike has stuck with the slogan 'Just do it' for good reason: it's direct, truthful and hard-hitting, and if you want to be financially independent, then you will need a time-based plan. Just do it!

Getting off the money-go-round

So many people live on the money-go-round and struggle in vain to get off. If this sounds like you, take heart. A good financial plan will allow you to take control of your finances, and use the banks to your advantage, so that you can get off the money-go-round sooner — and stay off it.

I suggest that you start by establishing three to five key goals, though there is no set rule. Here are some examples of the kinds of goals that people set for themselves:

- retire in 10 years' time, at age 55, with an after-tax income of $60 000 per annum
- retire in 10 years' time, at age 60, with assets of $1 million
- pay off the house within 10 years
- buy an investment property worth $500 000 with a 20 per cent deposit within two years
- establish a share portfolio worth $200 000 in five years through a regular savings plan and a conservative level of gearing (say, 50 per cent).

As you can see, these goals are all SMART goals. They are specific, measurable, achievable, realistic and timely.

Lifestyle versus financial goals

It's a good plan to have both financial and lifestyle goals. The purpose of having financial goals, after all, is to provide you with the freedom and choices to do what you want in life. If you simply want more money, you are unlikely to find this to be a very fulfilling pastime. On the other hand, if your financial success adds to your time with your partner and family or allows you to travel and meet new friends the world over, then your financial success will greatly increase your quality of life in the broadest sense.

Write down your goals

Now that you have given some thought to your goals, you need to write them down. You need to give them a physical form so that you can see and refer to them. Better financial management will give you more choices in life, but it won't happen by itself. Writing down your goals and objectives is the first step on the path to financial success. So do it now by filling in table 1.6. If your goals require you to make a financial commitment, you should allocate a value to them, and you also need to set a date by which you would like to achieve them.

Table 1.6: my goals and objectives

Goals and objectives	Value $	By when
1		
2		
3		
4		
5		

Are your goals SMART (specific, measurable, achievable, realistic and timely)?

Step 3: gap analysis

A gap analysis is designed to look at the gap between where you are now and where you want to be, and then work out how you can implement strategies and tactics to bridge the gap and thus achieve your goals over a given time frame. We can assemble the information gathered so far in your personal financial questionnaire and compare your current situation with your goals. Once you have educated yourself on the options available to you, this will help you to compile a set of strategies, and employ a subset of tactics for each strategy and thus achieve your financial goals.

Figure 1.2 (overleaf) shows a visual example of what a gap analysis and financial planning process should look like.

Figure 1.2: gap analysis and financial planning

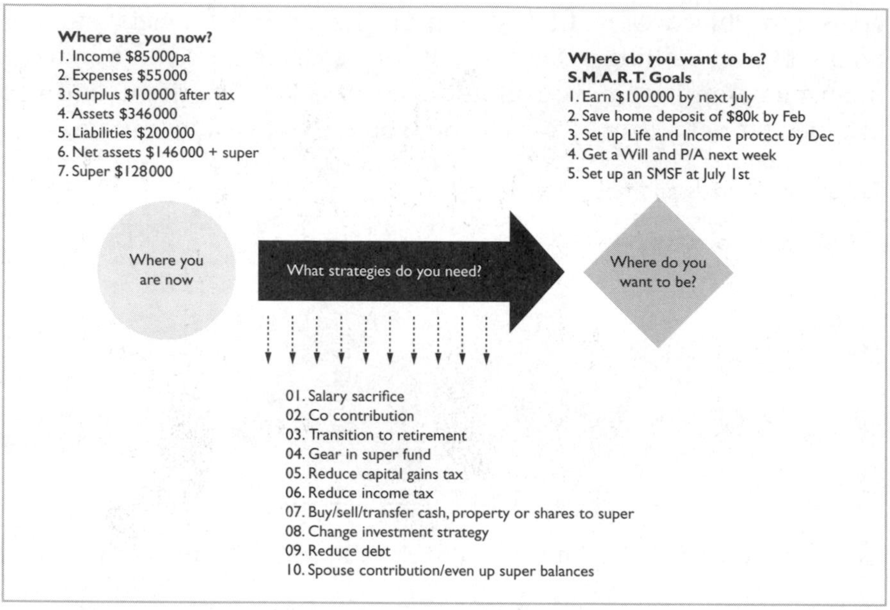

Where are you now?
1. Income $85000pa
2. Expenses $55000
3. Surplus $10000 after tax
4. Assets $346000
5. Liabilities $200000
6. Net assets $146000 + super
7. Super $128000

Where do you want to be?
S.M.A.R.T. Goals
1. Earn $100000 by next July
2. Save home deposit of $80k by Feb
3. Set up Life and Income protect by Dec
4. Get a Will and P/A next week
5. Set up an SMSF at July 1st

Where you are now

What strategies do you need?

Where do you want to be?

01. Salary sacrifice
02. Co contribution
03. Transition to retirement
04. Gear in super fund
05. Reduce capital gains tax
06. Reduce income tax
07. Buy/sell/transfer cash, property or shares to super
08. Change investment strategy
09. Reduce debt
10. Spouse contribution/even up super balances

Source: Henderson Maxwell.

Your SWAT team

In a police or military sense, a SWAT (special weapons and tactics) team is an elite team of paramilitary specialists used to manage high-risk situations. So, too, in your financial life, you may need a team of highly trained specialists to resolve your own high-risk situations — in a financial sense of course. For example, you may need an accountant, financial adviser, stock broker, real estate agent, buyer's agent, mortgage broker, solicitor, conveyancer, insurance broker or superannuation administrator, or possibly other advisers, to help ensure you can meet your goals and objectives.

While you may need to build your team over time, it may be helpful at this point to take an audit of who your specialists currently are and whether they are still appropriate for you.

You may also want to find a specialist who can help you in several areas to reduce both the costs and the number of professionals you need. I urge you to be cautious here, because not everyone or every company can specialise in everything — avoid the 'jack of all trades, master of none' situation.

Your list of advisers will feed directly into the one-page financial plan to ensure they are readily available to you when you need them. You may not need all of the advisers listed in table 1.7 (overleaf), and there may be some things you can do yourself, but you need to be honest with yourself and be prepared to pay a fair fee for a professional service. A true professional has worked hard to attain their level of expertise and if you are not prepared to put in the time or effort, then you should outsource that job to a professional who can do a better job for a reasonable fee. What is a reasonable fee? I always quote Warren Buffett, one of the most successful investors in the world and one of its richest men: 'Price is what you pay; value is what you get'.

Here are some tips to help you choose the right team for you. These five non-negotiable attributes of a good adviser must be fulfilled to ensure you can build a solid long-term relationship and you get the best advice you can:

- *Likeable or respected.* You need to like the person and respect them if you are going to work with them for the long term. Some people aren't necessarily likeable, but they may be highly respected in their field. I have met a few solicitors and surgeons who fall into this 'quirky but expert' category. You also want someone who listens to your needs, goals and objectives and then tailors the advice to your specific situation.

- *Education.* Advisers need to be well educated, at least to degree level. Ask for references for the last three clients they brought on and three clients that have been with the firm for at least three years. Call at least two of the people from each category. Also ask if they have won any awards, as this often indicates that they care enough about their business to compare themselves to other experts in their field.

- *Licensed.* Make sure your expert is in fact an expert. Check their credentials against association registers (such as the Financial Planning Association for financial planners, Chartered Accountants or Certified Practising Accountants for accountants, Law Society for solicitors and Finance Brokers Association of Australia for finance brokers). Also check the consumer website of the Australian Securities Investment Commission (ASIC) at www.moneysmart.gov.au or their scam site at www.scamwatch.com.au for tips on how to choose an adviser or notices of any scams that you should be aware of.

- *Experienced.* Experience in your field of need is essential and advisers should have at least five years' experience in the field in which you need assistance. There are many generalists out there, but a specialist in your particular area of need is likely to be more helpful.

- *Trust.* Probably the most important aspect of dealing with a professional expert is to ensure you trust them. If you do the background checks above and undertake your due diligence, that will help to reduce your risks — and always be aware of the complaints resolution process should things go awry.

So let's record your team, as it currently stands, in table 1.7.

Table 1.7: your current team of advisers, or SWAT team

Your team	Name	Phone	Email	Office address
Financial planner				
Accountant				
Solicitor				
Real estate agent				
Insurance broker				
SMSF administrator				
Mortgage broker				
Buyers agent				
Conveyancer				
Stock broker				

Step 4: strategies and structure

Strategies are the plans that will allow you to accomplish your goals. Strategies require your personal resources for achieving your key financial and lifestyle goals. You will need to establish a set of strategies for achieving different goals and satisfying different parts of your financial plan. Many goals require multiple strategies and, the more complex the goals, the more numerous the strategies may need to be. For example, one strategy may be to ensure your estate plan is in place and up to date.

It's a good idea at this stage to leave your strategies reasonably general and allow your tactics to provide the detail. Don't get too caught up in the detail of strategies. You should also feel free to change your plan and strategic direction as time progresses. As goals are achieved, they will be replaced by other goals and strategies, possibly more ambitious ones.

At the end of most chapters, I detail a list of five possible examples of strategies and tactics that you may find useful.

Step 5: tactics

Tactics are the individual and detailed activities you need to carry out to fulfil your strategy and thus achieve each individual goal. Using the strategy example of ensuring your estate plan is in place and up to date, tactically you will need to call a solicitor and have them prepare a will and a power of attorney for you. You will need to sign the will and keep a copy in a safe place, while also letting members of the family know that a will exists and where it is kept in the event of death. Fulfilling the goal of updating your estate plan will require some financial resources and some of your time. Each strategy may require several tactical activities, which need to be completed in order to satisfy the strategy.

Tactics are where the details lie and, as always, the devil is in the detail, especially when considering your financial matters. For that reason you may need assistance from professionals to carry out the strategic and tactical activities to allow you to effectively fulfil your goals. There are some things you just can't do without assistance. For example, you can buy a will kit from a newsagency for $25, but it is possible that it will be incapable of truly fulfilling your estate planning goals. Using a professional specialising in estate planning is likely to offer a better, more effective approach.

Making the planning process easier

I am in the process of building an online software program to make developing your financial plan easier. You can find out more about the software at www.samhenderson.com.au.

Step 6: your one-page financial plan

Your one-page financial plan will fall quickly and easily into place as you step yourself through each of the stages. From the time you start to complete your personal financial questionnaire you will start piecing together your financial plan and seeing where you can make improvements. Think about it: how much time do you really dedicate to improving your financial situation? Perhaps you can spend a little more time and effort to achieve a great result without having to make too many sacrifices.

Your one-page financial plan will provide you with a framework to improve your finances and make your life a little easier. It will bring awareness to your income producing activities and consciousness to your expenses. It will also give you confidence in your decision-making abilities as you take charge of your financial life and progress your asset building activities.

More importantly, the one-page financial plan will give you all you need to know in the palm of your hand. It will be easy to access and easy to update. Stick it on your corkboard or whiteboard, or carry it in your work compendium. You can stick it up on your study wall or post it on the bathroom mirror to keep it front of mind.

Figure 1.3 shows a sample of a one-page financial plan.

Figure 1.3: sample of a one-page financial plan

One-Page Financial Plan *for:* _____ Date: _/_/_

01 Team	02 Current Situation	03 Goals & Objectives	04 Strategies	05 Tactics	06 Implementation	07 Review of Plan
Who is going to help you?	Where are you at now?	What do you want to achieve?	What do you need to do to achieve your goals?	Your plan of action to implement your strategies	Your tactical action plan checklist	Your regular strategy review checklist
FINANCIAL ADVISER	TOTAL ASSETS $___	GOAL 1	STRATEGY 1	TACTIC 1	Contact ___ Forms Finished? Yes ○ No ○	Review What? ___ When? ___ In Diary? Yes ○ No ○
ACCOUNTANT	TOTAL LIABILITIES $___	GOAL 2	STRATEGY 2	TACTIC 2	Contact ___ Forms Finished? Yes ○ No ○	Review What? ___ When? ___ In Diary? Yes ○ No ○
SOLICITOR	NET WORTH $___	GOAL 3	STRATEGY 3	TACTIC 3	Contact ___ Forms Finished? Yes ○ No ○	Review What? ___ When? ___ In Diary? Yes ○ No ○
MORTGAGE BROKER	GROSS INCOME BEFORE TAX $___	GOAL 4	STRATEGY 4	TACTIC 4	Contact ___ Forms Finished? Yes ○ No ○	Review What? ___ When? ___ In Diary? Yes ○ No ○
INSURANCE SUPPLIER	TOTAL EXPENSES $___	GOAL 5	STRATEGY 5	TACTIC 5	Contact ___ Forms Finished? Yes ○ No ○	Review What? ___ When? ___ In Diary? Yes ○ No ○
SHARE BROKER	NET INCOME AFTER TAX $___	GOAL 6	STRATEGY 6	TACTIC 6	Contact ___ Forms Finished? Yes ○ No ○	Review What? ___ When? ___ In Diary? Yes ○ No ○
REAL ESTATE AGENT	SUPERANNUATION BALANCE $___	GOAL 7	STRATEGY 7	TACTIC 7	Contact ___ Forms Finished? Yes ○ No ○	Review What ___ When? ___ In Diary? Yes ○ No ○

Insurance Strategy

Client	○ Life $___	○ Income Protection $___	○ TPD $___	○ Trauma $___
Partner	○ Life $___	○ Income Protection $___	○ TPD $___	○ Trauma $___

Estate Planning Strategy

Client	○ Wills	○ Power of Attorney	○ Guardianship	○ Binding Death Nomination
Partner	○ Wills	○ Power of Attorney	○ Guardianship	○ Binding Death Nomination

Source: Henderson Maxwell.

Step 7: review and portfolio management

As we all know, life is full of change. Accordingly your financial plans need to be updated regularly to accommodate the changes in your life. Marriage, babies, divorce, new job, redundancy, retirement, death, disability, trauma, sharemarket fluctuations, interest rate movement, property sales — these are just some of the things that should prompt you to update your plan.

KEY POINTS

Your financial planning process could be summarised as follows:

- Step 1: discovery — working out where you are now

    (a) personal financial questionnaire — recording your details

    (b) budget — with seven questions to answer

    (c) risk profile — identifying your attitude to risk

    (d) tax returns — knowing your taxable income and deductions.

- Step 2: SMART goal setting — deciding what success will look like

- Step 3: gap analysis — working out the gap between where you are now and where you want to be

- Step 4: strategies and structure — deciding on the methods you will use to reach your goals

- Step 5: tactics — working out the ways you can implement the strategies you have chosen

- Step 6: your one-page financial plan — finalising the plan that suits your needs, goals and objectives

- Step 7: review and portfolio management — keeping things up to date.

CHAPTER 2

INCREASE YOUR INCOME AND MAKE THE MOST OF YOUR SALARY

> Invest 3 per cent of your income in yourself (self-development) in order to guarantee your future.
>
> *Brian Tracy, American motivational speaker and self-help author*

Now that you have established your goals and objectives, and developed an understanding of your assets, liabilities and net cash flow, I want you to consider one important thing you can try to change in the short term — your income. This is also a chance to consider a few quick tips that will hopefully give you a few quick financial wins. For a variety of reasons, some people may not have the potential to increase their income from their job in the short term, but just about everyone will be able to benefit from at least one or more of the strategies outlined in this chapter.

Before we begin, it's important to note that your income and your ability to earn income are your biggest assets when it comes to accumulating wealth. So don't take chances — protect your income (and your family's welfare) by taking out income protection insurance. Income protection insurance is not a luxury but a necessity for the vast majority of people. It will cover your expenses, and your family's ongoing expenses, in the event of your becoming disabled, falling ill or being injured. If you don't have income protection insurance, don't delay: start getting quotes immediately, and sign up before you need it! (See chapter 10 for more on this form of insurance.)

Small increase for a *big* difference

Clearly, the more you earn, the more you can save, and the more you can save, the more you can invest — and the faster you will reach your goals.

Even small rises in income can have a significant impact on your ability to invest. For example, if you are an employee earning a salary, and you invest your pay rises into assets that appreciate in value, such as shares and property, rather than goods that depreciate in value (such as most consumer goods), you will soon be well on the way to financial success. Too many people make the mistake of spending their pay rises on consumer goods that give them short-term gratification, and then wonder why they can't get ahead financially.

It will help to put things into perspective if I tell you that you could own a $500 000 investment property with a 10 per cent deposit for just $150 per week or around $7500 per year. In other words, a $5000 to $10 000 pay rise could fund an investment property or get you started on building a share portfolio that could have a major positive impact on your financial future and your lifestyle in a few years from now.

Tip

Whatever your income, here's something you can do right now. Make it a habit to pay yourself first! That is, set aside a portion of your income to be regularly paid into a savings account. This will dramatically improve your financial position over time. (The most effective way of doing this is explained later in the chapter.)

Let's take a look at the various ways you can invest in yourself with the aim of increasing your income — and the ways in which you can make the most of your income.

How to increase your salary

Month in, month out, your salary is paid into your bank account, and many of us accept what is given to us without considering ways of increasing it. This section is a reminder that you can take simple steps to increase your income so you will have some cash for investment purposes, allowing you to retire earlier and increase your choices throughout your life. Small increments in salary can make a difference to the end result.

Ask for a pay rise

As a salary-based employee, the first thing you can do to increase your income is to ask for a pay rise. If you don't ask, you don't get. Organise a meeting with your boss in an environment that is private and free of distractions so you can really flesh out the issues and discuss putting a written plan in place to improve your situation.

Ideally, you will be able to articulate how you have increased revenue or provided an efficiency improvement that your boss can relate directly to his or her hip pocket. If you haven't provided an obvious or direct business benefit to your employer, then perhaps have a chat to your boss about what you need to do to earn a pay rise. Again, if you don't ask, you won't get. You need to understand what the constraints are, what you need to do, and in what time frame you can achieve a pay rise.

This will allow you to set vocational goals and milestones that establish a point of reference for both you and your boss. You need to establish your career goals, in the same way that you established your financial goals in chapter 1. Go back to chapter 1 and reread the goals section with your career in mind.

Look for a new job

If your boss or your superiors don't recognise your achievements, another company will. Don't be afraid to talk to an HR consultant, a head hunter, recruitment agent or a personnel agent to gauge your skill level and salary potential. I highly recommend that you do this to give yourself a realistic assessment of your current position and your potential.

Also remember to discuss the benefits over and above a higher salary that a prospective employer may provide, such as days in lieu of overtime, extended holiday periods, rostered days off (RDOs), additional superannuation benefits, salary-packaging arrangements and motor vehicle usage, to name a few. These added benefits can be worth thousands of dollars every year or can simply free up time to allow you to focus on your investments.

Invest in yourself

Education is the best way you can invest in yourself. By going back to study, you can improve your qualifications or your skill set, and therefore your value to an employer. Don't be disheartened if you didn't do well at school. Some of the best students in later life are those who didn't excel at school — myself included. The only thing you will need to overcome in that case is your lack of confidence.

Post-school study is quite different from studying at school. There are no bullies, no annoying teachers micro-managing your every move, and no class clowns to disturb you. Talk to your local TAFE or university, or look at the options with the Open University and investigate what's possible. If you are working full time, you may want to look at studying by correspondence to save travel time and fit your studies into your own timetable, and many institutions offer intensive and short courses, too. Education is so much more flexible now.

Generally speaking, the more qualifications you have, the higher your income, and so the more you can afford to invest. It's worth noting here, however, that a high salary is no guarantee of financial success. Many highly paid people come unstuck when they take on a large mortgage and become a slave to it. I've come across plenty of would-be clients with an income of $250 000 who can't afford to invest outside their own mortgage.

If you can't afford to study, one option is to ask your employer to pay for your studies or salary package them (see the section on salary packaging on p. 29). Perhaps you could ask your employer to pay for your studies upfront and allow you to pay the costs off over many months with pre-tax dollars. If you are able to do this, it's like getting a 19 per cent, 32.5 per cent, 37 per cent or 45 per cent discount on the cost of your studies (depending on your marginal tax rate), because the ATO is subsidising the cost for you.

If you are thinking about doing this, be sure to check out your employer's study policy and make sure you understand it thoroughly before you make any commitment. Some organisations will only refund the cost of fees after you have passed each subject or completed a certain proportion of your studies, and some will require you to repay your fees if you leave the company within a certain period.

If you still can't afford to study, try the federal government's Higher Education Loan Program (HELP) scheme (www.goingtouni.gov.au).

Assuming your studies lead to an increase in your salary, this will make it easier for you to pay off your HELP debt over time. Invest in yourself!

Get a coach or mentor

One of the best things I ever did was to hire a business coach, and throughout my career with other companies I've always had a mentor or someone to bounce ideas off. A mentor is a trusted, respected and experienced colleague whose wisdom and experience you can draw on for career guidance and to help you make decisions. If you don't know of anyone who can perform this role for you, you can engage the services of a professional mentor, as I did.

Running with the premise that most successful sports people have a coach, so too most professional business people should have a coach to help them make better decisions about their business. If you are self-employed, a business coach can add huge value to your business and be tax deductible. Business coaching services vary dramatically, and as you progress you need to decide when it's appropriate to go your separate ways, but business coaches can add great value in the areas of financial management, marketing, people management and general operational efficiencies.

Just as a financial plan is designed to improve your financial situation, a written career plan will provide the impetus for you to articulate and track your career progression. Career counsellors and coaches can also assist you with this process.

This book is not about career planning, but in general terms a career plan will outline your strengths and weaknesses, your areas of interest, your preferred work environment, the type of people you want to work with, the amount of money you want to earn, the industries you are interested in, and where, geographically, you want to work. It should also clearly outline what education and skills you need to develop to reach your career goals.

A number of websites (including www.seek.com.au and www. mycareer.com.au) provide articles, tips and ideas on topics such as developing interviewing skills and writing résumés and cover letters, and also give other useful information about career development. They are an excellent resource for anyone wishing to advance in his or her career.

Start your own business

The truly rich generally run their own businesses. You can make good money as an employee in the position of a director or senior manager, but the consistently wealthy people I know are self-employed in good growth industries with a competitive advantage and scalable growth prospects. Entrepreneurial people often make more money from their business than from their investments and, in fact, their business becomes their investment when it is sold. Their business also becomes their retirement plan.

Running your own business is not for everyone and, given the high rate of business failures, it is far from a safe and secure option. However, despite the risks, it can be a very financially lucrative direction to take, augmented by lifestyle perks such as regular days off, more than four weeks of holidays and working from home or remote locations. For example, I try to work from home on Wednesdays and Fridays, and take about eight weeks of holidays each year.

The best businesses to own are those that offer recurring revenue, low competition, high barriers to entry, competitive advantage, unique selling propositions, high profit, scalability and good management. Businesses with these attributes sell for higher multiples of revenue, recurring revenue or EBIT (earnings before interest and taxes), maximising the value for the owners. For example, a real estate agency that offers a property management rent roll may sell for three times the recurring revenue of that rent roll. So if you have a rent roll producing $200 000 of income, it may sell for $600 000. So too, throughout its life it may produce $200 000 of revenue, minus costs, making a good living for you while also increasing the rent roll through marketing or word of mouth and augmenting income with sales commission revenue or home loans, or both.

Accountancy firms sell for one times their total revenue; financial planning firms for three times their recurring revenue; and many listed companies on the ASX sell for between 10 and 20 times their net profit. The added liquidity (the ability to sell individual company shares), from the ability to sell shares on the stock exchange, improves their value significantly; however, your business would need to be worth more than $20 million to even consider listing on the stock exchange, and much larger is ideal.

Should you be thinking about taking this path, make sure you are well capitalised (you have plenty of money to cover operating expenses for at least two years); you have plenty of experience; and you know your product, competition and industry intimately, particularly from a financial management perspective. You will need to plan and replan to ensure you are ready to make this commitment and to ensure you have the best possible chance of success. Also make sure you have read Michael Gerber's two iconic business books *The E-Myth Revisited* and *E-Myth Mastery* to learn how to systemise and operate a world-class small business.

How to make the most of your salary

So long as you are being paid every week, you may as well use your income as effectively as possible to reduce your tax and build your assets. This section is about changing the way you manage and use your income, and all of these suggestions can be implemented in the short term.

Salary packaging

Salary packaging allows you to purchase or lease an asset with pre-tax dollars. It's a way of purchasing certain work-related items with your gross salary (rather than your after-tax salary). Cars and education are two items that are commonly salary packaged. Laptops were another, until the government outlawed them in a recent budget.

If you want to undertake some work-related study and your employer agrees to pay for it up front, you can repay it over time using pre-tax dollars. The cost of the education is deemed to be an expense, and in effect it reduces your taxable income for the financial year in which you pay for it. This is a very efficient way to upskill yourself, as you are paying for your education with tax-effective dollars. The tax deduction will apply *only* if the study is relevant to the industry from which you derive your income (but your employer would be highly unlikely to be paying for it if it weren't).

Salary sacrificing

Salary sacrificing is similar to salary packaging, but it involves making superannuation contributions from your pre-tax, or gross, income. You will pay only 15 per cent contributions tax (paid inside your super fund) instead of your marginal tax rate, which could be 19 per cent, 32.5 per cent, 37 per cent or 45 per cent (depending on your income). If, for example, you are on the highest marginal tax rate of 45 per cent, you will be reducing your tax on the amount you salary sacrifice from 45 per cent to 15 per cent, representing a saving of about 66 per cent in tax. Moreover, under the current superannuation system, when you draw an income from your super after you reach the age of 60, this income remains tax-free and there is no capital gains tax. Salary sacrificing is a very tax-effective way of saving money.

For example, if you are earning $95 000 per year and you contribute $15 000 to superannuation through salary sacrifice, you will pay only 15 per cent tax (superannuation contributions tax) on that $15 000 instead of 37 per cent (the marginal tax rate that applies to salaries between $80 000 and $95 000). This represents a tax saving of $3300 per year, and this amount goes directly into your superannuation fund with the rest of the contribution.

Effectively you are sacrificing some of your cash flow for savings, and the government is happy to provide a tax incentive for you to do so, because if you are self-funded in retirement you will be less likely to require government benefits.

Among many rules and regulations governing superannuation, you are not allowed to touch your superannuation until you can meet a condition of release—which may be that you must be between the ages of 55 and 60, depending on when you were born—so make sure you read chapter 7 on superannuation so that you fully understand what you are allowed to do.

Salary sacrificing is a great strategy for reducing your tax and building your superannuation.

Regular savings plan

For years now I have had a regular savings plan with a major bank—not my normal bank, incidentally, but a different provider—in order to segregate the funds from my other accounts. My regular savings plan can be changed to accommodate my lifestyle and cash-flow requirements at any time, but generally it just sails along without interruption, accumulating over time.

I call my high-interest internet savings account a kick-start account, because so many times I have used the funds saved in it to make investments in shares and property.

I suggest you do something similar and arrange for a direct debit of between 10 per cent and 20 per cent of your salary, to be transferred from your bank account on the day you're paid into a separate online, high-interest savings account. You then have the freedom to spend whatever's left in your day-to-day account on whatever you want (after you've taken care of the necessities and paid your bills, of course), comfortable in the knowledge that you have savings put aside for a rainy day or, better still, investment.

The good thing about this strategy is that you can set and forget. It's usually easy to transfer money into your other accounts to pay bills and so on, and you receive end-of-year tax statements for your tax agent. The money really adds up over time, making this a very effective savings strategy.

Forced savings

When I borrowed money to buy my first house, I realised that the mortgage repayments were forced savings. I had to pay the bank before I paid anyone else, because if it didn't get its money it would repossess my house — it was simple. Two organisations should always be paid as soon as you have paid yourself: banks and the Australian Taxation Office (ATO). Neither takes kindly to late or missed payments.

The beauty of borrowing for investment (as opposed to borrowing to buy your principal residence), apart from the fact that the interest on the loan is tax deductible, is that it represents forced savings. Provided that you have been diligent in researching your investment and sensible in the amount that you have borrowed, the repayments will contribute to your equity in a solid asset that, in most cases, increases in value over time and produces a good income.

The power of compound interest

No matter what your job or income, you will be able to benefit from the principle of compound interest. Whether you invest in shares, property, fixed interest or cash, compound interest is a fundamental principle in the growth of your portfolio — but as with most, if not all, investments, you need to be patient.

It's commonly said in the financial markets that the important thing is time in the market, not timing the market. Timing your purchases to make a profit in unpredictable and volatile share and property markets is virtually impossible, but if you buy for the long term and assume your assets will increase in value over time, then time itself will be your best friend.

You are most likely familiar with compound interest. Compound interest is where you earn interest on top of your interest as your investment grows in value. For example, if you save $100 per week and you receive 5 per cent interest calculated annually, then you will have $5200 plus 5 per cent interest, which equals $5460, at the end of year 1.

In year 2, you receive interest on your initial savings, plus interest on your additional $100 per week, which adds up to $10 920. This process is repeated month after month, year after year, and slowly you accumulate wealth. After 10 years, you would have $54 600.

Table 2.1 illustrates the benefit of saving $50, $100, $150 or $200 per week over a 10-year period with interest calculated annually.

Table 2.1: compound interest — cash

| Year | Amount saved per week ($) at 5% interest | | | |
	$50	$100	$150	$200
1	2730	5460	8190	10920
2	5460	10920	16380	21840
3	8190	16380	24570	32760
4	10920	21840	32760	43680
5	13650	27300	40950	54600
6	16380	32760	49140	65520
7	19110	38220	57330	76440
8	21840	43680	65520	87360
9	24570	49140	73710	98280
10	27300	54600	81900	109200

Compound interest doesn't just work with cash in a bank. It works with shares and it works with property investment. In fact, as shares and property both have higher long-term returns, compound interest with these investments works much better than with cash. Let me give you a taste of what you can aim for if you are a little more ambitious and don't mind taking on some more risk — and I mean real risk, with real consequences if things go pear-shaped.

Compound returns for property

You could, for example, put this principle to work by buying a new property every three years. In this example, we are going to buy three investment properties over 10 years, for $400 000 each, using a 10 per cent deposit plus costs (say $50 000 in total) for the first property, and then use the equity you accumulate with each purchase to borrow 100 per cent of the two further properties, as shown in table 2.2 (overleaf).

As you can see, the difference between saving $150 per week in a savings account and investing $150 per week in a property investment portfolio is significant. Table 2.2 makes some assumptions, however, and must be viewed with caution. For example, we have assumed that property grows consistently at 5 per cent per year, but this is rare and unrealistic and is simply for illustrative purposes as property grows in fits and spurts, and while it may average out at 5 per cent over the long term, it will rarely rise consistently at that level, or any level for that matter. Property, like shares, is volatile, and you need to exercise due diligence when borrowing significant amounts of money.

Table 2.2 also doesn't take into account the expenses associated with properties, such as body corporate fees, management fees, refinancing expenses, rising interest rates, having properties untenanted and, of course, maintenance, all of which can potentially derail your plan. It's important to have a risk-management plan in place to ensure that you can comfortably afford your investment strategy as conditions change. And conditions can change rapidly, so be careful.

Table 2.2: compound returns for property at 5 per cent growth p/a

Year	Property 1 ($)	Property 2 ($)	Property 3 ($)	Asset's value ($)	Borrowings ($)	Equity ($)
1	400 000	–	–	400 000	360 000	40 000
2	420 000	–	–	420 000	360 000	60 000
3	441 000	–	–	441 000	360 000	81 000
4	463 050	400 000	–	863 050	760 000	103 050
5	486 203	420 000	–	906 203	760 000	146 203
6	510 513	441 000	–	951 513	760 000	191 513
7	536 038	463 050	400 000	1 399 088	1 160 000	239 088
8	562 840	486 203	420 000	1 469 043	1 160 000	309 043
9	590 982	510 513	441 000	1 542 495	1 160 000	382 495
10	620 531	536 038	463 050	1 619 620	1 160 000	459 620

Compound returns and shares

Compound interest on shares works in the same way as property. As you can see from table 2.3, if you invest $200 per week into a share portfolio and borrow to an equivalent amount of $200 per week (which is called gearing the portfolio), and receive a 5 per cent return annually, your investment will grow to $274 701 over 10 years. This represents a net equity of $170 701 (investment minus total level of borrowing, or gearing, of $104 000) at the end of the 10 years.

Table 2.3: compound returns for shares

Year	Saved amount ($)	Gearing ($)	Total ($)	Interest (%)	Total ($)
1	10 400	10 400	20 800	5	21 840
2	10 400	10 400	42 640	5	44 772
3	10 400	10 400	65 572	5	68 851
4	10 400	10 400	89 651	5	94 133
5	10 400	10 400	114 933	5	120 680
6	10 400	10 400	141 480	5	148 554

Year	Saved amount ($)	Gearing ($)	Total ($)	Interest (%)	Total ($)
7	10 400	10 400	169 354	5	177 821
8	10 400	10 400	198 621	5	208 553
9	10 400	10 400	229 353	5	240 820
10	10 400	10 400	261 620	5	274 701

As all these examples show, compound interest is a valuable means of increasing your savings and your investment income. An increased income, in turn, gives you more opportunities to invest, enabling you to achieve your goals sooner and increasing the choices you have in life. Remember, though, that all investments involve risk, and be wary of overcommitting yourself. When the sun is shining you don't think about rain — but it will rain some time.

KEY POINTS

- Insure your greatest asset — your ability to earn income — with income protection insurance.
- A small rise in pay can facilitate an investment strategy or savings plan and make a big difference to your life.
- Try one of these ways of increasing your salary:
  - Ask for a pay rise.
  - Look for a new, higher-paying job.
  - Educate to elevate yourself.
  - Hire a career coach or mentor.
  - Start your own business.
- Try these ways to make the most of your salary:
  - Salary packaging — maximise your tax deductions.
  - Salary sacrifice — reduce your tax and boost your super.
  - Open a high-interest kick-start account and start your regular savings plan.
  - Use forced savings by borrowing money to invest.
  - Harness the power of compound interest.

CHAPTER 3

LEGALLY REDUCE YOUR TAX

Begin with the end in mind.

Stephen Covey, author of The 7 Habits of Highly Effective People

We all want to reduce our tax and boost our savings, and the key to doing this is to understand the various structures under which you can invest your hard-earned dollars. Each of these structures attracts a different rate of tax, which can affect the amount of net income you receive from your investment (as dividends or rent, for instance) and the amount of money you have left after you sell the asset (capital gain). By diverting your income to the structure that is most tax-effective for you, you may save yourself a fortune over time.

Investment structures

You can buy an asset under any of the following six structures:

- individual name
- joint names: as joint tenants and tenants in common
- partnership
- company
- trust
- superannuation (accumulation or pension mode).

You need to have a thorough understanding of each of these structures in order to choose the one that will best allow you to meet your investment objectives. Comparing the various structures before you invest is not just recommended, it's an essential part of prudent investment management. You need to understand how you will be taxed under each structure, and you need to understand the capital gains tax rules that apply to each structure.

Think before you leap

Even as a professional I bounce my ideas off other advisers to make sure that I have covered all the bases and minimised my tax before I commit to buying an investment asset. It's always a good idea to speak to a trusted adviser before you sign on the dotted line in order to run through a number of scenarios and 'what ifs' and to ensure you have thought of every way to minimise your tax and boost your savings.

Features of each structure

Each structure has different features—making each more or less suitable in different circumstances—and different tax implications. Let's look at each in turn.

Individual name

This is where you simply put the asset in your own name. The individual's marginal tax rate applies.

The pros:

- An individual is eligible under capital gains tax law to receive a 50 per cent discount on capital gains tax (CGT) if the asset is held for at least 12 months before being sold.

- Assets can be passed on to others through a will.

- An individual can claim expenses as a tax deduction for the life of the asset (for example, interest on a loan is deductible when you are negative gearing a property).

The cons:

- The asset is taxed at the individual's marginal tax rate, which can be up to 45 per cent (the top rate of 45 per cent applies to income above $180 000 per year).

- It is not possible to distribute profit or capital gain to anyone else.

- The full amount of CGT is payable on assets sold before 12 months has elapsed from purchase.

- The individual carries the burden of any tax liabilities or losses on the asset.

- While directors of companies receive legal protection or limited liability in the event of a failed business, that protection is not afforded to individual investors, and they will be personally liable for all of their debts and liabilities.

The individual tax rates for the three financial years from 2012 to 2015 are shown in table 3.1.

Table 3.1: individual tax rates for 2012–13, 2013–14 and 2014–15

Tax bracket ($)	Tax rate (%)*	Amount of tax ($)
0–18 200	0	0
18 201 – 37 000	19	3 572
37 001 – 80 000	32.5	13 975
80 001 – 180 000	37	37 000
180 001+	45	Not applicable

*These tax rates are applicable for the 2012–13, 2013–14, 2014–15 tax years, excluding Medicare levy of 1.5 per cent.

Each person can also make use of the tax-free threshold of $18 200 per year. For example, if you are part of a couple and you have spare cash, the money should be held in the name of the person who has the lower income to ensure you are minimising the tax payable.

Joint names
Assets held jointly in the names of two or more people may be held as joint tenants or tenants in common.

Joint tenants
Under this structure, an asset is owned by two people in equal parts, and each person is liable for any debts. It's common for the family home, for instance, to be held in joint names, and documentation

can be established cheaply to ensure the surviving partner receives the family home instantly on the death of one partner. This is very important for effective estate planning. Each party pays his or her marginal tax rate on the income from the asset.

The pros:

- Each party shares the tax and ownership burden of the asset equally.

- When one party dies, the asset passes instantly to the surviving party and the asset does not become part of the estate to be distributed through the will and probate process.

The disadvantage is that you cannot choose to distribute a particular percentage of the profit or capital gain to one partner: all profits and gains are distributed 50–50. This can be a problem if one partner earns significantly more than the other and wishes to maximise his or her tax deduction and minimise his or her share of capital gains.

Tenants in common

Tenants in common is another way of two or more parties jointly owning an asset in equal or varying percentages. The parties can be individuals, companies, trusts or any other structures permitted by law. It is a structure commonly used in many cultures to establish family members financially.

Each party pays the marginal tax rate that applies to that person or entity.

The main benefit of this structure is that the income and capital can be distributed to owners according to the ownership percentages, which is handy when owners have different marginal tax rates. For example, if a husband and wife are tenants in common and one partner has a higher income, it may be appropriate to distribute most of the deductions and income to them.

The downside is that once you buy the asset in the percentages chosen at the beginning, any change will trigger capital gains tax on the percentage of the ownership that you want to change.

Partnership

A partnership is a legal arrangement in which each partner is jointly and severally liable for all debts taken on by the partners and profits are distributed through the structure to each member of the partnership. A limited partnership arrangement is a variation of this, in which each partner's liability and profit are limited to the extent of their ownership percentage. This is the more modern way of running a partnership, and it is a common structure for accounting and legal practices.

It is recommended that a written and very detailed partnership agreement be drawn up to deal with such matters as dispute resolution, dissolution of the partnership, ownership of clients in the event of dissolution, and dealing with debt and liabilities. It's best to discuss these matters, and the many other aspects of a partnership, with a specialist lawyer to ensure that your interests are properly protected and that any possibilities that could encroach upon your rights and obligations have been considered.

Each partner is taxed on income from the asset at his or her marginal tax rate.

The pros:

- The structure provides the ability to co-operate with other people to build a bigger business and operate in concert with others to share costs and obligations.
- The structure provides for the distribution of income among the partners.

The cons:

- Being jointly and severally liable means that you can be responsible for repaying a debt that you did not commit to.
- You are tied into working with one or more people and decisions have to be shared; there is therefore a high likelihood of disputes.

Company

A company is a legal structure limited by shares that is designed to carry on a business and provide protection for the entities running the company. Any type of entity, such as an individual or trust, can own shares in a company. Under Australian corporations law, the officers of the company have many obligations to run the company strictly according to the letter of the law to protect the public. The Australian Securities and Investments Commission (ASIC) regulates all corporations in Australia.

Companies are taxed at the rate of 30 per cent (this is expected to reduce to 28 per cent in future, subject to legislation). People who own a share of the company can receive franked dividends, meaning that the company pays 30 per cent tax and the individual pays the difference between the company tax rate and his or her personal rate (and is entitled to a refund if their personal tax rate is less than 30 per cent, as is the case with superannuation funds — that is, you can claim the tax credit back in your tax return).

The pros:

- Companies offer limited liability for individuals and company officers unless personal guarantees are made (which banks require in most circumstances when lending to companies).

- Small companies can receive a capital gains tax rollover, reduction or elimination if they are valued at less than $6 000 000.

The cons:

- There are regulatory and accounting costs to maintain a company.

- Directors have duties and legal obligations to regulators and shareholders.

- Unlike individuals and trusts, companies do not receive a 50 per cent reduction in capital gains tax when assets held for more than 12 months are sold.

Trust

In simple terms, a trust is a legal structure that allows the trustee to distribute income and capital to one or more beneficiaries. There are many types of trusts, but the following are the most common.

- *Discretionary trusts* (also known as family trusts) — in this type of trust, the trustee has discretion to distribute income and capital to the beneficiaries as he or she sees fit.

- *Unit trusts* — a unit trust is like a company in that the property of the trust is divided into a number of shares called units. The share of income and capital gains each beneficiary receives, and each beneficiary's voting power, is based on the number or percentage of units he or she owns.

- *Testamentary trusts* (also known as will trusts) — a testamentary trust is established on someone's death and is designed to protect and distribute tax-effective income and capital to children and other beneficiaries.

There are a number of parties to each trust, including an appointor, who appoints the trustee (and can be the trustee); a trustee, who makes the decisions in the best interests of the beneficiaries; a beneficiary or beneficiaries, the person or people for whom the trust is designed and who receive(s) the income and capital from the trust; and a settlor, the person who establishes the trust.

The appointor can appoint themselves as the trustee. A trustee can also be a beneficiary of the trust, and this is a very common arrangement.

Each trust member pays his or her marginal tax rate on the income that they receive from the trust. When an asset is sold, taxable capital gain is added to each trust member's income in the financial year in which the sale contract was entered into (*not* settled). A 50 per cent CGT discount applies if an asset was owned by the trust for more than 12 months.

The pros:

- Trustees can distribute tax-effective income to beneficiaries.

- Trusts provide some protection from legal action.

- A testamentary trust allows trustees to distribute income to minors without the minors having to pay very high rates of tax imposed on minors.

- Trusts protect the assets of beneficiaries.

- A unit trust allows two or more parties to collaborate and distribute income and capital in a tax-effective way.

The cons:

- Trusts have problems in passing on losses from negative gearing (see your accountant or financial adviser for details).

- Set-up costs paid to an accountant can be more than $1000.

- There are ongoing costs involved in administration and an accountant is needed for preparing tax returns.

- Trusts can last for only 80 years (although this seems to be long enough in most cases).

- Trusts are not eligible for the land tax threshold and must therefore pay land tax.

Superannuation

Superannuation is defined as a concessionally taxed savings environment designed to fund retirement. It is a legal tax structure that is designed with the sole purpose of funding your lifestyle after you retire.

If you earn more than $450 per month and you are aged under 75 (over 75 will be included after 1 July 2013), your employer is obliged to pay an additional 9 per cent of your salary into a superannuation fund — this is the superannuation guarantee. (The 9 per cent will rise gradually to 12 per cent over the next 10 years starting on 1 July 2013, when it increases to 9.25 per cent.) You can put more into superannuation if you wish — up to $25000. You can also put an additional $150000 per year into your super fund in the form of non-concessional (after-tax) contributions. If you prefer, instead of contributing $150000 each year for three years, you can make a lump sum payment of $450000 and average it out over three years. (In other words, you could contribute $450000 in year 1, after tax, and then make no more non-concessional contributions for the following two financial years. This is known as the bring-forward rule.)

Superannuation earnings are taxed at 15 per cent; capital gains are taxed at 15 per cent for assets held for less than 12 months and 10 per cent for assets held for longer than 12 months.

The pros:

- Super provides tax-effective savings, allowing you to reduce tax while boosting your retirement savings.

- There are plenty of available investment options in most super funds — even more with a self managed super fund.

- If you are aged over 55, you can set up a transition to retirement income stream, which allows you to boost your super contributions and reduce your tax (there's more about this in chapter 7 and chapter 14).

The cons:

- You can't access your superannuation until you meet a condition of release (for example, reaching age 55, or age 60 for people born after 1964, retirement, death, disablement, financial hardship).

- There are strict rules and regulations on how you can invest and in what assets you may invest.

- You may need a self managed super fund to invest in certain asset classes, such as direct property and direct shares.

Comparing the tax rates

Figure 3.1 shows how to choose an investment structure for receiving your income that is most likely to reduce your tax. It also illustrates how you can move money from one structure to the next in an attempt to reduce your income tax rate (remembering to take into account that to move assets from one entity to the next is a capital gains tax event — and possibly subject to stamp duty — and must be managed as such). We can see that:

- On an investment, you pay up to 45 per cent tax on assets that you hold in your own name, depending on how much you earn and, therefore, your marginal tax rate.

- You pay 30 per cent tax on assets held in a company name.

- Trusts simply distribute all their income to individual beneficiaries so marginal tax rates of up to 45 per cent are paid by individuals.

- You pay just 15 per cent tax on earnings and 10 per cent tax on capital gains on assets held for more than 12 months within superannuation

- If you are over the age of 60 and are drawing income from an account-based pension or a transition-to-retirement pension

(TRIS), you pay zero income tax, zero capital gains tax and zero earnings tax on assets held in an account-based pension (AP) within superannuation.

Based on current legislation, most people, particularly those moving closer to retirement, should be aiming to have a large portion of their investments inside the superannuation environment to reduce their tax to a legal minimum or, in many cases, eliminate it altogether.

Figure 3.1: tax rates that apply to each structure

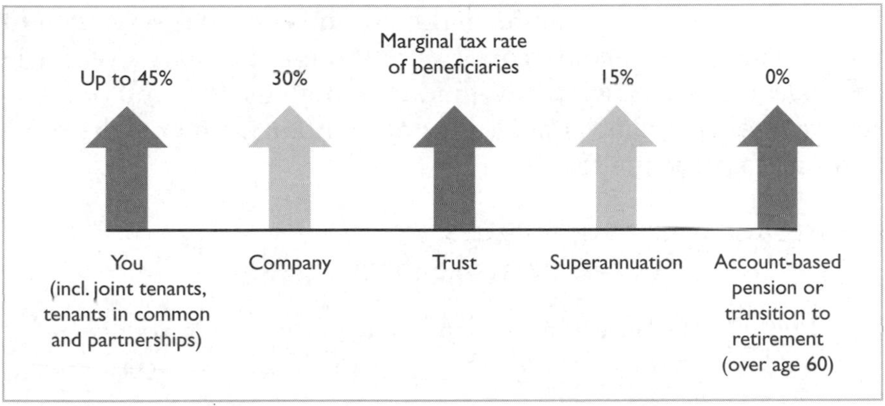

Up to 45%	30%	Marginal tax rate of beneficiaries	15%	0%
You (incl. joint tenants, tenants in common and partnerships)	Company	Trust	Superannuation	Account-based pension or transition to retirement (over age 60)

Source: Henderson Maxwell.

About capital gains tax

Any change to the ownership structure of an asset is deemed to be a capital gains tax (CGT) event. That means it's the equivalent of selling the asset or the part of the asset owned by the structure making the change. For example, if you want to move shares held in your personal name into your self managed superannuation fund, which you can do by an off-market transfer, the transfer is deemed to be a disposal for capital gains tax purposes, and you become liable for CGT.

The costs for each structure

It's simple and relatively cheap to establish any of these structures. At the time of writing, it costs nothing to put an asset in an individual name or joint names or to hold it as tenants in common. It costs about $500 to establish a trust, and about $600 to $800 to establish a company structure. Many superannuation funds are free to establish, but a self managed super fund costs about $500 to $1000 to establish, plus another $600 to $800 if you need to establish a corporate trustee. All of these structures require ongoing tax advice, tax returns, audits and other professional services and maintenance, which could cost several thousand dollars a year. The safest bet is to seek advice and a quote for both upfront and ongoing services from a financial adviser or accountant based on the most appropriate structure for you.

Five sample strategies

- Buy the next investment property in the name of your super fund (an SMSF) so when you sell it after retirement, there is no capital gains tax.

- Buy your principal residence in joint names for estate planning reasons: it does not have to go through the probate process (see chapter 13).

- Set up a trust for your small business so you can distribute the income more efficiently to multiple beneficiaries, thus reducing tax and gaining access to the 50 per cent capital gains tax discount.

- Maximise your salary sacrifice contributions to super to reduce your taxable income and boost your super.

- Leave your excess cash in the individual name of the partner on the lower income or if they are not working to reduce the tax payable on the interest, thus increasing the returns on your cash deposits.

Five sample tactics

- Set up a self managed super fund on 1 July to facilitate a property purchase.

- Ensure the contract on your house states 'joint tenants' and not 'tenants in common'. If it is currently tenants in common, have it changed (there is no stamp duty payable on this process).

- Talk to your accountant immediately about setting up a trust to run your business and distribute income more tax effectively.

- Organise a meeting with your payroll department or paymaster at work this week to maximise your salary sacrifice super contributions in order to reduce your taxable income and boost your super savings.

- Set up a bank account this week in the name of only the non-working partner to hold your excess cash. (If this cash is kept in a joint account, half of the interest earned will attract a high rate of tax if one partner works and the other doesn't.) This will make the best use of the tax-free threshold and the first $18 200 in interest will be tax-free.

KEY POINTS

- Depending on the structure under which you buy an asset you can save many thousands of dollars in tax over time.

- A different set of tax regulations applies to each investment structure.

- Make sure you understand all your options *before* you invest your hard-earned cash.

- Each structure needs to be considered in the light of your personal objectives and needs. Consider the effects of income tax, borrowing money, land tax and, importantly, capital gains tax in each structure.

- If you're unsure about the best structure for an investment, seek the advice of an accountant or financial planner who specialises in this area.

CHAPTER 4

ASSET CLASSES AND PORTFOLIO CONSTRUCTION

> Be fearful when others are greedy and greedy
> when others are fearful.
>
> *Warren Buffett, investment guru*

A multitude of investment choices is available to you. The magnitude of choice can cause what I call 'investor ineptness': a dangerous situation where you can be so confused by the sheer volume of choices that you end up doing nothing because doing something is simply too hard and time-consuming.

It's so important to bring your focus to the achievement of your needs, goals and objectives and select investments appropriate to your situation. If you already have investments, this is the time to reassess their appropriateness and perhaps make some changes.

In a recent Australian Securities Exchange (ASX) seminar I was asked to do, one of the presenters from the ASX projected a slide that showed that 98 per cent of your expected return from an investment was due to your asset allocation, not your stock selection. Ironically, much of what you read in the financial press focuses on whether Wesfarmers (which owns Coles) is a better investment than Woolworths, not whether shares are a better investment than bonds.

Each year, the best asset class returns will vary from shares to cash, or property or bonds and your allocation to each of these asset classes will have a greater effect on your returns than whether you buy Rio Tinto rather than BHP. After the GFC, many people became discouraged by the sharemarket because they had lost money, and had sold out of shares. But this was probably a time when they should have been buying because prices were so low — an idea summed up in the comment by Warren Buffett at the start of this chapter. Being contrarian, or doing the opposite of what everyone else is doing at the time, is often a successful strategy because assets are cheap when they are out of favour. However, quality is sometimes difficult to ascertain at these times.

The five asset classes

There are five main asset classes you can invest in. They encompass all of the possible investments someone can make except direct investments in a business that is not listed on a securities exchange (which is not discussed in this book). If you invest through a professional adviser or institution, they will always talk about investing and diversifying your investment among these five key asset classes to reduce risk and to optimise your investment returns over the long term.

The main asset classes in which people invest are cash, fixed interest, property, Australian shares and international shares.

Eight attributes of an investment

Before I delve into a description of the five key asset classes, I want to introduce you to the concept of the eight attributes of an investment, which will help you understand the features and benefits of each asset class. All investments have eight essential attributes (see figure 4.1, overleaf), and you need to think about these characteristics and how they interact with your personal needs, goals and objectives. The essential attributes of investments are risk, return, flexibility, volatility, liquidity, timing, cost and tax.

Figure 4.1: investment attributes

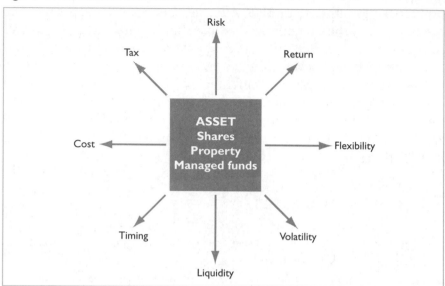

Source: Henderson Maxwell.

Risk

Risk is the potential to make a loss from an investment. The years from late 2007 until the end of 2010 saw a colossal paradigm shift in the way investors valued and assessed risk as global sharemarkets plummeted during the GFC, and the shift was perpetuated by fear. The risk profile of your portfolio of investments should suit your personal attitude towards risk. Cash and fixed interest investments, for instance, are considered to be lower risk assets than property or shares, so the more risk averse you are, the more cash and fixed interest you will want to hold. People who are not risk averse, will be happy to carry more shares, property and perhaps debt in their portfolios as they seek better returns over the long term. People are often happy to take a risk but very few will actually accept a loss. This means that people don't mind the idea of taking a risk, as their expectation is a rise in the value of an asset, but when an actual loss eventuates the reality can be a real shock.

Return

Return is the percentage or dollar value that you receive over and above your initial investment. Returns come in the form of income (dividends, interest or rent) or from capital growth (when an asset increases in value). Returns vary from asset class to asset class.

Generally speaking, the higher the risk the higher the return. But if an investment return looks too good to be true then it probably is. Make sure you research — do your due diligence on — the investments in which you want to place your hard-earned funds. History shows that an endless list of companies have made promises that were simply impossible to bring to fruition.

Importantly, think about your time frame and ensure that the types of assets you invest in are appropriate to your investment time frame. For example, many home buyers want to invest in shares to save money for their first home deposit. This is not always a viable solution because many first home buyers need their money within one to three years, and their tolerance for loss would not be high, given the importance of the house deposit. Sharemarkets can take years to recover after a fall in values, and a first home buyer would not be keen to deplete their deposit money if the sharemarket takes a dive. Shares would not be an appropriate investment for someone saving up for a house. However, if the time frame for investment was five to seven years, then investing in shares may be more appropriate, because the investment capital will have a longer time to recover from any downturns in value.

Flexibility

Flexibility is about having choice. Life is full of surprises so it's imperative that you incorporate a certain amount of flexibility into your investment strategy.

You can't sell the bathroom of an investment property to buy a caravan. So if you need lump sums, shares may be a good investment for you, because you can sell enough of the shares you own to fund your purchase. Cash is also a highly flexible asset and is ideal for funding your lifestyle assets.

Benjamin Graham's Mr Market story

In his famous book *The Intelligent Investor*, first published in 1949 and described by investment guru Warren Buffett as 'the best book about investment ever written', Benjamin Graham illustrates the irrational behaviour of the sharemarket by describing a fictional character called Mr Market.

Mr Market is an investor who offers to buy and sell your shares at a different price every day depending on his mood, which can range from very optimistic to highly pessimistic. His moods vary wildly. The price he offers can sometimes represent the exact price of a stock, but more often than not he is not a good valuer of company share prices because he is utterly irrational.

The global sharemarkets are very similar to Mr Market's moods. Share prices swing from wildly cheap to wildly expensive depending on the mood of investors, and not necessarily because investors fairly value shares every day. The sharemarket is inefficient and often provides great opportunities for savvy investors to buy good companies at low prices. The strategy, in Warren Buffett's words, is to 'be fearful when others are greedy and greedy when others are fearful'. Benjamin Graham describes this situation as 'an opportunity to buy wisely when prices fall sharply and to sell wisely when they advance a great deal'.

Volatility

Volatility is the potential of the value of your investments to rise and fall sharply in value. Investing has an intrinsic level of uncertainty as economic cycles can change quickly and catch out the unwary investor. Volatility can also provide some of the best opportunities for the purchase of new assets, when asset values are below their intrinsic values, and opportunities to sell, when assets exceed their true value. One thing you can guarantee about sharemarkets is that they never remain static: volatility is a reality of investing in any asset, except cash, whether it be shares, property or fixed interest.

To take advantage of volatility, you will need to have an understanding of asset values and a methodology for valuing investments that works for you. Historical averages can be a good benchmark for assessing the valuation of an asset. For example, the historical average price/ earnings (P/E) ratio of an Australian listed share is around 15 to 16. So if the average P/E ratio on the market is lower than this, then there may be opportunity to buy; if the average is much higher than this, then shares may well be overvalued and there may be an opportunity to sell and re-buy when asset values drop.

Liquidity

Liquidity is the ability to turn your investment into cash. Liquidity is very important during times of financial stress, such as the tech wreck of 2000–2001, the GFC (2007–2011) or the 1987 stock market crash, because when everyone wants to sell there are fewer buyers and valuations can plummet quickly. In ordinary times, a property may take about three months to sell, or liquidate, allowing four to six weeks to advertise a property for sale and approximately another four to six weeks to settle once contracts are exchanged. Shares can be sold on the internet via a broker and settlement will take place in three days, so they are far more liquid than property. In the case of cash, you can walk into a bank and withdraw your cash immediately. Cash is the most liquid asset. In the face of the GFC, liquidity became imperative as many funds were frozen and people were not allowed to withdraw their funds and many funds stopped paying dividends that investors were relying on to pay their bills, trapping the hard-earned assets of many investors.

Timing

Timing is the ability to choose the optimum time to buy or sell an asset to realise the best return in the fastest time. Timing the markets is very difficult and while many spruikers tell you they have the vital piece of software to let you know when the market bottoms, such an elixir doesn't exist, and even the world's best investors cannot pick market turnarounds. But having a good source of research helps with timing and gaining an understanding of long-term valuations so you can take advantage of opportunities when markets undervalue or overvalue an asset, or even a whole market.

You will never be able to pick the timing of a market perfectly, but remember Warren Buffett's advice: 'be fearful when others are greedy and greedy when others are fearful'.

The economic clock

The economic clock (shown in figure 4.2) provides a benchmark or rule of thumb for economic movements. Share and property markets often follow the same boom or bust cycle and the biggest money can be made when the economy is at its lowest level of production. That tends to be when interest rates are low and share and property prices are at the lower end of their valuations.

The issue, of course, is that at these times fear is also at its highest level and people tend to follow the crowd and hold back from investing, fearing that the worst is yet to come. The GFC was a great example: when the Australian sharemarket was at a low of 3100, some pundits were saying it could go to 1000. Fear was rife but that's when fortunes are made and it's why you need your own methods of valuation and understanding of share and property markets.

Figure 4.2: the economic clock

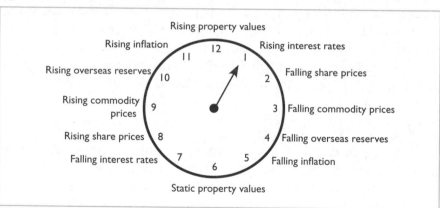

Cost

No-one likes to pay too much for anything and you always have to consider costs over and above the value of the asset that you are buying. Costs in transacting can be prohibitive when you are trading certain assets. For example, if you buy shares, you will need to consider brokerage costs; if you buy property, you will need to consider stamp duty and legal fees. Similarly, when selling assets you need to consider transaction costs and taxes such as brokerage, agents' fees, capital gains tax, and other statutory and regulatory costs.

Tax

In the purchase, sale and ongoing ownership of any asset, tax must be an immediate consideration. While you should never buy an asset primarily for tax benefits, it should certainly be a secondary consideration, and an important one. Understanding the tax ramifications and after-tax cost of an asset is essential. Many people were caught out in the collapse of Great Southern Plantations, a company that offered 100 per cent tax deductions on investment in its agricultural products. Investors did not adequately understand the integrity of the underlying investments and were swayed by the attraction of an instant tax benefit. The company went broke and took with it the investors' hard-earned funds.

Consider stamp duty, capital gains tax, depreciation and the income tax effect of your investment. You will also want to consider what name you purchase your investment in (such as an individual name or trust) and the tax consequences for that structure. Your key concern is to try to reduce the tax you pay and maximise the tax deductions you can receive to boost your after-tax earnings.

Asset classes

Now we're going to look more deeply at the asset classes and their advantages and disadvantages. The main asset classes are discussed in more detail in later chapters, with tips on how to invest wisely in each class.

Cash

While many professional investors don't classify cash as an investment, it does offer an element of security and stability within a portfolio and it can provide a regular income stream. Cash is a useful form of holding money in a bank in an at-call account, an internet high-interest account (with limited functionality) or in the form of term deposits. Cash has no chance of capital improvement, but it does offer a guaranteed income stream that is predictable and reliable. See table 4.1 (overleaf) for a summary of the attributes of cash investments.

Table 4.1: attributes of cash

Attribute	Rating
Risk	Low
Return	Low
Flexibility	High
Volatility	Low
Liquidity	High
Timing	Not relevant
Cost	Low
Tax	High

Cash is an ideal starting point for investors to put together a lump sum for investing in other assets, and it can be a fundamental tool for people saving for housing deposits or other essential lifestyle purchases. Cash is simple and easy to use. The fact that it is easy to understand and is reliable is an attraction to uneducated investors and those with a low tolerance for the rising and falling nature of shares and property.

The advantages of cash:

- provides certainty and reliability
- ideal for short-term saving
- suits investors who have a high level of risk-aversion, such as retirees or conservative investors who have a low tolerance for volatility
- provides a great start to investing
- not subject to capital gains tax.

The disadvantages of cash:

- not tax-effective, as interest is added into your taxable income
- offers no capital appreciation
- underperforms against other asset classes, such as Australian shares and property
- provides variable returns depending on the economy
- no ability to borrow money against to increase returns.

Fixed interest

Fixed-interest investments provide a regular income stream in return for an investment for a fixed period of time. Fixed-interest products can and will rise and fall in value depending on market conditions, but generally not to the same extent as shares and property, even though there have been times of rapid volatility in bonds. Table 4.2 summarises the attributes of fixed-interest investments.

Table 4.2: attributes of fixed interest

Attribute	Rating
Risk	Low
Return	Low
Flexibility	High
Volatility	Low
Liquidity	High
Timing	Low
Cost	Low
Tax	High

Types of fixed interest include:

- treasury bonds
- corporate bonds and hybrid securities
- mortgage-backed securities.

Treasury bonds

Treasury bonds are issued by governments at a set interest rate, called a coupon rate. The coupon rate is paid to you for the term of investment and at maturity you will receive your capital back, plus interest. Treasury bonds are not currently available to retail investors and are generally left to institutions to do the investing.

Many governments need to raise cash to fund public projects, particularly when they are in budget deficit because their tax revenues don't meet their expenses. Government bonds are a way for governments to effectively borrow money in return for providing you, the investor, with a fixed rate of return guaranteed by the government. The likelihood of the government defaulting on the loan is low, so they don't usually offer high coupon rates (rates of return for investors), so the return you receive on treasury bonds tends to be fairly conservative and close to the cash rate offered by the central bank (for example, the Reserve Bank of Australia, or RBA).

Treasury bonds have two distinctive forms of return: income and capital. The income tends to be regular in the form of monthly, quarterly, six-monthly or annual payments at a predetermined level or floating basis — which means that the rate rises and falls depending on the central bank's interest rate policy. If rates go up, so too does the interest rate paid. In the case of fixed-rate bonds, when interest rates go up, the interest rate stays the same for the life of the investment.

Most treasury bonds are fixed and are best bought in when interest rates are falling, because capital appreciation can be experienced. As interest rates fall, the capital value of the bond rises because your guaranteed rate of return is higher than what will be available in the marketplace. When interest rates are rising, the capital in a bond will be eroded because better rates of return can be found shortly after each issue, which creates competition among the returns available and pushes down the capital value of the bond being held.

Corporate bonds

Corporate bonds are like treasury bonds but they are issued by companies and not governments. They vary wildly in their attributes; just one example is the Commonwealth of Australia PERLS V listed corporate bond, which pays a floating dividend of around 4 per cent over the cash rate. So if the RBA cash rate is 4.5 per cent, then it will pay 8.5 per cent return (2 per cent over the best term deposit rates at the time of writing).

Some corporate bonds have fixed rates, but many provide a floating rate of interest. Like treasury bonds, the price of fixed-rate bonds decreases when interest rates are going up, and the price increases when interest rates are going down. At the end of the fixed-rate period, some corporate bonds convert to shares. These can be called hybrid securities or convertible securities. It is essential that you read the product disclosure statement (PDS) for every product you are considering buying so you understand how your product works, what happens at maturity, and how often you will be paid. It's also important to understand the income and tax consequences of the different corporate bonds as some provide franked income, that is, 30 per cent tax has been paid for you, and many provide unfranked income (taxed at your marginal tax rate).

Mortgage-backed securities

Mortgage-backed securities have been popular in the managed fund (unlisted unit trust) space for many years, as financial institutions package up large parcels of mortgages and sell them to investors. Typically they have a stable rate of return and lack volatility because most of the mortgages held are consumer home mortgages that have low default rates and interest rates several percentage points higher than the cash rate returns.

Mortgages can also be arranged directly through solicitors. That is, solicitors align a borrower with a financier and you can directly lend your money out to a mortgagee. Many of these work successfully for both parties. The investor receives both their capital and an interest-rate return and the borrower receives a loan that a bank may not provide for a variety of reasons. Needless to say, significant due diligence needs to be completed if you are considering lending money this way. It can be risky because you have only one borrower, whereas if you invest in a unit trust your risk is diversified among many mortgagees.

Different types of mortgages have different types of risk. In the years leading up to 2007 many were packaged up and sold to financial institutions under the guise of being very conservative, but the underlying mortgages were valueless because the mortgagees in America were often not working or under-employed, and never had a chance of repaying their loans. The people who received the loans became known as NINJAs (no income no job) and when a few mortgagees started defaulting, the domino effect took over and the result was the GFC. In most cases the properties financed were the only collateral that the banks had, and when the property prices fell below the value owed to the financial institutions there was no resale value in the homes for the institutions to repossess and the financial institutions simply fell over.

That being said, there are many good mortgage-backed securities offering good rates of returns on solid mortgages, but the industry will never be the same again.

The advantages of mortgage-backed securities:

- regular stable income
- better returns than cash
- low level of volatility (although history has shown periods of high volatility)
- capital preservation
- a low-risk investment.

The disadvantages of mortgage-backed securities:

- funds may not be accessible when you need them
- more volatile than cash
- corporate and mortgage bonds are only as good as the companies issuing them.

Property

You can invest in property in a number of different ways. They include:

- direct residential property — that is, buying a property
- direct commercial or industrial property
- listed property securities (Australian Real Estate Investment Trusts, or AREITs), which are listed on the Australian Securities Exchange (ASX)
- managed funds (unlisted property unit trusts).

Table 4.3 shows a summary of the attributes of property investment.

Table 4.3: attributes of property

Attribute	Rating
Risk	Medium/high
Return	Medium/high
Flexibility	Low
Volatility	Medium

Attribute	Rating
Liquidity	Low
Timing	Difficult
Cost	High
Tax	Low

Residential

Direct residential property is the most common form of property investment and it entails simply going out and buying a residential unit or house. You will have two key objectives for buying a property:

- you want the property to increase in value (capital gain)
- you want to rent the property to provide income to meet the property's expenses and give you some cash flow (rental yield).

Your property: an asset or a liability?

If your property is going up in value and it provides a solid rental return, then you have a reasonable investment. If neither of these two objectives is being met, then you have a problem. If only one objective is met, then you need to assess the viability of your investment, as it is possible that you have a liability and not an asset. We discuss property further in chapter 5.

The advantages of residential property:

- a tangible asset
- can be improved through renovation or building to increase value
- banks will often lend up to 90 per cent of the value
- Australians love property and its values held up well through the GFC
- an average return of 9.0 per cent for the past 20 years (according to research undertaken by Russell Investment to June 2012)
- may be a very tax-effective investment.

The disadvantages of residential property:

- need to save for a deposit or borrow against another property
- net yields (yield after expenses have been deducted) often significantly lower than the yield from shares
- expenses can add up (for instance, interest, council rates, maintenance, strata and management fees)
- not a liquid asset — it can take months to sell
- not a flexible asset — you cannot sell part of your investment, say a bathroom, to raise cash
- possibility of extensive and expensive damage by tenants, and the law favours tenants over property owners.

Commercial, industrial or retail property

A commercial property is simply a property that is used for commercial purposes, that is, running a business from the premises. You may have heard the expression *industrial property* and this simply refers to a type of commercial property, often in the form of a manufacturer or large storage warehouse, where factories or industrial units are needed to carry on a business. *Retail* simply refers to property whose tenants are in retail businesses such as shops and malls.

The advantages of commercial property:

- high yields and good income
- reasonable capital growth
- can be held inside your super fund while you tenant your own building, and a sale can be free of capital gains under certain conditions (CGT concessions for small business).

Tip

Small business owners receive some relief from capital gains tax on the sale of their business goodwill or active business assets. If you are in small business then some essential reading for small business owners can be found on the ATO website at www.ato.gov.au/sbconcessions.

The disadvantages of commercial property:

- expenses can be high (for instance, strata fees, sinking fund and repairs)
- can be vacant for a long time while you try to find a tenant
- can be sensitive to economic influences
- banks lend less and charge higher interest than for residential property
- financial incentives to tenants can often be 20 per cent of three to five years' rent, which may be the equivalent of giving a year's rent for free
- can be very illiquid — may be difficult to find a buyer.

Listed Australian Real Estate Investment Trusts

Listed property investment trusts are property companies that are listed on the ASX. They are specialist companies that operate businesses that buy, sell and manage commercial property. Examples include Westfield and Stockland, which own many shopping malls around Australia and the world.

Shares in Australian Real Estate Investment Trusts (AREITs) can be bought and sold on the stock exchange under three-letter codes. For example, Westfield's share code is WDC. That makes AREITs quite liquid and you do not have to invest a large amount of money in the company to own a small piece, compared with investing in residential property, where you need to save a large deposit before a bank will lend you money.

The advantages of AREITs:

- liquid (you can sell them easily on the stock exchange)
- generally offer good income yields
- well diversified across many properties, reducing specific property risk
- large sums of money not needed for you to have exposure to the sector — you can invest with just a few hundred dollars
- information on the companies is readily available.

The disadvantages of AREITs:

- heavy losses were experienced in the GFC
- banks lend less on commercial property
- very sensitive to economic conditions
- investors have no control over the investment strategy, as AREITs are internally managed.

Property managed funds

Property managed funds are unit trusts in which you can purchase units instead of shares. Like shares they also pay dividends and can distribute capital gains if a property is sold. You do not own a direct property: rather, you own units within a trust and your funds are pooled with other investors. That trust in turn owns properties that are managed by the managers of the fund for the benefit of the unit holders. Many property managed funds own AREITs and international real estate investment trusts.

Property managed funds invest both in Australia and overseas, and different funds specialise in specific global locations, such as an Australian property fund, a European property fund or even a US retail property managed fund. They fell out of favour during the GFC because many property companies' share prices were slammed by bank failures and slowing economies, which meant tenants were going broke and vacancy levels were rising.

That being said, property managed funds are a good way to gain exposure to a diversified portfolio of properties, which often reduces risk and increases income returns.

The advantages of property managed funds:

- you don't need a lot of money to get started
- generally provide good income yields
- diversified pool of assets, thus reducing specific property risk
- reasonably easy to buy and sell units.

The disadvantages of property managed funds:

- open to the whims of management, who can alter dividend policy and distribute capital gains tax when you do not expect it

- may freeze your funds, so they can be illiquid

- charge ongoing fees up to 2 per cent, and may charge entry and exit fees

- you own units in a trust not the underlying stocks

- they can take weeks to sell.

Australian shares

When talking about Australian shares, I am referring to shares in Australian companies that are listed on the Australian Securities Exchange (ASX), which means they are available for any member of the public to buy and sell. For example, BHP Billiton (ASX:BHP), Commonwealth Bank of Australia (ASX:CBA) or Telstra (ASX:TLS) are companies that are listed on the ASX.

Table 4.4 summarises the attributes of Australian shares.

Table 4.4: attributes of Australian shares

Attribute	Rating
Risk	High
Return	High
Flexibility	High
Volatility	High
Liquidity	High
Timing	Difficult to get right
Cost	Low (cheap to enter market and invest)
Tax	Low (can be very tax effective)

By using a broker that has been approved by the ASX, you can readily trade any of the 2500-odd companies listed on the ASX. You have the choice of using full-service brokers, which charge between 0.5 per cent and 1 per cent of the value of the trade (or more) or an internet broker, which will charge anything from $14.95 per trade. A full-service broker will generally give you advice on what to buy and sell, while an internet broker will provide you with limited research, so you have to make your own decisions.

Companies listing a proportion of their shares or all of their shares on the ASX give investors the ability to take a small ownership in the company. Shares do not give investors any rights to the assets of the company—for instance, you can't walk into the company and take a computer because you are a shareholder. Share ownership *does* entitle you to vote for management at annual general meetings, make decisions by poll, receive capital distributions when they become available and receive part of the company profit in the form of a dividend.

Did you know?

For information on any Australian listed assets you can log onto www.asx.com.au and download education booklets, book to attend seminars or watch webinars, and learn about the various product types that can be bought on the ASX.

Sharemarkets can be volatile and investing in shares can be an emotional rollercoaster. Share prices change daily and can fluctuate by several percentage points per day, giving you a profit or loss situation that can change rapidly. If you are investing in shares, I suggest that you take a long-term view. Most younger people or those who try their first foray into the sharemarket tend to gamble by trying to make large amounts of profit from small trades or small companies. While the impression may be that many people make millions quickly by trading—buying and selling shares regularly—very few people actually make a consistent and sustainable profit from this sort of activity.

A sophisticated investor takes a long-term view and understands the volatility of the market. In fact, when other people are selling when the market is falling, a sophisticated investor is looking to buy good companies at good prices and using the volatility to their advantage, knowing that most share prices will rebound when markets and economies stabilise. Sophisticated investors focus on good companies, as many poorly run companies can be taken over or go broke when economies slow and their risks are highlighted.

Unsophisticated investors make rash decisions and follow the crowd based on emotional and uncalculated responses to the media and friends. They tend to have no system in place and no way of knowing whether overall markets or listed companies are overpriced or underpriced. They are soon parted from their money and then change their focus to simpler asset classes, such as cash and fixed interest. Often these are the people who denigrate share investment because they were given shares in companies such as AMP that have not performed well and apply that experience to their impression of share ownership as a whole, when in fact there was no decision-making process in the ownership of those shares and no system in place to assist them in buying quality shares at the right price.

Often unsophisticated investors — I was one once, and was caught particularly during the tech wreck in 2000–01 — will gamble by buying low-valued stocks in companies that have low or no earnings. They speculate that the company share price will rise because of a trend in demographics, technology, biology or some other trend, which they think will exponentially raise the price of the share, allowing them to sell at a massive profit (known as a stag profit). This approach is common, but the ability to generate large stag profits is uncommon.

The wealthiest people I see are those who invest in blue-chip shares or property for the long term, and use their income to keep building tax-effective investments over their lifetime. Blue-chip companies are those companies that are the largest and best-performing companies listed on the ASX. Ultimately, like property, you want to own Australian shares for two reasons: so they go up in value and so they can pay you some income. If they fail these tests, then you own a liability and not an investment.

The advantages of Australian shares:

- very liquid
- offer tax-effective regular income or you can reinvest dividends to grow your shareholding
- increase in value over time (by an average of 8.5 per cent over the past 20 years)

- easy to buy and sell small parcels of good companies
- possibility of borrowing against shares to increase your shareholding (leverage)
- can be owned through a self managed super fund.

The disadvantages of Australian shares:

- can be volatile, with prices rising and falling rapidly, causing uncertainty
- prices can fluctuate on information not specifically related to the company, such as economic news
- borrowers can get a margin call, requiring them to urgently pay more to secure their holding
- dividend policies can change or cease, affecting income levels
- no strategic management control or decision-making ability
- smaller companies not very liquid
- many investors gamble with their investment and come to grief.

International shares

Like Australian shares, you can own shares in international companies that are listed in Australia or overseas. Typically, the term 'international shares' refers to companies listed on overseas sharemarkets and can be bought on those exchanges, such as the New York Stock Exchange (NYSE), the London Stock Exchange (LSE) or the German or Japanese Stock Exchanges. See table 4.5 for a summary of the attributes of international shares.

Table 4.5: attributes of international shares

Attribute	Rating
Risk	High
Return	High
Flexibility	High
Volatility	High

Attribute	Rating
Liquidity	High
Timing	Difficult
Cost	Low
Tax	Medium

An index is a basket of companies listed on a particular stock exchange and used as a benchmark measure. For example, in Australia a commonly used index is the ASX 200, made up of the top 200 stocks listed on the ASX. Here are some international sharemarket indices used to measure overseas movements in share prices:

- MSCI — Morgan Stanley Capital International, which is the index of 1500 worldwide stocks excluding developing nations

- Dow Jones Industrial Average — top 30 stocks on the NYSE

- S&P 500 — top 500 stocks on the NYSE

- FTSE 100 — top 100 stocks listed on the London Stock Exchange (pronounced 'footsie')

- Hang Seng — top 45 companies listed in China's Hong Kong

- Nikkei — top 225 stocks in the Japanese Stock Exchange

- DAX — top 30 stocks in Germany listed on the Frankfurt Stock Exchange.

The international stock exchanges have many more companies listed and available for purchase than the ASX: Australia has less than 2 per cent of the world's listed companies, so many would argue that there are opportunities overseas to purchase good companies and receive solid returns. But overseas markets are fraught with danger and even the best professional stock-pickers struggle to get it right. In fact, according to Morningstar research, most international managed funds underperform their respective indices.

One way of gaining the benefits of investing in overseas markets while reducing the risk is to buy international exchange-traded funds (ETFs). ETFs represent an index or a basket of companies internationally that you can buy on the ASX under a three-letter code just like a normal share. ETFs are available on a host of indices such as the S&P 500 (ASX:IVV); BRIC countries — Brazil, Russia, India and China (ASX:IBK); world's top 100 companies (ASX:IOO) and even China (ASX:IZZ). EFTs offer diversification, which reduces the specific company risk involved in investing overseas. It also reduces the amount of international company research required to make the right decisions.

Managed funds set out to outperform the benchmark indices they choose, but many do not achieve that for a variety of reasons. Investing through managed funds can also be expensive, because it simply costs more to run an international managed share fund.

The risks in investing in international shares are numerous and include:

- sovereign risk (the risk of investing in another country, such as Greece in recent times)
- company risk
- market risk
- currency risk.

If you are considering investing overseas make sure you understand who will be making investment choices on your behalf. For example, most fund managers closely monitor international growth in gross domestic product (GDP), interest rates and unemployment to gauge the economic health of the country or region in which they are investing. You should also try to gauge value by assessing international price/earnings (P/E) ratios and other market data indicating whether a market is overvalued or undervalued. You can crossmatch that with further data from a number of research houses that specialise in asset allocation and international investing.

Once you have compiled that information, you may be better placed to make an informed investment decision. Once a decision has been made, your investments must be very closely monitored and, as information comes to market, you can then make the decision to buy, sell or hold stock.

Did you know?

A number of websites and companies specialise in research on overseas investing may be helpful. They include:

- International Monetary Fund, www.imf.org

- FTSE All-world, www.ftseall-world.com

- Alta Vista Research, www.altavista-research.com

- PennyWise investment, www.pennywiseinvestment.com.au

- Farrelly's Handbook, www.farrelly.com.au; the handbook is available for a fee, but it is a great read for asset allocation for both domestic and international investing.

The advantages of international shares:

- access to the world's biggest and brightest companies

- growth and income

- diversification

- exposure to other currencies

- exposure to emerging nations that have high GDP growth and growing companies.

The disadvantages of international shares:

- volatility can be higher than in Australia

- people may lack an understanding of overseas markets and indices

- currency risk—the average investor is unable to hedge currency

- many companies unknown and difficult to research

- trading may be difficult from Australia, so an overseas bank account may be necessary, for example in Singapore

- brokerage may be more expensive

- ETFs have management/expense ratios (management fees to the companies that run them).

Risk assessment

Risk assessment is a fundamental process in deciding where your money should be invested and the appropriateness of the investments you have chosen. Given that investments can and will rise and fall in value, you need to understand the effect that the rise and fall will have on your lifestyle and of course your ability to sleep at night. I call it the 'eat well, sleep well theory'.

Here's the line of thinking: you may eat well if investments go up in value, but you may not sleep well if you are worrying about when they may fall in value. You may also sleep well knowing that your investments are sitting in cash, but will you eat well in retirement when you need some growth in your assets to fund a long and fruitful retirement lifestyle? The point is that your savings and investments are really there to fund a lifestyle for you now and in the future, but you need to be aware and comfortable in the asset classes in which you are investing.

Figure 4.3 illustrates the maxim of 'the higher the risk, the higher the return'. As you move up the risk–return continuum, risk increases depending on the asset class in which you invest. Cash offers a low risk, but it has low returns. Property has medium risk and medium returns, and shares can be high risk but offer high returns. More commonly a diversified investment approach across all of the asset classes is recommended to reduce risk and optimise returns based on a financial planning client's individual attitude towards risk.

Figure 4.3: risk–return continuum

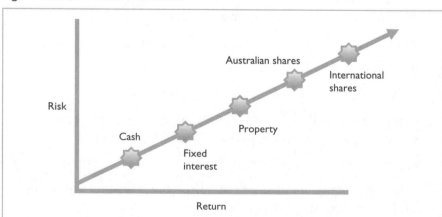

Your task as an investor is to choose a starting point and begin investing. If you have a modest income or assets, or the thought of taking a loss is simply too much to bear, then cash is a perfect place to start. Retirees typically need a low level of volatility, as they are trying to ensure that their investments can provide an income stream for the rest of their lives. So, too, if a person is saving for their first house, then taking a loss on a potential home deposit is generally too much to bear, so investing in cash makes sense.

As you build your assets, you start diversifying your investments among the various asset classes. This is designed to lower risk because the different asset classes can be negatively correlated. That means when one asset class is going up in value, another is going down; diversification smooths out your returns.

The GFC effect

Things may never be the same after the GFC. The GFC, which started in 2008, involved many failed investment companies — capped off by the ultimate risk-taker, Bernie Madoff, who lost $85 billion of his clients' money in a devious and complex Ponzi scheme (paying existing investors' dividends with funds paid in by new clients, while fraudulently spending the capital on himself). Suddenly the chance of loss became a huge reality for many investors.

Word of these events swept around the world quickly and we experienced a GFC as banks suddenly wanted to recall all the loans that they had made. Unfortunately, many of those loans were to people who could not afford to repay the funds and the security for the loans dropped in value, leaving very little for the banks to reclaim. The result was that many banks went broke and many investors went bankrupt. It also saw share and property markets plummet the world over.

For your information

To check out the current scams and banned products or licensees, go to the government's financial consumer watchdog site at www.moneysmart.gov.au, and click on the Scams tab.

The hard facts—long-term returns

A recent research paper by Russell Investments for the Australian Securities Exchange showed that long-term returns (more than 10 and 20 years) for shares and property exceeded cash returns by about 3 per cent—despite the impact of the GFC up to the end of 2009. The graph of results is shown in figure 4.4.

Figure 4.4: long-term returns of shares and property

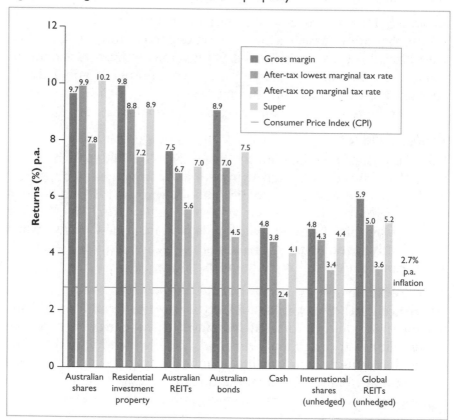

Source: Russell Investments/ASX Long-Term Investing Report.

Avoid the boom–bust mentality

When you're investing, try not to get caught up in the latest gimmick or fad of investing. A short period of inflated asset prices can be a sure-fire way to lose a lot of money quickly and get yourself into all sorts of trouble. There are untold examples of people who borrow money to jump into trends of growing asset values only to be caught out when markets inevitably fall in value and they are left owing more than they own. This behaviour can seriously stunt your personal economic growth.

Here are some examples of such boom–bust scenarios:

- *The 1987 stock market crash*, described as Black Friday, was fuelled by rampant inflation, high interest rates and a junk bond feeding frenzy that went horribly wrong when investors started finding out that their bonds were worthless.

- *Property spruikers of the 1990s*, who flew interstate investors up to Queensland to invest in properties with inflated prices above market value, left many investors holding loans worth more than the property's value for many years and well into the 2000s.

- *The 2000–01 tech wreck* (dotcom bust) saw the sharemarket listing of technology companies seeking seed capital that didn't have income, only potential income, rocket in price on speculation of one day having massive earnings, market share and sky high profits. Such prosperity never eventuated and share prices crashed.

- *The GFC*, when many banks lent money to property investors, often known as NINJAs who, by sheer volume, pushed up the values of properties across the United States. The loans were then packaged up and sold to institutions, who onsold them to private investors, governments and other institutions as collateralised debt obligations (CDOs). Those CDOs became valueless when the value of the collateral (the houses) fell below the value of the debt, and the financial institutions holding the products started falling over. The financial domino effect affected financial institutions and investors the world over and will be felt for years to come as governments grapple with the debt.

There have been many periods in history when asset values have vastly exceeded their true intrinsic value. Way back in 1637 Tulip Mania gripped Dutch investors when the prized tulip bulb price rose to 10 times the annual wage of a skilled Dutchman. When prices collapsed a short time later, one of the first boom–bust scenarios was written into history and the Dutch lamented a brutal lesson in market volatility.

Another well-known historical event in 1720 was the South Sea Bubble. Stock in the South Sea Company skyrocketed on the back of speculation (possibly fraudulent) when it was granted a monopoly right to trade in South America after it assumed a portion of England's national debt. The stock was given to politicians, allowing them to make a quick buck when the stock continued to rise on the back of unscrupulous promotion of the company. The stock eventually plummeted in price, taking the personal of wealth of many with it. Paradoxically, the company restructured and continued operating for another 100 years, although it had left thousands in financial ruin.

People rarely learn and history has a habit of repeating itself. Keep an eye out for boom–bust events and remain vigilant to the temptations of participating in a bubble. If you do find yourself in a bubble situation, make sure you take profits regularly to repay any debt, make a reasonable profit and ensure you regularly assess your worst-case scenario in order to minimise your potential loss. One methodology for success is to sell 50 per cent of your stock holding, when your capital growth exceeds your expectation, to cover your initial investment, any debt and for a bit of profit. You can repeat this process if the price keeps rising exponentially. You will never go broke making a profit — just don't get too greedy because you may be left with nothing.

Risk tolerance and asset allocation

Now that you have a basic understanding of the various asset classes available in which to invest, and some of the risks, it's time to test your own attitude towards risk. It's important to understand your risk tolerance and your partner's attitude towards risk to help you build a portfolio that is appropriate to your risk profile.

A risk profile questionnaire will help you work out your risk tolerance and then assist you in the asset allocation decisions that are so important when you are investing your retirement savings or when you are looking to establish a portfolio of investments from cash. A questionnaire is available to download from www.samhenderson .com.au.

We talked earlier about the 'eat well, sleep well theory' — risk profiling puts a formal procedure around the asset allocation decision-making process to allow you to match your investments with your attitude towards risk. You can visit www.myrisktolerance.com to complete the questionnaire and purchase the results of your risk profile.

Everyone has a different attitude towards risk and even partners in a couple will have different attitudes towards risk depending on their education, experience, time frames, family history, and a whole host of external factors that go towards developing an individual's appetite for risk. The results of the questionnaire will indicate a possible (but not certain) portfolio that may be appropriate for you. The final decision will be your own, but you should probably talk through your decision-making process with an independent financial adviser and your partner to ensure the appropriateness of your investment decisions.

KEY POINTS

- The trend in investment can be your friend, but being contrarian, or acting in the opposite direction to the trend, can be a successful investment strategy under the right circumstances.

- Make sure you understand the eight attributes of an investment before you invest: risk, return, flexibility, volatility, liquidity, timing, cost and tax.

- The economic clock can be a helpful economic forecasting guide.

- Choosing an asset class to invest in can be difficult, so start with cash and seek to diversify your investments once your confidence and your assets build.

- Consider the risk–return continuum and make sure you understand that the higher the risk, the higher the return.

- If an investment looks too good to be true, it probably is.

- Avoid the boom–bust mentality, and don't gamble with your hard-earned dollars.

- There is no such investment as a 'sure thing'.

CHAPTER 5

PROPERTY INVESTMENT IS EASY

> An investment in knowledge pays the best interest.
>
> *Benjamin Franklin, US statesman and inventor*

About 20 per cent of Australians own investment properties, and many Australians have been building their wealth through rising property prices for many years. But it's important that you get the right education before starting to invest in property: too many have been caught up in the hype of receiving their investment advice from property spruikers who have limited credentials and build their investment strategies on the premise of speculation and fast-rising prices.

Like any investment, there are no guarantees and no substitute for doing your homework, but a well-researched and planned property portfolio can set you up for life. With a growing economy and increasing wages, Australian property is well placed for continued price increases.

Why invest in property?

Property investment can be hugely rewarding, both financially and personally. Property, like shares, has risen an average of 8.5 per cent per year for the past 20 years, including the years of the GFC. If you add the benefit of gearing, coupled with the tax deductions available to negatively geared property and building depreciation, investors can in fact benefit more from property investment than any other investment.

I often say, 'Property to build wealth and shares to retire with'. The reasoning behind this comment is that property offers the ability to gear (borrow) to a higher level than shares, without the volatility of shares. Coupled with tax benefits, particularly for higher income earners, property is a great way for patient and intelligent people on a reasonable income and with an ability to save to grow their asset base.

Property offers an additional benefit through the possibility of making capital improvements to the asset in the form of renovations. If you can undertake renovations yourself, or partly do them yourself, you can save a fortune and add significant value to your property. For example, if you have $50000 and buy a portfolio of shares, there is no way to instantly improve the share portfolio and increase its value. However, if you have $50000, you can put down a 10 per cent deposit on a $350000 unit, pay stamp duty and still have some money left over for a tin of paint, some carpet and blinds. If you have some extra money saved, you can renovate the kitchen and bathroom too. All of this adds value instantly and boosts the rent your investment will attract.

The attributes of consistently rising property prices, tax incentives and the ability to obtain cheap loans have catapulted the net wealth of many property investors. Combine these attributes with the fact that property is simple, easy to understand and tangible, and you can understand why Australians are particularly enamoured of property as an investment. Owning property also brings with it a great sense of pride in the ability to drive past a physical asset that you own.

As property values increase, you also have the ability to use the equity in your property as security for further lending, thus increasing your exposure to property. Most seasoned investors do this. But the key here is increasing values and, unfortunately, like shares, property does not increase consistently over the medium term. The consistent increases are over the long term, and you need to understand that patience and persistence are often required to make a decent profit from property. So, too, you need to know when to cut your losses.

Make sure you do your research. Most of the property investment magazines include monthly data in the back pages covering past returns, vacancy rates and other property information for each area and postcode across Australia. Magazines can be a great resource for research.

Property values in different locations move at different paces for a variety of reasons, but inner-city property in all of the major cities has been consistently moving up for more than 20 years. My own strategy was to buy terraces in the inner city of Sydney, renovate them myself and then either sell or hold them depending on my situation at the time.

Buy and hold

The best thing to do with any good appreciating asset is to keep it. When many Europeans migrated to Australia after the Second World War, they bought property for themselves and for their family. They helped other family members repeat their investment strategy in subsequent generations, and they have accumulated masses of wealth through property investment as a result of not selling and allowing the assets to grow in value over time. More of us should take notice and be more community-minded in helping our families get ahead through investment.

Time is your best friend if you are a property investor. If you need money you can always take out a loan against one of the properties to provide you with liquidity. You can always borrow against a property to buy another property, and the banks will gladly lend you more money in these situations.

The only problem with never selling property is that one day you will need cash flow and, generally speaking, the purpose of accumulating wealth is to retire and live happily ever after. If you keep buying property, you will probably have a lot of equity, but you may also have a lot of debt. That debt needs to be retired and you will probably have to — one day — sell a property or two.

Or you may want the equity put into a tax-free haven, such as superannuation, so it's important to either buy your properties inside super (only possible in a self managed super fund) from the beginning, or sell property and contribute to super to create a tax-free income stream. That being said, the ability to purchase and gear property within superannuation is only a recent change to superannuation law and very few people are actually taking advantage of this yet.

Can you afford property?

The problem in Australia is that our property prices have continued to rise, and many people will never be able to afford to buy unless they receive a windfall or inheritance.

Getting the deposit together is the most important start to the property investment cycle. I often recommend a regular savings plan for saving the property purchase deposit in the form of a high-interest internet account (a kick-start account) or a regular contribution to a conservative share portfolio, if you have a savings time horizon of more than three years. Once you have actually bought property, the best thing is that it is forced savings. Since the bank direct debits your accounts, you have no choice but to prioritise the mortgage payment before every other item in your budget.

So when you are saving for a property, it's best to get into the same habit and establish a regular savings plan with a high-interest internet bank account that takes the money straight out of the bank account that receives your salary each month. Think of this as paying yourself first. In the classic book about managing your finances through a series of parables, *The Richest Man in Babylon* by George Samuel Clason, one of his first principles is to teach you to pay yourself first. It sounds so simple but most people can't grasp the concept because they say that they can't afford to save. But you can. Pay yourself some savings before you pay the phone bill, the electricity bill, the credit card and all the other monthly payments you may have. This is a really important principle.

The other option for coming up with a deposit is to get some help from family. Most banks have a specific loan product to allow parents to act as guarantor; that is, your parents provide a guarantee to the bank that if you can't afford the property, they will pay it off.

Naturally, the risks are high for the guarantor. A retired client of mine provided such a guarantee for his son. The son then lost his job and declared bankruptcy, and the bank sought a remedy from the client by making him repay the $200 000 loan. The $200 000 had to be withdrawn from his superannuation retirement fund and repaid to the bank immediately. While the bank delayed the process for some months to enable other remedies to be sought, the client had no option as his son had no other assets for the bank to repossess. Be warned, and be sure you know exactly what you are doing and what the potential consequences are if you enter into such an arrangement.

Using another property as a deposit

If you already own a property and the property has gone up in value, then the bank may lend you the money (up to 100 per cent or even more) to buy another property for investment. This is called cross-collateralisation. This means that the bank will take into account the value of both properties when it undertakes its finance assessment before making the loan.

For example, if you have bought a property worth $400 000 and have a loan of just $200 000, then you can effectively use the equity of $200 000 as a deposit for a second property by combining the values and loans of both properties. If you want to buy another $400 000 property, you could effectively use $80 000 from your equity in your original home as a 20 per cent deposit against the investment property. Your total property values would be $800 000, with a total loan of $600 000, assuming you use savings for the purchase costs, such as legal fees.

A specific bank loan product, called a line of credit, will allow you to do this efficiently and repeatedly, but the bank will need both houses as security against a possible default. You will also need to clearly assess whether you can afford to repay the debt before you undertake such a large loan. But this is a common method of gearing up (borrowing) to buy property.

Property investment costs

Once you have a deposit saved, you're well on your way to acquiring an investment property. There are, however, other costs involved in buying and owning a property and it's essential that you understand what those costs are and how they apply to you.

These costs include stamp duty (different in every state), mortgage stamp duty and mortgage establishment costs, lender's mortgage insurance (LMI) — insurance that covers the lender in the event of your defaulting on the loan (discussed on pp. 100–101) — building inspection fees, property research fees from Residex (www.residex. com.au) or RP Data (www.rpdata.com.au), conveyancing or solicitors' fees, land tax, strata fees, maintenance, rates (council, water, electricity, gas) and agents' management fees.

Stamp duty

Stamp duty is a one-off, lump-sum state-government tax that is imposed on all purchases of property. It differs from state to state depending on where you live and the purpose of the property purchase, that is, principal residence versus an investment property. In New South Wales and Queensland, the relevant department is called the Office of State Revenue; in Victoria and Tasmania it is called the State Revenue Office; in Western Australia it is called the Department of Treasury and Finance; in the Australian Capital Territory it is called the ACT Revenue Office; and in South Australia it is called RevenueSA. An online search will take you to the relevant department where you can view the stamp duty rates for your state.

Mortgage stamp duty and establishment costs

Mortgage stamp duty has been abolished Australia-wide.

Some banks charge fees to set up your mortgage for you and this is called a mortgage establishment cost. I suggest you negotiate a fee-free deal before you sign anything, as this fee is often discretionary and may be dropped.

Building inspection fees

Before you buy a property I strongly recommend you spend the money to have a building inspection carried out by a professional. A number of companies specialise in pre-purchase inspections that will give you an idea of the condition of the property, whether there are any termites or other pests, and create a list of building defects and any other building issues that you should be aware of before you buy. An inspection should cost you around $500.

The Royal Australian Institute of Architects can give you some design ideas through its referral program for a very reasonable sum. It also has a do-it-yourself fact sheet that you can download from its website (www.archicentre.com.au) for a pre-purchase inspection.

Property research fees

You can access research report about the suburb you are buying in from providers www.realestate.com.au, Residex (www.residex.com.au) or RP Data (www.rpdata.com.au). It will cost less than $100 and allow you to check the prices from recent sales. There's more about these reports in the case study on page 88.

Conveyancing or solicitors' fees

Conveyancing is the act of confirming the title of the property as it transfers from one owner to the next. It can be carried out by a specialist conveyancer or a solicitor for around $1000 to $1500. The process requires property title searches to confirm the seller is the real owner and has clear title of the property in order to sell it.

A conveyancer will also check the special conditions of the contract, including encumbrances or easements on the property, which may include drains running through your property, fences inside your boundaries or pieces of neighbours' houses hanging over or built on your land, to name just a few.

A conveyancer will also ensure all rates, fees and charges are up to date, and that the appropriate parties pay the correct fees before you buy the property. These final payments can be taken from the purchase price if there are any arrears and debts so the purchaser doesn't end up with unpaid council rates, for example.

Land tax

Land tax is an ongoing annual payment applied by state governments to the value of property, excluding your own home. It will therefore differ from state to state depending on the location of the property. My opinion is governments taxing land-holders to simply hold land is another disincentive to investing and saving for future generations. Nevertheless, investors have an imposition of land tax and it must be paid.

An online search will take you to the relevant land tax rates for your state.

Strata fees

Strata fees are payable to body corporates or owners' corporations (groups of owners that manage the maintenance of properties) of units and townhouses to maintain the common areas of property between units. Fees are usually quoted in dollar terms per quarter and can range from a few hundred dollars per quarter to many thousands per quarter, depending on the property. Strata fees are tax deductible for investment properties.

Maintenance

This is the process of keeping your property in reasonable order for someone to live in. What is required is a subjective judgement and can therefore vary from owner to owner, but I have always had a theory that I would never own a property I wouldn't live in myself. That theory has kept the properties I own in good rentable order and I never have trouble finding tenants. Vacancy periods can be expensive for property owners, so it's important to keep your property in good 'marketable' order.

Allow around $2000 to $3000 per year to maintain a house or unit. This may include a paint job, kitchen repair, hot water system, electrical issue or some plumbing. There is always something to do and an expense to meet, so it's best to expect it and have the cash flow to pay for it. Maintenance is also tax deductible for an investment property so you can claim back the expenses.

Rates

Rates include water, electricity, gas and council. Tenants are usually responsible for paying the water usage charges (but not the rates portion), electricity and gas rates, as they are consumable items under the tenancy agreement. The landlord usually pays the council rates. These are tax deductible to the owner for investment properties.

Agents' management fees

Real estate agents who manage a property for you charge an annual fee of between 4 per cent and 7 per cent of the annual rent. This amount can usually be negotiated depending on how much work is required, but often 5 per cent is the figure most agents will accept. I'd start at 4 per cent when you are negotiating.

The advantage of having an agent manage your property is that you don't have to be bothered by calls late at night to unblock drains, deal with complaints about noisy neighbours or fix leaking taps. This can be a real drag in the middle of winter and if you have no idea how to maintain a property or you don't live nearby you will have to organise tradespeople to undertake work when you are not qualified or experienced in managing tradespeople. Real estate agents usually have regular tradespeople who can attend to problems quickly and cheaply. I certainly recommend having an agent manage your property.

If you are handy and have plenty of spare time, then managing the property yourself may be a good and cheaper option, but it's not for everyone. Property management fees are tax deductible for property investors.

Depreciation

Depreciation is the ability to claim an expense on the falling value of the building on the land that you have purchased. For example, a kitchen may have a useful life of 15 years. It can be written off over 15 years, so you can claim a portion of the original value each year as the kitchen deteriorates. The real benefit arises when you add up all of the depreciable assets within the property to give you a lump sum, and each year you can write off that lump sum as a tax-deductible expense.

Interestingly, you have not actually expended the amount that you write off so we call this a 'non-cash cash-flow expense'. The benefit is the ability to claim an expense for money that you did not spend in the year that you claim it on your tax. The result is an increase in your cash flow from money that you didn't spend.

The newer the property, the higher the depreciation available, so sometimes it's best to buy a newer property to obtain a better level of depreciation. If you are looking at a new unit and an older one, once you do your cash-flow analysis, you may be better off going for the newer investment unit.

Companies specialise in providing assessments for depreciation. The professionals that work on the calculation of depreciation are called quantity surveyors. Quantity surveyors are in the business of providing 'depreciation schedules' for property owners, which show how items in their property are depreciated over time.

Most will charge around $600 to $800 per property and they often offer a guarantee that, if you can't claim back at least the amount of the cost of the depreciation schedule, then they will give you a refund. It's hard to go wrong under those circumstances and I certainly recommend you call a quantity surveyor.

What is the cash flow?

Now you know about the costs of buying a property, you can calculate the upfront and ongoing expenses to assess a property's viability for purchase. Many people don't undertake this process properly (or at all) and it can mean the difference between a long-term success and a short-term disaster — or, even worse, a long-term disaster. I see plenty of people who invest in the wrong property and hang on to it for far too long, waiting for it to rise in value, which never happens.

The 5.2 per cent rule

On the income side of the equation, we know there is just one source of income on an investment property: rent. It is often said that you should receive a weekly rent equivalent to the value of a property, less the last three zeros. For example, a property worth $400 000 should rent for $400 per week.

Using these figures, if we multiply the weekly rent by 52 we come up with the figure of $20 800: $20 800 ÷ $400 000 = 5.2 per cent. That's the rental return you will receive from your property before expenses, assuming your property is fully leased for the 12 months. If you try the calculation with other amounts, it works out the same. For example, if I own a property worth $675 000 and I rent it for $675 per week, the calculation is $675 × 52 weeks = $35 100; $35 100 ÷ $675 000 = 5.2 per cent.

The 5.2 per cent is what is known as the gross yield or the gross income for the property. If your property's gross yield is much less than 5.2 per cent then one of two things must be true:

- the property is undercapitalised — that is, it needs to be developed or improved in some way to release its true value

- the property may be overpriced.

The question is, how can you tell? The answer is simple: if you do a cash-flow analysis, it will lead you to your answer. If the property costs you too much to own, then don't buy it. However, if it is affordable and in a good growth area, then you may want to proceed with the purchase.

Investment property case study

Brad and Susan want to buy an investment property in Sydney. A renovated, two-bedroom unit is for sale in Sydney's inner west, in Leichhardt (comparable to Prahran in Melbourne or Kelvin Grove in Brisbane). It is a fast-growth area, close to the city, and the agent says it will sell for $400 000 and probably rent for $400 per week (5.2 per cent gross yield).

Brad and Susan are already paying off their own house, which they bought 10 years ago. It is worth $900 000, with $500 000 of equity and a $400 000 loan. They can use the equity in their own home to purchase the investment property.

Generally I recommend that buyers put down a 20 per cent deposit, so you can avoid having to pay for lenders' mortgage insurance (LMI). LMI insures the mortgagor if you cannot repay the loan and can cost $2000 to $4000. It does not insure you and your repayments, so I also recommend that you take out income protection or life insurance when you take out a mortgage or use any other types of debt. The lender will require you to take out LMI on any loan with less than 20 per cent deposit or equity.

Brad and Susan want to put down a 20 per cent deposit, so they need to release equity from their own house of $80 000 (20 per cent × $400 000). Let's assume they have saved some money and will use their own money to pay for the stamp duty and legal costs involved in buying the investment property that will equate to $14 767. Total upfront costs for the property will therefore be $80 000 plus $14 767 = $94 767, but $80 000 of that will be borrowed, meaning Brad and Susan only need $14 767 to buy this property. They may ask themselves why they didn't do this sooner.

The recommended property investment steps would be as follows:

Step 1. Refinance the existing principal residence to increase the loan by a further $80 000 (or even increase lending up to 80 per cent of the value of the principal residence in case you want to purchase more property). This is best done through a line of credit, which allows for two sub-accounts (one for the existing residence and one for the new investment purchase). The sub-accounts will separate the non-deductible debt from the tax-deductible debt: the debt against the investment property, including the $80 000 deposit, will be fully tax deductible. It is recommended that the debt against the investment property be taken on an interest-only basis for five years to increase Brad and Susan's cash flow and allow them to buy further properties sooner.

Step 2. Obtain a research report from www.realestate.com.au, Residex or RP Data (which will cost less than $100) on the area of Leichhardt. Check and compare all recent sales to make sure that the purchase price is reasonable and the rent is realistic.

Step 3. Order a building and pest inspection to ascertain the state of the building, the costs of any repairs, the timing required for any repairs and to ensure there are no termites or other pest infestations.

Step 4. Order, from the strata managing agent, a copy of the past minutes of the meetings of the body corporate to ensure that there is no intention to increase expenses in the sinking fund or increase strata fees to pay for unexpected items. This will also give you a good understanding of the operations of the body corporate and who is involved, and to see if there are any issues that you should be aware of.

Step 5. Assess the upfront affordability of the property, as shown in table 5.1.

Table 5.1: calculation of upfront property purchase expenses

Purchase expenses	Value ($)
Price	400 000
Deposit	80 000
Stamp duty and costs	14 767
Amount borrowed, including borrowing against principal residence	400 000
Total costs required upfront	14 767

Step 6. Assess ongoing cash flow from the property, as shown in table 5.2.

Table 5.2: calculation of ongoing cash flow

Income	Value ($)
Rent @ $400 per week	20 800
Total income (A)	20 800
Less expenses:	
Interest on $400 000 @ 7%	28 000
Strata fees at $600 per quarter	2 400
Agents' fees	1 456
Depreciation (C)	1 233
Maintenance	2 000
Rates	1 200
Total expenses (B)	36 289 pa
Net income (before tax) (A – B)	–15 489
Net income after depreciation is subtracted (A – B + C)	–14 256

Table 5.2 shows that this property in Leichhardt will cost Brad and Susan $15 489 per year—which equates to $289 per week—to own. That means this property is cash-flow negative and so Brad and Susan would be negative gearing the property: that means the after-tax cash flow is negative and they have borrowed money to buy the house. If the cash flow after tax is positive, then it is referred to as positive gearing or positive cash flow.

There is only one reason that they would want to own this house. That reason is that it *must* go up in value by at least 3.87 per cent per year ($15 489 ÷ $400 000 = 3.87 per cent), otherwise there is no point in owning it. By researching house price growth in the area of Leichhardt (on www.realestate.com.au), I can see that the average price increase has been 5.2 per cent on units and 7.2 per cent on houses, and it seems reasonable to assume that this will continue if all other economic conditions remain constant.

As shown in table 5.2, the depreciation amount of $1233 is not an actual cash-flow expense, so the annual cash-flow requirement is reduced by $1233 per year.

Further, as the investment is creating a loss, the loss amount is 100 per cent tax deductible under Australian taxation law, which means that 100 per cent of the loss amount for each individual is deducted from their total income and their normal marginal tax rates then apply. We have assumed the property is in joint names and each will deduct 50 per cent of the total loss (50 per cent × $15 489 = $7744.50). Brad is on a 37 per cent marginal tax rate, earning $100 000 per year after any other deductions and Susan works part time earning $45 000 per year, and is on a 32.5 per cent marginal tax rate. In Brad's case, $7744.50 is deducted from his taxable income and he is taxed on an income of $92 255.50 ($100 000 – $7744.50), thus reducing his tax payable and providing him with a tax rebate if he paid tax from his employer on a salary of $100 000. Another way to think of it is that Brad gets a 37 per cent discount on his loss and Susan obtains a 32.5 per cent discount on her loss. This is shown in table 5.3.

Table 5.3: tax summaries

Item	Cost ($)
Brad's tax summary	
Brad's income from work	100 000.00
100% tax deduction from the loss on the investment property	7744.50
Brad's taxable income	92 255.50
Susan's tax summary	
Susan's income from work	45 000.00
100% tax deduction from the loss on the investment property	7744.50
Susan's taxable income	37 255.50

The total cost of the property after tax falls from $15 489 per year to just $10 296 per year, a saving of $5193, because of the combined tax deductions available to the couple. This means the total actual cost per week after tax deductions are taken into consideration is $196, as shown in table 5.4 (overleaf).

Table 5.4: calculation of actual cost per week

Item	Cost ($)
Actual cost per week ($15 489 ÷ 52) before tax	298 per week
Income loss split 50/50 because the property is owned in joint names:	
Loss to Brad (50% × $298)	149
Less 37% tax deduction for half of loss (joint names)	55
Actual loss to Brad ($149–$55)	**94**
Loss to Susan	149
Less 32.5% tax deduction	48
Actual loss to Susan after tax deduction	**102**
Total actual after-tax cost (combined)	**196 per week**

Who pays for your investment property?

Figure 5.1 shows who pays for your investment property. According to figure 5.1, 66.66 per cent is paid by the tenant; 16.66 per cent is paid by the taxman via tax deductions; and the remaining 16.66 per cent is paid by you. While the percentages will vary from property to property and the diagram serves simply as a benchmarking and illustration tool, the essential rule of thumb illustrated by this diagram is that you pay a minority (just 16.66 per cent in this case) of the cost of the property, assuming you borrow 100 per cent of the value of the property.

Figure 5.1: who pays for your investment property?

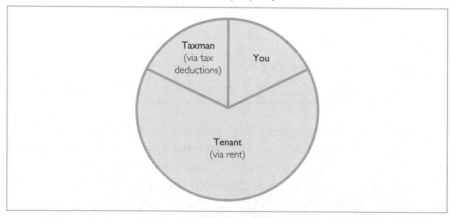

The key point is that you are using someone else's money to buy a property and using another person's money to make the repayments.

An example of the rule of thumb

If you borrow 100 per cent of the value of a property worth $400 000 (assuming you pay for the stamp duty and legals with your own money) using your existing property as collateral for the bank loan, your interest at 7 per cent will be $28 000 per year. If we include costs of $3000 per year to cover rates, maintenance and strata fees, the total costs for the property are $31 000 per year.

Assuming the property has a 5.2 per cent gross income yield ($400 000 minus the last three zeros equals $400 weekly rent), you would receive $400 per week from the property, which equals $20 800 per year (assuming a 52-week rental period and zero vacancy). These calculations are summarised in table 5.5.

Table 5 5 investment costs

Item	Cost ($)
Cost of property	400 000
Interest at 7%	28 000
Maintenance and rates	3 000
Total costs	31 000
Income (rent)	20 800 (67%)
Loss	10 200
Claimed tax at 45%	4 590 (15%)
Total cost to investor	5 610 (18% of total cost)

The tenant pays 67 per cent, the taxman pays 15 per cent and you pay just 18 per cent of the total annual costs. Assuming the property is increasing in value by more than 1.4 per cent per year ($5610 ÷ $400 000 = 1.4%) this is a viable long-term investment.

In this example, if you were on a 32.5 per cent tax rate, then your claimable amount would drop to $3315 or 10.7 per cent of total costs.

The amount that you would have to pay out of your pocket would increase to $6885 or 22.2 per cent of total costs.

How is my cash affected?

And also, how do I claim my tax deduction and when can I get my claimable amount back? These are very pertinent questions that you must ask when undertaking your research for a property. Your cash flow will be negatively affected if you are making a loss on the property, and despite the fact that you may be eligible for a tax deduction, you will probably need to fund the full loss with your after-tax income. The tax deduction will ordinarily come back to you when you do your tax return.

If the ATO owes you money, then it's best to do your tax return immediately after the end of the financial year. If you owe the tax office money, then it's best for your cash flow to do your tax return as late as possible before incurring a penalty.

You may even be allowed to pre-pay your interest for the coming year on 30 June (of any financial year) and then do your tax return the next day (1 July) to claim back the interest pre-payment. This also improves cash flow, but you must have the money for the interest payment available in a cash account or similar liquid form.

If you do not have enough cash flow to meet the expenses of the property, then you can apply for a *tax variation* through the ATO; that will result in your salary increasing, because a lower tax rate will be applied by your employer. It's important to seek tax advice on this matter as the added cash flow can really help, especially when interest rates are rising: talk to your tax adviser for information on tax variation.

Tip

The ATO provides a multitude of information on rental properties. Go to the ATO website (www.ato.gov.au) and type 'residential rental property' into the search engine in the top right corner for more information. The ATO regularly runs webinars for property investors.

Property speculation and development

Short-term property speculation is best left to the developers, but if that's what you want to do, then make sure you understand how property taxes, capital gains tax, income tax and other transaction costs such as agents' fees and legal costs will affect your final outcome.

During the GFC this area was one of the hardest hit, so be aware, get educated and make sure you understand the true costs of a property development and sale. Many so-called experts have gone bust trying to make what seems like a quick dollar only to be shot down by holding costs (such as interest), development risk (council rezoning, funding, neighbours' objections) and regulatory costs (capital gains tax, income tax, land tax).

Warnings and risks

Every investment has risks. Your job is to do your research and make sure you are confident that you will receive the capital growth that you anticipate from the property. Capital growth is always inconsistent and prices may also fall. The risk is that the value does not increase (or decreases) and you keep losing money on the property—that simply does not make sense.

The worst thing that can happen is if property prices decrease and you end up owing more than you own. This is the situation many Americans ended up in during the GFC, and in fact was one of the catalysts for the GFC.

While working out cash-flow scenarios is sensible, and looking at past research is very helpful, economics can throw unexpected curve balls. Always make sure you can afford your decision to invest into property or any other asset and make sure you take the necessary precautions to protect yourself against the worst-case scenarios, such as recessions (by ensuring you have spare cash and job security), or health issues such as death, disability and disablement (by using insurance products).

You can reduce risk by buying in the best areas where there is consistent demand for both sales and rent so your property is liquid, if you need to sell it, and easily rentable if your tenant leaves.

Interest rates can go up and lending can become very expensive very quickly. Always make sure you allow for 2 per cent or more on top of your calculations for interest rates to ensure you can afford the loan for the long term, not just for today's economic conditions.

While properties are not particularly volatile, they can be inflexible and illiquid. You can't simply sell part of a property to release equity to create spare cash or buy something, but you can increase or dip into your line of credit to increase your flexibility. By comparison, share ownership allows both more flexibility and liquidity: you can sell some of your shares to raise funds very quickly when needed. Timing property markets can be difficult and the cost of both purchasing and maintaining property can be high, so some savings planning will be needed.

Properties can be a very tax-effective investment as we've seen in the previous example. Look back to table 4.3 (see p. 60) for a summary of the attributes of property.

Property is not an automatic win

Increases in property values never occur at a steady rate and in fact, values can fall to a point where people can owe more than they own. This is a very dangerous situation to get yourself into, so undertaking thorough research is imperative for the property decision-making process. Properties in the wrong area can also stay at the same value for many years, producing negative cash flow, and negating the investment purpose of negative gearing. Risk management is fundamental and when done properly you can profit very handsomely. When executed incorrectly it can be very costly. Property is not automatically a winning investment.

If you sell a property, you will also need to take into account your costs and capital gains situation as well as other compliance costs, such as accounting and land tax, when undertaking all of these calculations.

What's wrong with property?

One of the key problems with property if you are an average wage earner, or even an above average earner, is that at some time you will hit your limit on how much you can borrow and how much you can comfortably pay back.

In addition, carrying a lot of debt and a few properties can create stress and your investments can become a financial and mental burden: be careful not to binge on debt and be too greedy. It may be your downfall when the economy slows.

In theory, you are investing for the bad times, not the good. The good times look after themselves, but you have to look after the bad times and it can be difficult to always do your homework and make sure you can afford your property purchases. If you add the responsibilities of managing and maintaining your properties to the mix, property ownership can be a real pain. I often have clients coming to me in retirement wanting to sell all their properties to alleviate the pressure of holding them. They also want to put the money into a tax-free environment inside superannuation, which wasn't available to them when they first bought. Super is a great way to buy property, but it's only available through a self managed super fund.

Property versus shares

Property is a good tool for building wealth because you can effectively borrow someone else's money (the bank's) to buy the property and then have someone else (the tenant) pay it off for you. This only makes sense when you have a reasonable income to meet the difference between the expenses and the rental income. So retirement, or the years just before retirement, are not necessarily the best time to gear into property investment through super, because you need free cash flow to pay pensions in retirement unless you have the ability to repay the debt.

The best friend of a property investor is time: when people retire they need an income to support their lifestyle and they no longer have the time to let the property increase in value and pay down the debt. When you take into account property rental yields, council rates, water rates, maintenance, agents' management fees and all the other costs of maintaining a property, often it makes little sense to own investment property in retirement. Add the burden of interest on an investment property loan and the equation rarely makes sense unless you have a very positive cash flow property or have nearly paid off the property.

Shares and cash or fixed interest often make a better investment for retirees because the yield is higher after expenses (there are few expenses with share ownership and dividends can offer tax refunds, increasing the income yield) and you can specifically pick stocks that have high tax-effective income.

That being said, I have seen clients with good commercial properties that have been paid off producing excellent income for retirement. Commercial properties typically return 6 per cent to 10 per cent per year.

The key here is to do your homework and stay focused not on the actual investment but on your life goals and financial objectives. If you need a certain income from your investments, then it may make sense to sell a property and put the money into superannuation where it will be tax free in retirement and produce a good income to sustain your lifestyle. Thus, property works well for creating wealth, and shares and their low ongoing costs and good income work well for wealth management.

Other things to consider

Before you buy a property, or any investment, you should give a great deal of thought to what name (entity) you want to buy the asset in. As I said in chapter 3, 'Begin with the end in mind'. For example, will you buy the asset in your own name, as joint tenants, as tenants in common, as a trust, as a company, as a partnership, within your super fund, or in someone else's name such as a spouse or sibling.

As discussed in chapter 3, the structure in which you buy will affect your tax situation. Think about the end goal, which may be selling the property, and that means thinking about the income and capital gains tax consequences of the sale before you buy. You will also need to consider possible scenarios in which you may need to sell early, such as death, disablement, fire, divorce, insolvency or legal proceedings.

Other issues to be considered in property investment include negative gearing, positive gearing, loan-to-value ratios, lenders' mortgage insurance, interest only or principal and interest, vacancy rates and costs, capital improvements and capital gains tax.

Negative gearing

If you are borrowing to buy property, the rent will meet a significant portion of the interest payable on the loan and the difference will be tax deductible. This is known as negative gearing. If you have a high income, then the tax deduction provides a valuable saving on your annual tax.

Like any investment, you want your property to be a good investment and go up in value. If you own a poorly performing property that has not gone up in value (and is unlikely to) and it is negatively geared, then your investment lacks integrity and is not realising your desired objective, which is for the property to increase in value so it will increase your wealth. In this case, the property should be sold.

In the examples above, if you buy a property worth $400 000 and rent it for $400 per week ($20 800 per year) and your costs are $31 000 per year, then this property is *negatively geared*: *negative* because the cash flow is negative (it's costing you $10 200 per year), *geared* because you have borrowed money (geared the property).

Given the fact that the property is costing you $10 200 per year, it needs to be increasing in value to be a good investment. While the $10 200 is claimable as a tax deduction, if you are in the 32.5 per cent tax bracket, you receive a tax deduction of only $3315 per year and the property will still cost you $6685 per year ($129 per week).

However, people buy property because it has increased in value by an average of 9.0 per cent per year for the past 20 years (according to research undertaken by Russell Investments, June 2012). If we apply that to the example above, the property of $400 000 is increasing in value by $34 000 per year and it's costing you just $6685 per year. You are therefore $27 315 per year better off. It is extremely difficult for most people to save this sort of money from their after-tax incomes when they take into account the cost of living in the 21st century, not to mention the discipline required to actually put money aside and not touch it — hence the popularity of negative gearing for many Australians to build their wealth.

Positive gearing

Positive gearing is where you borrow money against a property, and the interest and other expenses are met by the rent. Simply, the *positive* portion of the expression means that the property is cash-flow positive: that means you are making money in a cash-flow sense. The *gearing* portion of the expression means that you are borrowing money. Simply, you borrow to buy an investment property and it earns you more than it costs you. Some commercial and many regional residential properties are positively geared. Often positively geared properties do not increase in value as much as negatively geared properties, but that generalisation may well relate to city property versus country property. Of course, the ideal situation is to have a positively geared property that goes up in value. This is hard to find but not impossible.

Mining towns with low availability of properties and a high demand for living quarters are a good example of such a situation, but prices have probably already moved, so be careful when doing your research.

For example, if a property purchased for $400 000 in a small mining town of New South Wales is rented to miners at $750 per week, the annual rent equates to $30 000 per year. Assuming the investor borrowed 100 per cent of the purchase price, the interest rate was 7 per cent, and expenses were $1000, giving a total expenses cost of $29 000, then the investor would still be ahead by $1000 per year. This is called positive gearing.

Further, because the property is positively geared, the investor will pay their highest marginal tax rate on the $1000. That is, 0 per cent if you earn less than $18 200; 19 per cent tax if you earn less than $37 000; 32.5 per cent tax if you earn less than $80 000, 37 per cent if you earn less than $180 000 and 45 per cent if you earn more than $180 000 per year.

For retirees or those on low tax rates, positively geared property makes sense.

Loan-to-value ratio

A loan-to-value ratio (LVR) is simply the total amount of money lent to buy or develop the property divided by the total value of the property (as assessed by the bank). For example, if you borrow $320 000 on a $400 000 property, then your LVR will be $320 000 ÷ $400 000 = 80 per cent. It is always a good idea to put up a deposit for a property so you have less to pay off over time.

Lenders' mortgage insurance

You may hear bankers talking about lenders' mortgage insurance (LMI). LMI is insurance that you pay for to protect the bank if you default on the loan. It is *not* insurance that covers you for not repaying the loan.

As a rule of thumb, a lender will require you to pay LMI when the loan-to-value ratio of your purchase is greater than 80 per cent. For example, if you buy your first home or investment property and put down a deposit of just 10 per cent, then the bank will require you to pay lenders' mortgage insurance, which could be another $3500 on a $400 000 loan. It's important to factor this into your research when you are looking for a property to purchase.

See chapter 10 for information about other types of insurance.

Interest only or principal and interest

Generally speaking, for high-income earners it is often best to pay interest only on your investment properties to free up your cash flow to buy more property, which maximises your tax deduction and your exposure to property as it increases in value — assuming it does go up in value.

If you are on a lower income, interest only also works well to free up your cash flow to cover the costs of living.

But if you can afford to, it's always best to repay the loan, too, because when it comes to retirement you don't have to meet the cost of the loan, which means that you do not have to sell the property and you can live off the rent. So principal and interest makes sense if you can afford it, but always try to pay down the loan on your principal place of residence first to eliminate your non-tax-deductible debt.

Vacancy rates and costs

Vacancy rates are the percentage of rental properties that are available for rent but without tenants. If you are looking at purchasing an investment property it is always helpful to know the vacancy rates in a state and in a specific area to assess the potential for you to actually find a tenant for your property.

The mainstream property investment magazines print the latest data for vacancy rates on the back pages of their magazines. The Property Council of Australia or your state Real Estate Institute (for example, REINSW) also offer reports for you to purchase, but you may have to join as a member to obtain the reports.

If vacancy rates are high, then you will have less chance of finding a quality tenant, and there will be little pressure on rental income to improve, as demand will be low. If vacancy rates are low, as they are at present owing to a housing shortage, then rental income is likely to rise steadily and finding quality tenants should not be a problem.

Three to 4 per cent is considered a low vacancy rate and post-GFC rates in Sydney, for example, were well below that level, indicating upward pressure on rental yield, which is positive for investors.

Capital improvements

One of the best things about property is that you can renovate the property and increase its value. If you do the work yourself, and do a good job, then you can save on the improvement cost and profit when you sell it or rent it for more than it was worth when you first bought it.

If this is your plan when you buy an investment property, it's very important that you cost the renovations realistically. Renovations can be a disaster if you attempt them without the requisite skills, and finding a buyer for a property that has been ruined by an inexperienced renovator may be difficult.

For most of my twenties I bought and renovated properties around Sydney's inner west, North Shore and northern beaches. I can assure you that it is hard work, and gaining the skills can be time-consuming. Lessons learnt can be expensive, as I found out by trying to cut corners sanding or tiling floors when I didn't have the skills. I should have paid a professional to sand my floors in one house rather than having a floor that looked like it was pocked with moon craters. Know your limits.

That being said, I bought my first house in Wilson Street, Newtown, for $155 000 with a $15 000 deposit and rented it for $280 per week after painting, carpeting, replacing the blinds and installing a new kitchen and bathroom.

Capital gains tax

The final thing you will want to know about property is capital gains tax (CGT). This is not a separate tax, it is part of your normal income tax. So if you make a gain in a particular financial year, the taxable gain is added to your taxable income in that financial year.

CGT applies to all assets purchased after 21 September 1985 and subsequently sold. You have to realise the gain to pay CGT, which means you have to sell or transfer the asset to another name. Both activities are triggers of CGT. If you don't sell (or transfer) an asset, you do not pay capital gains tax.

If an asset has been owned for more than 12 months then a 50 per cent CGT discount applies to the sale if the asset was in an individual name, as tenants in common, as joint tenants or in a trust (super funds receive a 33 per cent discount). The discount does not apply to assets held in a company name and companies therefore pay CGT at the company tax rate (currently 30 per cent). There is also an outdated indexing method that helps reduce CGT, but I have never seen it outpace the 50 per cent discount method.

Here is an example of how CGT works. An investor purchases a property in April 1992 for $200 000. The property is sold in 2011 for $600 000 and is subject to CGT. The CGT calculation is shown in table 5.6.

Table 5.6: calculating CGT

Item	Cost ($)
Purchase price	200 000
Sale price	600 000
Capital gain	400 000
50% discount	200 000 taxable gain

If the asset is owned by just one person, then $200 000 is added to their taxable income in the financial year that contracts are exchanged on the property, and the normal tax rates apply. For example, for the property shown in table 5.6, if this person was earning $60 000 per year then the $200 000 taxable gain is added to their taxable income for that financial year. In the 2014 financial year, their tax would be $90 546 (excluding Medicare levy) and they would take home $569 454 excluding the real estate agency and legal costs, as shown in table 5.7 (overleaf).

Table 5.7: calculating net proceeds from the sale

Item	Cost ($)
Taxable income	260 000
Tax payable (A)	90 546
Normal income (B)	60 000
Proceeds from house (C)	600 000
Less tax	90 546
Net proceeds after tax (B + C − A)	569 454

If the property is owned in joint names or as tenants in common, then the taxable gain amount would be split between the owners, depending on what percentage of the property they own. If a property is owned by a couple as joint tenants, then the taxable gain is split 50/50 between the two owners; in this example, the taxable gain of $200 000 is split 50/50 between the two owners, so $100 000 is added to each owner's taxable income for that financial year.

When to sell and reducing CGT

Based on the distribution of capital gains tax, the timing of the property sale is very important. It is always best to sell a property when your taxable income is at its lowest. That may occur after retirement or in a year that you are not working for some reason.

Another way to reduce your taxable income is to make sure that, in the year in which you are selling your property, you maximise your concessional superannuation contributions (15 per cent tax is applied and the amount you can contribute is limited to $25 000 per year). This can be done through salary sacrifice arrangements at work or if you are self-employed by simply making the contributions to your super fund.

For your information

Make sure you seek advice if you are planning to sell a property, or take a look at the video on www.samhenderson.com.au on how to reduce your CGT.

CGT does not apply to assets inside superannuation for superannuants who are in account-based pension mode—that is, drawing money from their super. If you buy a property inside your self managed super fund and sell it after you retire, then you will not pay CGT. Always give consideration to the name in which you buy your investment assets.

CGT and your principal residence

Your principal residence is free from capital gains tax. Under tax law you are allowed one principal residence; any other residence, such as an investment property or holiday house, will be subject to CGT when you sell it.

If you rent your house for a period of time, then the calculation for capital gains tax is pro-rated for the number of days that it was your principal residence versus the number of days it was an investment property. So, too, if you move into an investment property for a period of time and it becomes your principal residence, then the time spent in the house or unit will be deemed to be CGT-free on a pro-rata basis.

It is always recommended that if you live partially in one property you should obtain a valuation from a licensed professional valuer, not a real estate agent, to ascertain the value at the time you moved in or moved out to assist with calculating your cost base for capital gains tax purposes.

Your cost base is the value of the property plus the cost of any capital improvements you have made to the property. For example, if you paid $300 000 for a property and spent $50 000 on a renovation, then your cost base will be $350 000. Anything you make on the sale of the property above the $350 000 will attract CGT.

I have had many clients say that a friend told them that they could live in a house for a period of six to 12 months and it would not be subject to capital gains tax. No such law exists. However, there is a law ('the six-year rule'—section 118-145 of ITAA 97) that allows you to move out of your principal residence for up to six years and rent it out. If the house is sold, it will remain free of CGT within the six-year period. This law is designed for people who move overseas or interstate because of work and have to rent, or even buy somewhere else. If you buy somewhere else, only one house can be your principal residence and free of CGT.

I would advise you to seek a professional opinion if you have any questions surrounding CGT issues because there is a plethora of case law outlining exemptions and situations where homeowners were deemed to have a rental property as their principal residence, therefore negating the application of the six-year rule.

Be careful when attempting to calculate your CGT liability and seek professional advice from a licensed and experienced adviser if you need help.

Return on equity

The real secret to property investment — any investment for that matter — is to consider the factors affecting your return on equity. Your return on equity is your actual return on the money that you put into the investment. Here is a simple example. I put a deposit down on my first property in 1994 of $15 000 and spent $30 000 renovating the property over five years. The property value increased from $155 000 to $360 000 over that period, and I sold the property in the late 1990s.

The total amount of equity I put into the property was $45 000 ($15 000 deposit and $30 000 in renovations) but I sold the property for a profit of $175 000 ($360 000 − $155 000 − $30 000 in renovations and other costs). The return on my equity was $175 000 ÷ $45 000 = 388 per cent over five years or an average of 77.6 per cent per year on my equity, representing my internal rate of return. That was a good investment.

A more complicated and up-to-date example could look like this: I buy a two-bedroom apartment by the beach near Sydney today for $700 000, put down a 10 per cent deposit and rent it for $700 per week. I expect a property price growth of 8.5 per cent per year. With a loan of $630 000 at 7 per cent interest and stamp duty and legal costs of $30 000, my equity would be $100 000 ($70 000 deposit plus $30 000 in costs). Interest on $630 000 at 7 per cent would be $44 100 per year plus strata fees, rates and costs of around $3000 per year, so the unit would cost me $47 100 per year to maintain.

Rent would be $700 per week and assuming a 52-week rental cycle and full occupation for the period, which is ambitious, I can expect a total annual rental return of $36 400 per year. If the property increases in value by 8.5 per cent per year then it is increasing by $59 500 in the first year and then the increase is compounded thereafter. So my total return in the first year will be $36 400 + $59 500 = $95 900.

If I deduct my annual costs from this figure, I arrive at a net increase of $48 800 ($95 900 – $47 100) in the first year. Think how long it would take you to save that sort of money each year — that's almost $1000 per week.

My return on equity would be $48 800 ÷ $100 000 = 48.8 per cent.

This is a good result, but remember property never increases consistently at 8.5 per cent per year, or any other percentage level. It rises and falls in bursts and the key to a successful experience is time and sitting through the various cycles.

Not only would I have a high return on equity but I would also be able to claim a tax deduction for the difference between the rent and the annual costs. So I must be able to afford to pay the difference, which, in cash-flow terms, would equate to $10 700 per year. This cash-flow loss is 100 per cent tax deductible. That is, 100 per cent of the $10 700 is used to reduce my taxable income for the financial year.

Ten steps to success

There is no shortage of people who are only too willing to sell you property, finance or any other services associated with property investment, so you need to decide what you want before you embark on your project. You will also need to be well researched so you can identify value, potential and opportunity when you see it.

There are so many options in property that it can be overwhelming; devising a process methodology will overcome many of the pitfalls associated with buying. The following 10-step process will provide such a methodology for you and serve to incorporate all of your objectives, requirements, restrictions, costs, research and options so you can make an informed decision.

The following 10 steps are a sure-fire way to better property investment:

- List your objectives and goals.
- Compile a list of costs.
- Set your budget and what you can afford.
- Obtain finance.
- Undertake research for the desired areas within your budget.

- Start looking for the right property.
- Research and run a project assessment sheet.
- Negotiate on the property.
- Time to buy.
- Settlement and project commencement.

Five sample strategies

- Start saving now to achieve a deposit of $30 000 by December next year.
- Research areas to buy property.
- Obtain a depreciation schedule for investment properties.
- Calculate your after-tax cash flow as part of your planning to buy a property.
- Obtain finance approval *before* you start looking for a property.

Five sample tactics

- Set up a kick-start internet high-interest savings account and put $500 per week into the account.
- Have a look at the Residex, RP Data or Australian Property Monitors website for research on areas where you would consider buying a property.
- Contact a company that specialises in depreciation schedules such as Depro, Depreciator.com.au or Washington Brown to obtain an estimate for a depreciation schedule.
- Do a budget calculation on the after-tax cash flow of the property you are about to buy before you buy it to make sure you can afford it.
- Call a broker or your bank to obtain a quote on finance and put your application through before you start looking for a property.

KEY POINTS

- Property is not a guaranteed way to make money, but with the right education and research, you will be better prepared and have a greater chance of success.

- Never sell property unless you have to or you can make more money elsewhere.

- Always think about the most tax-effective name in which to buy your investment property and, importantly, think about the effect of capital gains tax before you purchase.

- Make sure you understand your cash flow intimately for every property investment, and allow for contingencies such as vacancies and damage by tenants.

- Understand the effects of tax and the possibility of changes to tax laws — the investment must stack up with or without the tax benefits.

CHAPTER 6

SHARES FOR INTELLIGENT INVESTORS

> We can go further and assert that in an astonishingly large proportion of the trading in common stocks, those engaged therein don't appear to know — in polite terms — one part of their anatomy from the other.
>
> *Benjamin Graham, author of* The Intelligent Investor

Shares have proved to be a solid investment over the years and historically have always outperformed cash over the long term. Much like property, you will want to own shares for two key reasons: they increase in value and they provide income — which in the case of shares is called a dividend.

While shares have the attraction of offering a (potentially) high return, like all such investments they also carry a high risk. Look back at figure 4.1 and table 4.4 (p. 50 and p. 65) to remind yourself of the attributes of Australian shares as a form of investment.

What are shares?

Shares are simply part ownership of a company, which entitles you to a share of its equity and profit as decided by the board of the company. Some companies distribute all of their profit and others don't distribute anything — rather, they reinvest their profits back into the company to make it grow. Hence the term 'growth stock' versus 'income stock' (also known as a 'value stock'). A good example of a growth stock is BHP and a good example of a value stock are the big four banks.

The role of the ASX

Australian shares can be bought and sold on the Australian Securities Exchange (ASX), which is the body that facilitates and regulates the buying and selling of shares in listed companies in Australia. This buying and selling provides much-needed liquidity for companies and investors, and it's the liquidity that pushes up the share price of a company — a company is worth more if it is liquid, meaning that its shares can be converted into cash quickly. One of the biggest issues for private, non-listed companies is that they cannot readily sell their shares in exchange for cash.

What do brokers do?

Businesses that trade in shares on the ASX are members of the ASX. These businesses are called brokers and they are responsible for placing trades on behalf of investors, allowing them to buy and sell shares on the ASX. There are many different types of brokers but the two main types of brokers are full-service brokers and internet brokers.

Full-service brokers provide research on companies and recommendations on which companies to buy and sell. They tend to charge more because they provide more. Full-service brokers usually charge between 0.5 and 1 per cent of the value of each trade (you can usually negotiate them down to 0.5 per cent). Many full-service brokers also provide general financial advice. Full-service brokers include Bell Potter, UBS, RBS and Wilson HTM, but there are many others.

Internet brokers are for self-starters and self-directed investors who know what they want to buy and sell. Internet brokers provide a cheap execution-only (buy or sell only) service, and provide limited or no specific advice about your circumstances. Often third-party advice and recommendations are provided as part of the service on their websites. Expect to pay between $15 and $50 per trade depending on the value of the trade. Internet trading companies include CommSec, E*TRADE, NAB and Bell Potter, to name just a few.

Some companies are not listed on the ASX

Companies that are listed on the ASX are known as public companies because the public can buy and sell their shares on the stock exchange. Not all companies are listed on the stock exchange and many remain privately owned companies (also called unlisted). When a company needs to raise capital by selling a portion of its equity, it can do so privately, or list on the ASX and do so publicly.

There is a cost to listing a company on the ASX and there are very stringent rules to be met, such as financial and regulatory requirements; listed companies are therefore subject to more scrutiny than unlisted, private companies. These requirements also mean higher costs to regulate the company. This is one of the reasons many companies remain private and unlisted.

Ways to own shares

The two ways to own shares are directly and indirectly.

This chapter will concentrate on direct share ownership, that is, owning shares in your own name or in an investment structure that you control, such as individual names, joint names, a self managed super fund or a family trust. You can own shares indirectly via managed funds, listed investment companies (LICs), exchange-traded funds (ETFs) and other unlisted trusts.

Shares versus property

Table 6.1 compares the attributes of shares and property.

Table 6.1: shares versus property comparison summary

Attribute	Property rating	Shares rating
Risk	High	High
Return	High	High
Flexibility	Low	High
Volatility	Low	High
Liquidity	Low	High
Timing	Difficult to get right	Difficult to get right
Cost	Expensive	Low entry point
Tax	Tax effective	Tax effective

Both shares and property provide similar returns that will vary at different times depending on what dynamics are playing out in each investment market at different stages in their cycles. It's important to determine the right asset class (shares versus property) or level of diversification that suits you.

When you begin your investment program it makes sense to invest in cash — that is, to save money and invest it in a high-interest account. The reason for this is that cash is not volatile and it serves a purpose for building a base that can be used for buying shares or property later.

The beauty of property, as we discovered in the previous chapter, is that a bank will lend you money to buy it, and property tends to be less volatile than shares. Property is also tangible and can be improved by undertaking renovations; for those who are happy to put in the time and effort, property can be very rewarding financially.

Shares are also a popular method of wealth creation, but many people start out by gambling in two-cent stocks, start-up companies, tech or bio stocks, or two-bit resource companies in an attempt make a fortune overnight. Often younger people employ this approach because their perception of the sharemarket and share investors is that fortunes are made overnight by taking high risks on low value stocks that will hit the big time.

Nothing could be further from the truth, although there are many professional traders who make a fortune from either being paid by institutions to undertake large trades or by working for small boutique trading firms that specialise in trading specialist and complex financial products such as futures or commodities, for example. If that's what you want to do, you will need to be very good at maths, be prepared to study hard and start at the bottom to work your way up. I've seen plenty of traders earning more than half a million dollars a year, with bonuses of the same amount, or even much more. But these people are the exception, not the rule.

For the rest of us who don't want a career in trading but just want somewhere to invest, the sharemarket should play a vital role in wealth creation, wealth management and, when you have significant assets, diversification of investments.

As with property, the best friend of a sharemarket investor is time. Like all investments, shares trend upwards over time, albeit with some volatility, because shares are priced daily — property is only priced when it's bought or sold and any other pricing mechanism is merely speculation. A property is worth what people are prepared to pay for it at the time.

The types of shares you decide to buy should match your risk profile and your investment objectives. My company invests our clients' money only in blue-chip, top ASX 200 companies that have a growth profile or good, tax-effective dividends. We also invest into term deposits and property, because these are investments that we can easily understand. We do not invest client money in CFDs or similar products, because these are products that are more difficult to understand and riskier, and they are only as good as the companies selling them: a few of those have fallen over, taking all of the investors' money with them.

Unlike property, shares have no maintenance costs, agents' fees, land tax, strata fees or pesky tenants who ruin your property. For these reasons alone, many people prefer shares over property. Property can be a headache, particularly if you borrow money and can't find a tenant.

Many shares offer better after-tax, after-expenses net income because the cost of maintaining them is virtually nil (and therefore much less than property). Many property investors don't calculate their after-expenses rental yields and focus too much on the possibility of the property rising in value, which may not happen for many years.

Many shares also offer franked dividend income. Franking indicates that company tax of 30 per cent has already been paid by the company before they send any income to you. The 30 per cent is paid to the ATO only once and therefore the 30 per cent tax benefit is passed on to you as an owner of the company. If you are in the 30 per cent tax bracket you will pay no additional tax on a fully franked dividend.

Tip

Not all companies pay fully franked dividends. In fact many companies listed on the ASX pay partial or non-franked dividends to their shareholders. Property trusts or Australian Real Estate Investment Trusts (AREITs) don't pay franked dividends at all.

For example, if you own a Commonwealth Bank (ASX:CBA) share and it produces a 5.2 per cent dividend that is fully franked, then you only have to pay tax on the dividend if you earn more than $80 000 per year under the current tax rates. If you do earn more than $80 000 per year, then you pay only the difference between the company tax and your personal tax rate, which will be an additional 7 per cent (if you earn between $80 000 and $180 000 per year) or 15 per cent (if you earn more than $180 000 per year), depending on your marginal tax rate, or the top rate that you pay (for the financial years 2012–2015).

One of the key advantages of shares is the low barrier to entry. That is, you can buy shares with just a few hundred dollars and buy more over time. I recommend that you start with at least $2000 so the brokerage doesn't eat into your capital too much, but unlike property you don't need hundreds of thousands of dollars of borrowed money to enter the sharemarket.

Capital growth is similar to property, dividends can be highly tax-effective and the net income can be much higher than you would get from property, all without the headaches of property ownership.

Margin lending and margin calls

Share investors can also borrow money to buy shares and use the benefits of gearing, as with property. Effectively, this is negative or positive gearing for shares.

Banks will lend money against many different types of shares for you to invest in. In the event that you can't repay the loan, the bank repossesses the shares. This is called a *margin call*, where the bank calls in the shares and they are sold to repay the loan. You can generally obtain a loan for 60 per cent to 70 per cent of the value of a share, and the interest rate will be a couple of percentage points higher than that for a home loan.

If you are interested in margin lending, contact a lending institution and find out how much it will lend you against each stock and what its interest rates are for doing so. All the major banks offer margin loan products. Each lending institution has a list of shares that it is willing to lend money against and the percentage of the value of the share it will lend (loan-to-value ratio, or LVR). You should be buying, not selling, when share prices are low, so be careful with margin loans and make sure you fully understand the dynamics of the loan structure. The GFC reshaped the margin lending industry and risk was re-priced by margin lending providers, making it more expensive when LVRs are lower.

> ## Tip
>
> If you are thinking about a margin loan, it may be worth visiting the ASX website (www.asx.com.au) to find out more about margin loans or visit one of the banking websites to read one of their product disclosure statements (PDS) on margin lending.

If you own property, a better way to borrow money to buy shares is via a line of credit or redraw facility against the property because the interest rate will be lower and you will never get a margin call and be forced to sell your shares. Make sure that you only take out a loan against the best blue-chip shares and that you diversify to lower your risk.

Risks with shares

Like all investments, investment in shares has risks. It's important to understand the risks and how they affect your investments at different times. Your goal is to reduce risk while maximising returns. Some of the types of risk to be aware of are:

- economic risk, including interest rate risk

- country, or sovereign, risk, including political and legislative risk

- market risk, including general market fluctuations and influences

- industry risk, including legislative, political and industry-specific events

- company risk, which relates to specific company issues and performance

- management risk, which is the effect of management expertise and ethics.

Qualitative versus quantitative research

Qualitative research is all about working out *why* you want to invest in certain companies over others and the reasons relating to the quality of a company, such as the quality of its product, the integrity of management or the way in which management has a history of committing to its announcements and shareholders. My research would include understanding the remuneration model of management of a company; understanding the industry in which the company operates (is it growing or shrinking); researching the company's staff experience and the qualifications of senior management; and gathering an understanding of the trends of the market in which a company operates (is it competitive and price conscious, for example).

Some of this is logical; for example, the banks have little competition, high barriers to entry, excellent management and good recurring revenue from home loans, so they make a good investment. Some industries, such as the resources or media industries, are more complex to research quantitatively, because of the nature of a company's structure or industry. Companies such as Newscorp or Macquarie Bank can be difficult to understand because of these complexities.

If you can't be bothered with doing any of the analysis or don't have time, you can get yourself a full-service broker, so you have access to their research and advice, or subscribe to a broker newsletter or simply buy a managed fund or an exchange-traded fund to give you general exposure to the sharemarket.

The attributes that I seek in an ideal company are:

- *Economic resilience.* Companies that still perform well and their revenue and profits are not materially affected in tough economic times, such as Woolworths (ASX:WOW), and Invocare (ASX:IVC). Woolworths is in the grocery industry and people will always buy groceries, even in challenging economic times because we all need to eat. Invocare is in the funeral business, and death rates are unaffected in tough economic times so revenue is likely to be unaffected.

- *Recurring revenue.* Companies, such as banks and financial institutions, that have constant revenue, such as Commonwealth Bank (ASX:CBA) or Platinum Fund Management (ASX:PTM).

- *Good management.* Companies that have good management; for example, BHP (ASX:BHP) or Lend Lease (ASX:LLC) consistently outperform those with a high turnover of CEOs.

- *Market leaders.* Companies that are market leaders and high-growth companies have a timing advantage or technology advantage over their competitors, for example, Seek (ASX:SEK) or Realestate.com.au (ASX:REA).

- *Monopolistic tendencies.* Companies that have a much better chance of success simply because competition is low, for example, AGL (ASX:AGL) or Telstra (ASX:TLS).

- *Operate in industries with high barriers to entry.* Companies would include the banks, such as Westpac (ASX:WBC) or ANZ (ASX:ANZ).

- *Exposure to long-term global trends.* Companies that, for example, have high exposure to China's burgeoning demand for resources as their infrastructure expenditure continues to grow rapidly, for example, BHP (ASX:BHP), RIO (ASX:RIO) or Woodside Petroleum (ASX:WPL).

If you use this list as a test for assessing stocks for your portfolio, you will have a much higher chance of success and obtaining better returns over time.

Quantitative research

Quantitative research requires more empirical study of companies and industries to obtain a better understanding of the numbers behind a company. Looking at the numbers and making comparisons with past performance, competitor companies, shareholder returns, sales and revenue, and share-price growth are some of the areas that you will need to understand.

Here are just some basic examples of quantitative attributes of a company that are important to know if you're going to invest into shares:

- share price
- dividend income — to reinvest or take the cash
- franking percentage
- grossed-up dividend
- earnings per share (EPS) and EPS growth
- price/earnings ratio (P/E ratio)
- return on investment (equity)

- return on assets

- net tangible assets (NTA).

Share price

The share price is a simple function of the value of the company (market capitalisation) divided by the number of shares on offer. For example, Commonwealth Bank of Australia (CBA) has a market capitalisation of approximately $100 billion and around 1500 million shares issued. So the share price is $100 billion divided by 1500 million, which is $66.66.

Dividend income

Dividends are the income distributed by a company to investors. The amount of dividend is determined by company management and may vary depending on the company's performance in any year.

Franking percentage

Dividend income is likely to have some or all of the 30 per cent company tax already paid, providing you with a tax-effective income. That 30 per cent has to be paid only once to the ATO so you don't have to pay that initial 30 per cent tax again; you only have to pay the difference if you are on a higher effective tax rate. If you are on a lower tax rate than 30 per cent, which may include retirees or non-employed people, then you actually get a rebate.

For example, if you own a CBA share that is fully franked (100 per cent of the 30 per cent company tax has been paid by the company before the dividend is distributed to you) and you are in the 45 per cent tax bracket (earning more than $180 000), then you pay only an additional 15 per cent tax on the dividend. If you are in the 30 per cent tax bracket, then you pay no more tax; and if you are on 15 per cent tax, then you are eligible to claim a 15 per cent rebate when you complete your tax return at the end of the financial year. If you are on a 0 per cent tax rate, then you can claim back the full 30 per cent tax credit.

Grossed-up dividend

To calculate the grossed-up dividend, divide the dividend by one minus (the franking percentage multiplied by the company tax rate).

Note that fully franked equals 100 per cent franking. This will give you your pre-tax dividend amount so you fully understand the level of income that you are entitled to receive.

That is:

$$\text{Dividend} \div (1 - [\text{franking percentage} \times 30 \text{ per cent company tax rate}])$$
$$= \text{grossed-up dividend}$$

For example, if CBA has a 5 per cent dividend that is fully franked, using this equation will help you calculate the full dividend before tax:

$$5\% \div (1 - [100\% \times 30\%]) = 5\% \div (1 - [30\%])$$
$$= 5\% \div 0.7\% = 7.14\%$$

Once you have worked through this equation, you can then apply your marginal tax rate to the dividend to calculate your after-tax dividend.

In this CBA example, give some thought to the fact that a bank such as CBA probably has a lower term-deposit rate than the after-tax dividend. For example, at the time of writing the term deposit rate was 4.6 per cent, but the before-tax dividend from CBA shares is about 7.14 per cent. I grant you that the share price is far more volatile than a term deposit rate, but the average rate of return from a term deposit over the past 10 years has been 5 per cent, whereas the average rate of return from a CBA share over the past 10 years has been 16.7 per cent — even after the GFC! Now that's a good investment.

Moreover, the earnings or profit made by CBA are forecast to grow, and as a result the forecast dividend is expected to grow by 5 per cent next year and again by 5 per cent or more the year after. These figures are subject to change, but anyone who owns these blue-chip shares will attest that this is a great investment.

Earnings per share

Understanding earnings per share (EPS) is important because it gives you an indication of the company's profitability and how that profitability changes over time. Earnings per share is simply the total dollar value of company profits divided by the number of shares issued in the company. Finding this information is relatively easy: the annual report is a good place to start, or reports such as those in figures 6.1 (overleaf) and 6.2 (see p. 123) from Morningstar — in figure 6.2 we can see CBA shares issued is about 1.570 billion, and it shows the earnings per share history for the past 10 years as well as dividend history.

The dividend forms part of the earnings that are distributed to the investor and the remaining portion is reinvested into the company. The dividend is a percentage of the earnings per share.

For example, if CBA has earnings per share of $4.34 per year and distributes $3.34 each year to investors, the remaining sum ($4.34 – $3.34 = $1.00) of $1.00 is reinvested back into the company, which will help the company grow.

In the CBA example, you have a company with a good dividend yield (that is highly tax effective) and a company that grows over time. This is an ideal investment and free from the headaches of managing a property with high-maintenance tenants and high property taxes. The average investment return on CBA shares has been around 12 per cent over the past 10 years (depending on price fluctuations since the time of writing).

It's important that earnings per share grow so that you know the company is not stagnant or even going backwards. You will notice in table 6.2 and figure 6.1 (overleaf) that earnings for CBA have risen consistently, albeit with some volatility between 2001 and 2003, as a result of the tech wreck and the 11 September 2001 terrorist attacks on the United States, and the GFC in 2009. So, too, dividends have grown in line with earnings. In fact dividends have grown by between 5 per cent and 30 per cent per year. Wouldn't it be nice if rents for property went up by the same amounts? Needless to say, CBA looks like a good long-term investment based on this information, assuming it meets your requirements, goals and objectives.

Table 6.2: CBA earnings and dividend growth for 10 years (2013 and 2014 are forecast figures only)

	2005	2006	2007	2008	2009	2010	2011	2012	2013	2014
EPS	3.03	2.96	3.39	3.44	2.93	3.70	4.39	4.34	4.71	4.97
DPS	1.97	2.24	2.56	2.66	2.28	2.90	3.20	3.34	3.57	3.77

Source: Morningstar (www.morningstar.com.au).
Note: 2013 and 2014 are consensus forecasts.

Figure 6.1: Morningstar report—CBA

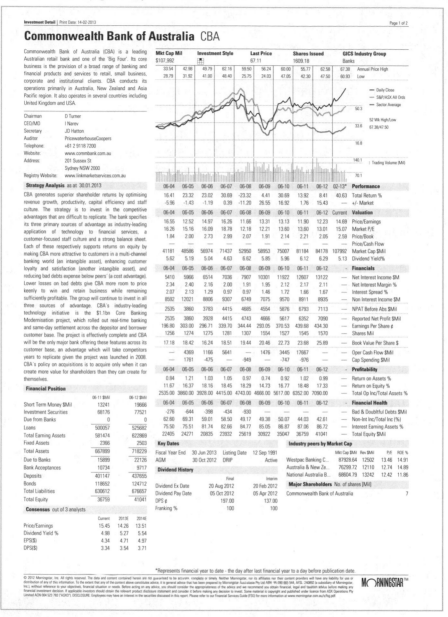

Source: Morningstar (www.morningstar.com.au) 14 February 2013.

Figure 6.2: Morningstar report—NAB

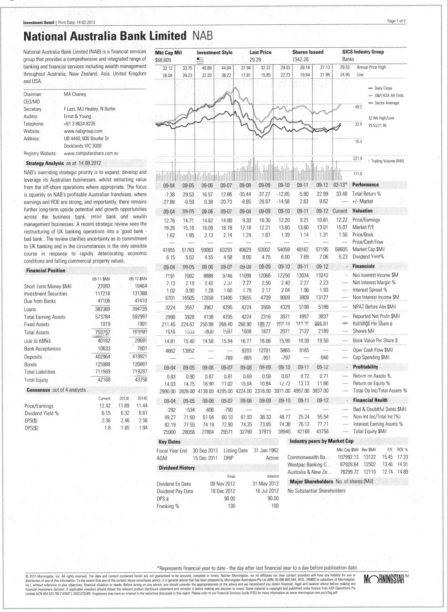

Source: Morningstar (www.morningstar.com.au) 14 February 2013.

Figure 6.3 shows that the trends for earnings per share and dividends per share are both headed in the upwards direction. The effects of the GFC in 2007-2010, and the tech wreck and effects of the September 11 terrorist attacks from 2001 to 2003 are noticeable. Companies try to leave dividend trends in place for a number of reasons unless their earnings are severely affected, because changing dividend policy can create wild swings in share prices and destabilise a company's shareholders, who rely on that dividend. If dividend policy changes, then investors are likely to drop the shares in that company and seek other havens or tax-effective income.

Figure 6.3: CBA graph of 10 years of earnings and dividend growth to 2014

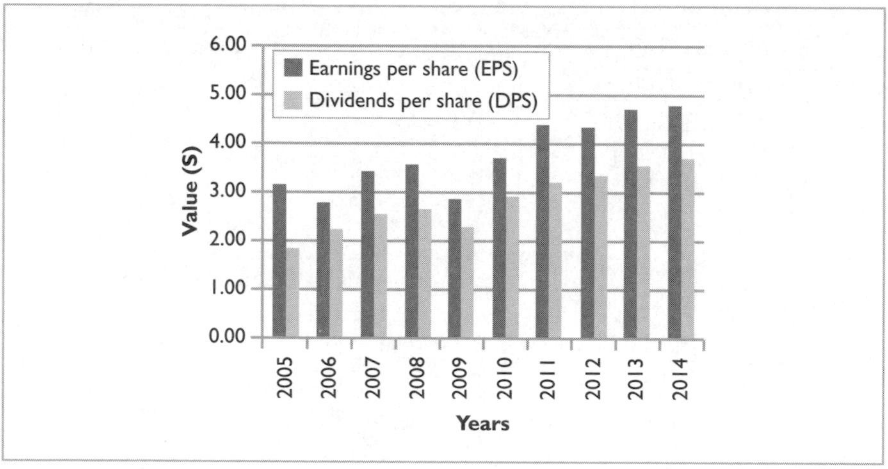

Source: Morningstar (www.morningstar.com.au).

Price/earnings ratio

The price/earnings (P/E) ratio is one of a number of benchmarks that you can use to measure the value of a company, or even the value of the whole sharemarket.

To work out the P/E ratio you simply divide the company's share price by its earnings per share. In our previous CBA example, the share price at the time was $67.11 and the earnings per share were $4.71: $67.11 ÷ $4.71 = $14.24.

The average long-term P/E ratio for the market is around 14 to 16, but in recent years it has fluctuated wildly from a high in 2003 of 23 to a low in 2009 of just 8 (it didn't stay there long). If you are interested in buying shares in a company that has a reasonably low P/E ratio, but with a solid growth outlook, it *may* be a buy signal. Certainly if you see wild fluctuations in blue-chip companies, when share prices are down but earnings are not substantially under pressure, common sense may suggest this is a buy signal for the company's shares.

This happened in March 2009 when company share prices across the entire sharemarket dipped as GFC fear reached a peak. Share prices plummeted, and so did P/E ratios, because people didn't know what the future held. Earnings appeared to be mildly affected, but the economic forecast was unknown, and so people sold off shares on the expectation of severe economic conditions, which did not happen. Those who purchased shares at times when P/E ratios were just 8 saw the sharemarket increase in value by more than 50 per cent and some shares by more than 100 per cent over the following months. CBA, for example, rose more than 120 per cent in the 12 months from late January 2009 to January 2010, when it rose from just $25 to close at $60 in just 12 months.

Be careful when using the P/E ratio to make buying decisions, because the denominator (earnings) can change for a number of reasons, highlighting the risks of using only P/E ratios to measure value. Share prices also fluctuate, so you need to make sure you set a price at which you want to buy and stick to your system. You want to buy low, but you will never know how low the price will fall, or how high it will get, so it's important that you have a system for valuing the market and a stock.

Subscribing to publications from a sharemarket research house such as Morningstar or Fat Prophets or simply using a credible full-service broker or financial adviser may also assist.

Return on equity

One of investment guru Warren Buffett's favourite measuring sticks for buying shares is return on equity (ROE). As I discussed in chapter 5, return on equity is the actual return you receive on the money that you contribute to the investment: your equity. It excludes the return on borrowed money, but includes its interest, because borrowed money magnifies your returns or losses, but is not part of your equity.

If an investor buys a company's shares for $10 000 (equity) and they return $1000, the return on equity can be calculated as follows:

Net profit after taxes ($1000) ÷ total shareholder's equity ($10 000)
= return on equity (10 per cent).

However, if the investor contributes only $5000 to the investment and borrows $5000 at 7 per cent and the interest is $350 per year, then the formula would change like this:

Net profit after taxes minus interest expense ($1000 – $350) ÷ total shareholder's equity less the borrowed funds ($10 000 – $5000)
= return on equity (13 per cent).

This simple example shows the instant effect of borrowing money for a successful investment.

Warren Buffett also likes to invest in companies that invest well into their own operations, which allows them to grow over time. That reinvestment is the catalyst to growth and ROE provides the evidence of such a practice in companies. So ROE is a good yardstick to measure value and compare other companies that you are thinking about investing in.

Did you know?

Warren Buffett is considered one of the world's most successful investors. He is worth around $50 billion and runs an investment business called Berkshire Hathaway. You can buy his A-class shares for around $150 000 per share or his B-class shares for around $100 at the time of writing. He draws a salary of just $100 000 per year and will give away 99 per cent of his wealth to charity when he dies. He is 82.

Had you invested $10 000 when Buffett started out in 1965 at Berkshire, your investment would be worth around $80 million, now. Not a bad run!

In our CBA example, ROE is listed as one of the final ratios in figure 6.1 (see p. 122) and most research reports will do the calculations for you to save you the effort. CBA's ROE for the past 10 years has fluctuated from about 10.2 per cent to 18.4 per cent.

National Australia Bank's (ASX:NAB) lower ROE (see figure 6.2 on p. 123) indicates it does not employ its equity as well as CBA. This may be an indication that despite NAB's higher dividend and lower P/E ratio, CBA may in fact be a better investment because of its ability to better employ its equity and thus grow the business faster over time. That means your share price will grow and so will your dividends. This is what you need to look for in a good company and this example illustrates how a good dividend and a low P/E ratio do not necessarily represent good value.

Another indicator that we used earlier was growth in earnings per share. NAB has not grown its earnings or dividends anywhere near as consistently as CBA over the past 10 years and therefore one may conclude that CBA is a significantly better investment than NAB. So if you are a long-term investor, you would be best to invest in a CBA share than a NAB share on this basis.

Return on assets

Return on assets (ROA) is a simple calculation of the net income produced by an investment divided by the total assets of the company: net income ÷ total assets = ROA.

The aim of this calculation is to show how well the company uses its capital (assets) to produce an income. So it's an efficiency tool used to measure how well management deploys the assets available to the company to produce its profit. As you can imagine, management has no end of options in deploying its capital, so the types of shares you will want to own will be in companies that employ their assets at optimal levels.

ROA can fluctuate wildly from company to company so it's best to compare companies' ROA from year to year or compare similar companies from a similar industry. If we compare CBA with NAB again, we can see from the research reports that CBA's ROA has stayed at about one, with a low of 0.73 (see figure 6.1 on p.122), whereas NAB has fallen over the years to a recent low of just 0.59 and a high of 0.72 in 2011, although it was as high as CBA's more than 10 years earlier (see figure 6.2 on p. 123). This is an indication that NAB has not employed its capital as well as CBA and in fact its management of capital may be getting worse. Earnings and dividends are unlikely to grow if capital is not well employed. Therefore, over time, it is not likely that NAB will be as good an investment as CBA because it is not as well managed, based on the evidence of these research reports.

You may want to keep checking ROA over time because changes in these metrics could indicate a recovery in NAB shares, and growth in earnings and dividends could present an opportunity to investors to buy the shares if management gets its act together.

I invest in the CBA shares because they have a long history of good management and good performance. That is, both their *quantitative* and *qualitative* data point to a solid long-term investment.

As you can see, from a quick comparison of some readily available research we can decide between investing into one company over another and see how to compare companies. A little research will pay dividends and it's well worth obtaining good advice or subscribing to a research house to assist you with your homework on shares.

Net tangible assets

In a simplified definition, net tangible assets (NTA) represents the value of the company's assets minus its liabilities. It is also known as book value, net asset value or balance sheet value. You can calculate this figure yourself by looking at the balance sheet of a company's annual report. From the total shareholders' equity you can subtract goodwill, trademarks or other 'non-hard assets' or intangibles. To bring that to a figure that relates to the share price of the stock, you can then divide that figure by the total number of shares in existence to arrive at a NTA per share figure.

For example, if CBA had a book value of $40.6473 billion and had $1.570 billion shares outstanding, then the NTA per share of CBA is $25.89. These figures can be gleaned from the CBA research in figure 6.1 on p. 122.

It can often be said that the closer a share's value is to its NTA, the better the current value. Keep in mind that the market does a reasonable job at pricing shares, so always question why a stock may be cheap or expensive. If the general market is not pricing many companies near their NTAs, then caution may be needed. The answer for a low valuation may lie in the company's earnings outlook. Sometimes shares can fall below their NTA, possibly indicating a bargain price. This has been experienced in extreme market fluctuations and for large company stocks, and is often not seen until a crash occurs, as at the height of the GFC. Smaller stocks more often sit around their NTA levels, but NTA generally can be used as a benchmark for stock price valuations in combination with other valuation methods.

Other ways to own shares

Other ways to own shares include managed funds, managed accounts, exchange-traded funds (ETFs), options, warrants and contracts for difference (CFDs).

Managed funds

A managed fund is a unit trust structure (see chapter 3) run by a professional share manager that invests in shares on your behalf. You own units in the trust and not the underlying shares. Managed funds charge a fee of between 0.3 per cent and 3 per cent of the value your investment per year. You should be able to invest in a wholesale managed fund for less than 1.5 per cent per year for an international fund and less than 1 per cent per year for an Australian fund.

Tip

Many wholesale funds will require a minimum investment of $500 000, although many are now accessible through wrap platforms such as Colonial First State, BT Wrap or Macquarie Wrap. Many managed funds are also dropping their minimum investment levels as industry fee pressures reduce pricing.

Managed funds tend to be an expensive way to own shares as they charge buy and sell costs as well as management expense ratios (MERs) or total cost ratios (TCRs). Managed funds also distribute capital gains, and you have no control over the timing of these distributions and you can be disadvantaged. For example, during the GFC many managed funds had to distribute their capital gains from the previous year at a time when sharemarkets were depressed, resulting in owners having tax bills at the same time that they were experiencing substantial losses. Many managed funds also froze redemptions or lost a lot of money during the GFC, reducing consumer confidence in them.

Managed funds do, however, provide a cheap and effective means of investing into a basket of shares using a professional manager to do the investing on your behalf without the time and effort required by you to manage your own portfolio. You could invest into a fund with as little as $2000 to $5000 with the ability to regularly add to the fund over time. They can offer a great means of investing.

Managed accounts

A managed account is basically a basket of assets that is managed for you by a professional manager. It is similar to a managed fund, but the investor does not own units in a trust — instead, they actually own the underlying assets. A managed account is more transparent than a managed fund, and the investor remains the owner of the assets, but the professional manager can actively manage those shares on the investor's behalf. Like all professional money managers in Australia, operators must have a financial services licence, which helps to protect the investor's assets.

Different types of managed accounts include the following:

- *Separately managed account (SMA)*. A professional portfolio manager runs a templated list of assets, such as shares and term deposits, so every investor has a similar portfolio.

- *Individually managed account (IMA)*. The manager runs a portfolio unique to each investor's needs, goals and objectives.

- *Unified managed account (UMA)*. This can be either an SMA or IMA, and can also include assets external to an individual share portfolio, such as a property, under the wing of the professional manager. This is particularly handy for clients running self managed super funds who need efficient asset management and administration.

I use managed accounts to manage my clients' money because they are very transparent and also suit fee-for-service financial advice. They also tend to be cheaper for the client and offer the ability to actively manage a client's money — in other words, my staff have the ability to sell out of a stock, or buy into a stock, as soon as information is released to the market and they can make the trade across the client base in seconds, so no client is disadvantaged.

Exchange-traded funds

Exchange-traded funds (ETFs) are simply a basket of shares that represent a particular index. So owning an ETF is like owning that basket of shares but the basket is represented by a single three-letter stock code for ease of trading. For example, you can buy a stock with the code STW, which represents the entire ASX 200. That is, you can buy a small part of the top 200 companies listed on the Australian Securities Exchange by market value, providing great diversification, at a cost of just 0.286 per cent of the value of all those stocks, which is less than one-third of the cost of most wholesale managed funds.

After fees, around 80 per cent or more of managed funds underperform the index. That means if you buy an Australian shares managed fund, there is an 80 per cent chance that it will underperform the ASX 200 index, after fees have been deducted (and international funds have an even lower success rate). That means owning ETFs can provide diversification, risk minimisation and exposure to international markets without the cost of a poorly performing and expensive managed fund.

I manage around 40 per cent to 60 per cent of my clients' money using ETFs because they offer a cheap and well-diversified method of investing across a number of key asset classes. Henderson Maxwell uses a 'core satellite' approach in which the core is made up of ETFs and the satellite portion of the managed account is made up of direct shares, term deposits, hybrid securities and other fixed interest–type products. We even have a managed fund or two to give us exposure to particular asset classes or to increase income in the fields of commercial property and fixed interest.

Tip

According to statistics issued by the Australian Taxation Office (ATO) about the asset allocation of SMSFs, Australian investors put the lion's share of their money into fixed term deposits or Australian shares. Their diversity is low, increasing risk. ETFs are a relatively new method of gaining exposure into international sharemarkets by providing diversity at a reasonable cost without you having to do the research on overseas companies.

Exchange-traded funds are gaining popularity here in Australia and one of the best sources of information on ETFs is the ASX website (www.asx.com.au). Table 6.3 shows examples of some exchange-traded funds that are available to be traded in Australia.

Table 6.3: exchange-traded funds

Fund type	Code	Description
ASX 50	SFY	ASX top 50 companies
ASX 200	STW	ASX top 200 companies
ASX 300	VAS	ASX top 300 companies
ASX high dividend	RDV	ASX top high-dividend companies
ASX property	SLF	ASX top 200 commercial-property companies
ASX resources	AII	ASX resources index
S&P 500	IVV	S&P USA top 500 companies
Global 100	IOO	Global top 100 companies
China 25	IZZ	Xinhua 25 (top 25 Chinese stocks in Hong Kong)
BRIC countries	IBK	Brazil Russia India China
Gold (currency hedged)	QUA	Pure exposure to gold without currency fluctuation influence
Gold bullion	GOLD	Pure exposure to gold price and currency

Options

Options are a derivative that can be traded like a share on the stock exchange. The concept of an option is that you may buy an option to buy or sell a particular stock. If you buy the option to sell a stock, it's called a put option. If you buy the option to buy a stock, it's called a call option.

For example, I can buy an option to sell CBA shares at $60. If CBA shares are currently $65, but there is speculation that the economy may fall back into the doldrums and the stock could dip to $50 again, then buying an option to sell the stock at $60 is like buying insurance for your shares. If you exercise the option, then you can sell the shares for $60 each. If the sharemarket never drops and the stock continues to rise, then your option will expire and become worthless. That could be a loss of around $1 to $2 per share or so, depending on the stock. That's what happens in most instances, but the option can serve as an insurance policy nonetheless.

There are a number of different types of options and you should get more information about how they work from the ASX website (www.asx.com.au) and download some of its free booklets to educate yourself on options if you are interested in them. Brokers will not let you trade options unless you have read the ASX booklets on options owing to their high risk, so a predetermined level of knowledge is expected given the high risk of these types of instruments.

Warrants

Like options, warrants are derivatives that represent a listed share. Warrants allow you to leverage or protect or diversify into markets or certain stocks. There are a number of different types of warrants, such as instalment warrants, put warrants and call warrants. Warrants often bring the added benefit of share ownership, such as access to dividends.

Self-funding instalment warrants allow you to buy part of a share with a deposit and then pay the remainder over time — a bit like the Telstra instalments many years ago. For example, you can buy an instalment warrant over CBA shares from Royal Bank of Scotland (RBS) over a five-year period (this was originally a 10-year period but the period reduces with time). You can choose how much you put down as a deposit and how much you want to borrow to buy the warrant. For example, you can put down 50 per cent now and you can use the dividends to repay the loan to RBS over the next seven years. At the end of the five years you take full ownership of the shares at their market value, with full shareholder rights.

If the market falls substantially, then the institution that offers the warrant has a stop-loss in place to ensure you don't owe any more than your initial deposit. That is, they will simply sell the shares if it looks like they are going to go close to losing money. Your invested money would be close to gone, in this situation. Effectively, this is like issuers having insurance in place for themselves.

Instalment warrants are great for self managed super funds because most people can't touch their super for many years and the instalment warrants allow for using gearing, the interest is repaid by the dividends, and the investor receives full ownership once the shares are fully paid for.

Again, it is best to look at the ASX website (www.asx.com.au) publications to gain a better understanding of warrants if this is an area of interest.

Contracts for difference

There has been a lot of hype around contracts for difference (CFDs) over the past few years owing to a number of providers going bust and taking with them the investment savings of their clients. CFDs are an agreement between a buyer and a seller of an asset. A seller will pay to the buyer the difference between the current value of an asset and its value at a future contracted time. They are risky. For this reason alone it is best to ensure you are fully aware that the providers of CFDs need to be treated with care, as well as fully understanding the underlying investment integrity of the product they sell. The ASIC consumer website (www.smartmoney.gov.au) has warnings on it about CFD providers: do be careful.

CFDs are specialist investment instruments that allow you to buy into shares, indices, commodities, currencies or futures. CFDs are highly leveraged and can be very risky. Traders can also take positions on rising or falling markets, depending on what their research or understanding of a particular market, share, commodity or currency may be.

Given the high risk rating of CFDs, some people have made good money from trading them, and trading such an instrument in volatile times can be highly beneficial, but again I must emphasise they are not for everybody and can be very risky.

I advise you to invest in only the ASX-listed CFDs or those of companies that you feel 100 per cent confident in, so you have all the transparency and credibility of a good operator without the company and credit risks associated with other providers.

Summing up on shares

Investing into shares can be a very rewarding experience. It can be fun, challenging and highly profitable. But you should avoid speculating in companies that you do not truly understand, as that will only fuel the gambling bug and lead to losses. It will also prevent you from investing further.

Sharemarkets will always change, sometimes for the worse and sometimes for the better. Those changes provide opportunities at times that may challenge your thinking and emotions, but it's at those times that money can be made — when the market misjudges the future. Don't be afraid to be a contrarian when all the other sheep are following a trend.

It's paramount to maintain your own investment strategy and philosophy. Stay strong and true to your research. If you have done your research thoroughly and base your decisions on a sound foundation of research instead of speculating, then you can remove the emotion that can lead to hasty and poor decisions.

Five sample strategies

- Set up an online trading account for investing long-term into shares.

- Establish a regular monthly deposit straight from your monthly pay into your share trading account for regular investing.

- Review your share portfolio every six months.

- Invest into 15 to 20 stocks for ample diversification.

- Remember transaction costs, management fees and tax can eat into your returns.

Five sample tactics

- Call E*TRADE or CommSec to open an account and get them to send out some information on how to trade and operate the account.

- Go onto the ASX website (www.asx.com.au) and download some information brochures on trading and understanding the market. Consider attending their seminars, webinars or educational programs.

(continued)

Five sample tactics *(cont'd)*

- Once your trading account is established, set up a monthly direct debit from your personal account to your trading account and ensure it is invested at the same time every month or every quarter, depending on how much you can afford to invest. This is dollar cost averaging.

- Review your share portfolio at the end of the reporting season (February and August in Australia) and take a look at net tangible assets, return on assets, return on equity, earnings per share, dividend policy and the company's outlook for the half year ahead.

- Before you buy or sell a share, always calculate your desired return, taking out transaction costs, management fees and taxes. Always do your numbers before you trade and consider the most tax-effective entity through which to invest, such as super, if appropriate to your situation.

KEY POINTS

- Shares are small parcels of equity in large companies traded on the stock exchange by share brokers.

- Shares have very different attributes from property and often produce better income and have lower transaction costs, and you can invest with smaller amounts of savings.

- Qualitative research looks at a company's management, the market in which it operates, the industry's barriers to entry and other competitive environmental issues.

- Quantitative research is all about assessing a company's performance data and using it to compare it with its past performance and its competitors' performance in similar or other industries. Metrics, such as dividends, price/earnings ratios and return on equity, will give you a method of comparison with other companies.

- In addition to direct ownership, you can invest in shares through managed funds, managed accounts, ETFs and a variety of derivatives, such as options, warrants and CFDs.

BOOST YOUR SUPER AND REDUCE YOUR TAX

> In an uncertain world, [superannuation] can only strengthen Australia and make the outlook for its citizens much more secure.
>
> *Paul Keating, former Australian Prime Minister and former Australian treasurer, and the chief architect of superannuation in Australia*

Superannuation provides one of the greatest opportunities for investing in the most tax-effective environment. Despite the complexities of the superannuation system and the regular tinkering by governments, it remains a low-tax investment structure that presents significant opportunities for making more money than investing in other structures. Admittedly, superannuation can be difficult to understand with its constantly changing legislation, but a small amount of research or advice can make a big difference to the type of retirement you will enjoy.

A recent survey has indicated that at least one-third of Australians are ill prepared for retirement; another indicated that we have a one trillion dollar retirement savings gap. The fact is that Australians need to do more to ensure they will have a comfortable retirement and, as you will see in this chapter, superannuation presents fantastic opportunities to reduce or eliminate tax and invest your hard-earned dollars in a more tax-efficient environment to give you the retirement you dream of. Small changes to the way you distribute your income or invest your funds can make substantial differences at retirement. This chapter aims to give you some clarity and guidance around the issues surrounding superannuation.

What is superannuation?

Superannuation is a savings environment that offers concessional rates of taxation specifically to fund your retirement. It is in fact a trust, a bit like a family trust that is designed to hold assets and distribute income to various beneficiaries. However superannuation fund trust has some significant differences.

Superannuation is controlled by a number of laws, including the *Superannuation Industry (Supervision) Act 1993* (SIS Act), *Income Tax Assessment Act 1997* (ITAA97), *Corporations Act 2001*, *Tax Administration Act 1953* and the usual variety of case-law precedents that have influenced the outcome of specific cases. To confuse things further for the consumer, some new changes to superannuation law seem to be announced with every budget — some of them make it through parliament and become law, and some never become law for a variety of reasons.

Superannuation also has its own tax rates. For example, tax on superannuation earnings is just 15 per cent and capital gains tax (CGT) on an asset held for more than 12 months inside a superannuation fund is just 10 per cent. If you are over the age of 55, retired and in pension phase, or transition to retirement mode, you pay no CGT in your super account or tax on the fund's earnings. You may pay some income tax until you are age 60. However, once you are age 60 and you are drawing an income from your superannuation, your fund pays no CGT, and you pay no tax on your income from super, or on the investment earnings in your super pension account.

The special tax rates make super a very attractive structure under which to invest.

Superannuation is a very flexible structure, allowing you to invest in a host of assets, including cash, fixed interest, Australian shares, international shares, options and warrants, or even physical assets such as gold or commercial or residential property.

Some of these assets also have attractive tax features, allowing you to further benefit from the concessional tax system. For example, some shares, such as Commonwealth Bank of Australia (ASX:CBA), produce income in the form of dividends, on which the bank has already paid 30 per cent company tax. That means that if your tax rate inside your superannuation fund is 15 per cent, or even 0 per cent if you are drawing an income stream, then you can actually receive a tax refund from the ATO when they complete your tax return for your fund. This occurs whether you have a fully managed superannuation fund or a self managed superannuation fund.

What superannuation isn't

By definition, superannuation is not a managed fund. It is not a specific investment. It is simply a tax-effective structure under which you invest.

If you ever hear someone say, 'I don't like superannuation', then they may as well say that they don't like family trusts. It doesn't make much sense, but I hear it all the time because people lost money inside their super funds during the GFC. What they are really expressing is a dislike of the investment strategy or performance of their investments inside their fund, not necessarily a dislike for the investment structure.

Given that most people have a choice of super fund, people who are suspicious of superannuation should make different choices that match their risk profile, which flows on to their asset allocation. That is, if they feel insecure, they should change their investments to include more cash and fixed interest.

Why do you need superannuation?

If you want to maintain your standard of living when you stop working, you should be putting some real thought into how you will be able to fund your retirement.

Australia has an ageing population and at the moment the dependency ratio (the number of people working versus the number on social security) is about ten to one. That is, there are about ten workers for every person on social security payments. If current trends prevail, that number could fall to as low as three to one by 2050, that is, only three workers to each person on social security. That means less tax revenue will be available to pay social security benefits, including the Age Pension: people who want a decent standard of living will have to be self-funded. For example, the full Age Pension for a couple is currently around $30 000 per year, while the annual survey produced by the Australian Super Funds Association (AFSA) suggests that for a comfortable retirement, a couple will need around $56 000 per year or $1075 per week.

Superannuation is complex

Superannuation laws change regularly and it's very hard to keep up with those changes unless you work in the industry or have a penchant for reading superannuation law. Many people don't keep up to date with the changes to super and so don't understand how those changes affect them. This lack of understanding breeds contempt and the result is that people are disengaged from their own retirement savings — possibly their biggest asset outside their own home.

Superannuation is an attractive investment structure because of the tax concessions afforded to it. Many investments should be considered under the structure of superannuation because of the tax concessions available. For example, you can now borrow money inside your self managed super fund to buy property, and when you sell the property, there is a likelihood that the fund will pay no CGT. While self managed super funds aren't for everyone, there are some fantastic opportunities afforded to those who choose to invest via a superannuation structure, whether you have an SMSF or not.

If you do not have the time or inclination to manage your superannuation, then I strongly suggest that you seek advice from an independent financial adviser who will be well placed to give you expert advice. Your accountant or self managed super fund administrators may also be able to assist you. Take ownership of your superannuation and seek advice when you have questions.

No silly questions

There is never a silly question when it comes to your own money. Too many people don't ask questions because they worry about seeming ignorant. Since most people have a very poor understanding of superannuation and taxation, you should never feel uncomfortable about seeking information or asking questions. It's your money: you should never feel silly asking questions about it!

Superannuation is your opportunity to supercharge your investments. It provides a fantastic opportunity to grow your asset base faster because one of the greatest inhibitors to investment growth, tax, is significantly reduced or eliminated. So your assets will grow faster because the income they produce is concessionally taxed. As you would expect, lower tax rates do not increase the capital growth of an asset—that's up to the market forces in which you are invested. However, when it comes to selling the asset the CGT is either reduced or nullified. This means more money in your bank account at the end of the day.

Defining the terms

Governments keep changing the names of things in superannuation, making defining terms more difficult. Here are some of the most important current terms:

- *Taxable portion*. This was formerly known as post-1983 contributions. It is made up of your superannuation guarantee (SG) amounts (9 per cent) and your salary sacrifice contributions or concessional contributions that were taxed at 15 per cent when they went into your super fund. When these funds are passed on to non-dependants after the death of the owner of the super, they are taxed at 15 per cent, and when they are passed on to financial dependants, zero tax applies.

- *Non-taxable portion*. This was formerly known as a combination of the pre-1983 and undeducted contributions. This is made up of your after-tax contributions to super, also known as non-concessional contributions. No tax is payable when these are passed onto any beneficiaries after the death of the super owner.

- *Preserved*. Preserved funds inside your super fund cannot be touched until you meet a condition of release (these are described later in the chapter). Most of your super will fall into this category.

The following two categories are not common:

- *Restricted unpreserved*. These are funds that can be withdrawn from super under certain rules. These funds are very rare—ask your fund if you have any of these restricted unpreserved funds in your account, but they should be shown on your regular superannuation statement.

- *Unrestricted non-preserved*. Also very rare, these funds can be withdrawn from your super fund at any time.

Types of superannuation funds

There are different types of superannuation funds, including self managed super funds, retail funds, corporate funds, industry funds, defined-benefit funds and small Australian Prudential Regulation Authority (APRA) funds. Each type of fund has its advantages and disadvantages and your role is to find the one that best suits you and your financial goals.

Self managed superannuation funds

Also known as a DIY (do it yourself) super fund, a self managed superannuation fund (SMSF) is a superannuation fund with four or fewer members that is managed by the members, who are also trustees for the fund. The members construct the investment strategy and manage the assets in the fund. There are about 90 rules and obligations that must be met by the trustees of SMSFs. These funds are regulated by the Australian Taxation Office (ATO), whereas other funds are regulated by APRA, and they are governed by the terms set out in the fund's trust deed.

SMSFs have the most involved and engaged members, and hold the largest proportion of funds in superannuation in Australia. Indeed, while only 4 per cent of people (490 000 funds) are members of an SMSF, the sector makes up more than 35 per cent of all funds held in superannuation. The average fund balance is currently around $900 000, and the average member balance is $450 000. The median fund balance is around $534 000, so a few large funds distort the averages somewhat. The ATO recommends that anyone starting an SMSF should have a minimum amount of $200 000 in super.

Trustees of SMSFs have a number of regulatory obligations, including preparing annual tax returns, accounts, managing pensions, getting the fund audited and meeting investment management obligations. A fund may cost between $1000 and $5000 or more in annual compliance costs, in addition to any advice and investment costs.

The advantages of an SMSF:

- investment fee savings
- control of your retirement savings

- flexibility to do what you want (within the superannuation laws)
- greater choice of investments than in other funds
- ability to gear into investments
- ability to transfer shares and commercial property into the fund
- access to investment in direct shares and property, and other physical assets, such as gold.

The disadvantages of an SMSF:

- compliance obligations and cost
- need to be involved (to some degree)
- penalties if the fund does not comply with the rules
- lack of investment expertise of members.

SMSFs are discussed in more detail in chapter 8.

Retail super funds

Retail super funds are available to everyone and may be supported by financial advisers and financial institutions. They have an internal trustee and are regulated by APRA. Retail super funds include old-style legacy retail superannuation funds (which pay trail commissions to advisers), and master trusts and wrap accounts that allow investors to access wholesale managed funds and direct shares without having to set up an SMSF. Retail funds do tend to be a more expensive option than corporate and industry funds, but they may come with advisers and plenty of investment choice. Examples of institutions offering retail funds include BT, Colonial, MLC, Asgard and Macquarie Wrap.

Tip

Trail commissions and incentive payments paid to financial advisers will be banned for all new clients (and possibly grandfathered for existing clients) through the operation of the *Future of Financial Advice* legalisation to take effect from 1 July 2013.

The advantages of retail super funds:

- choice of investments and access to wholesale managed funds (wholesale funds are cheaper versions of retail, and have no entry fees or trail commissions)
- access to financial advisers who can help to reduce tax and boost your super
- tax reporting
- online daily access to your accounts.

The disadvantages of retail super funds:

- cost — they tend to be more expensive than other funds
- no access to direct assets such as investment property
- most advisers use a set-and-forget strategy, by which you don't receive active portfolio management
- can underperform just because of cost of fees.

Corporate super funds

Usually associated with your employer, corporate super funds have their own trustees and are regulated by APRA. Many are now simply outsourced master trust services. Master trusts are investment software platforms that allow for the administration of the superannuation funds. Corporate funds have developed more choice and reduced fees over the years and some also have a defined-benefit structure, through which employees are eligible for superannuation payout based on a multiple of their final average salary at retirement plus any additional contributions they have put into the fund. These can be fantastic funds and a huge boon for retirees because they are not affected by the sharemarkets, but very few employers run these now because of the expense; most employers have transformed themselves into public offer funds, running like an industry fund or a retail fund. Examples include master trusts run by Mercer and Plum; Telstra Super is now a public offer fund, accepting non-Telstra employees as members.

The advantages of corporate super funds are that the defined-benefit component can be a huge advantage, far outweighing any or all of the disadvantages, and some funds offer choice of investments. The disadvantages of corporate super funds are cost, limited service and advice offerings and restrictive investment choices.

Industry super funds

Industry funds are not-for-profit superannuation funds that were originally associated with and run by a specific industry with an internal trustee that is regulated by APRA. They tend to have low fees and limited service (although many now offer access to advisers) and appear to be appropriate to those members associated with a particular industry. They may also attract members who have lower account balances and who may be disengaged or disenfranchised from the superannuation industry and do not seek advice. Examples of industry funds include Australian Super, CBus, HESTA and REST.

The advantages of industry super funds:

- low fees
- financial advice is now offered by many funds
- diversified investments mean a reasonable return and a lowered risk of losing everything
- they are not for profit.

The disadvantages of industry super funds:

- limited or general advice offerings (although many funds now do offer a full suite of financial advice)
- limited choice of investments
- limited control of the investments and asset allocation.

Government funds

Often older state and federal government funds offered defined benefit super, which provided a guaranteed lump sum or pension available at retirement to their members (like the defined benefit corporate funds mentioned above). These are fantastic, as few guarantees are available inside superannuation owing to many funds' exposure to the sharemarket. For example, a member may be entitled to 8.25 times their final average salary over the three years prior to retirement. Alternatively, they may be eligible for a set amount each fortnight, indexed at the

Consumer Price Index (CPI) for life, and, if they die, their spouse receives 66 per cent of the deceased's pension until their own death.

Government funds have an internal trustee and are regulated by APRA. Many government departments, both state and federal, used to offer these superannuation products to their members. They are not financially viable for the government, so they have been trying to move clients out of these products for years, and current employees belong to funds that are similar to retail and corporate funds, in offering benefits based on employer and employee contributions and investment earnings. If you have one, they can be a huge benefit: rarely would I tell someone to exit the program unless they have a large debt that can be repaid by a lump sum or if they are gravely ill. Perhaps an alternative for some owners of defined-benefit pensions who need lump sums to repay debt is to cash out a portion to repay debt, and then continue to receive a smaller defined benefit.

Examples include Commonwealth Superannuation Scheme (CSS), ESSSuper (Victoria's Emergency Services & State Super fund) and State Super Scheme (SSS) (New South Wales government super).

The advantages of government defined-benefit funds:

- guaranteed lump sum or income stream at retirement, so no retirement financial planning required
- no fluctuation caused by volatile sharemarkets
- income streams are usually indexed to inflation (UK pensions, as received by Australian citizens, are not indexed)
- lump sums are often augmented by member contributions for those who choose to salary sacrifice.

The disadvantages of government defined-benefit funds:

- after death only the spouse can receive a defined-benefit income stream (of 66 per cent or similar); other dependants, such as children, are not eligible to receive income streams from the deceased, and the benefits are lost forever
- lump sums obtain no benefit from a rising sharemarket
- some are not indexed or fully indexed
- you often cannot make additional contributions or investments to the fund.

Small APRA fund

While rarely used, a small APRA fund (SAF) is like a self managed super fund, but it has an external trustee and is regulated by APRA. They may be appropriate for SMSF members who are going overseas and do not meet the SMSF regulatory requirements for residency, or for someone who wants the investment choice of an SMSF without the compliance obligations.

The advantages of small APRA funds:

- good for people with legal disabilities, such as compensation recipients
- allow SMSF members to move into a comparable fund if they move overseas
- estate planning (spouses can receive tax-free reversionary pensions)
- disqualified members of SMSF can be members
- low compliance risks.

The disadvantages of small APRA funds:

- trustee has to sign all cheques and documentation
- limitations on investments
- additional cost for an external trustee
- not widely used because most people meet the requirements to maintain an SMSF.

Moving from one fund to another

It is simple to move your money from one super fund to another — this is called a superannuation rollover. A rollover is not considered a contribution to super as the funds are already inside the superannuation system. Most funds will have a standard rollover form for you to complete to allow you to roll your money in or out of their fund.

Superannuation choice was introduced some years back and unless you have an employment contract that prohibits choice or are a member of a defined benefit scheme that is exempt from the super choice legislation, then you will be eligible to choose a fund for your super.

You employer is supposed to give you a superannuation choice form to allow you to choose your fund, giving you more freedom as to where your work superannuation is directed. To get a copy of the form you can visit the ATO website (www.ato.gov.au), and type 'superannuation choice form' into the search engine.

Find your lost super

You can undertake a super search on the ATO website (www.ato .gov.au/superseeker). You'll need your tax file number (TFN), name and date of birth. More than $20 billion in lost super is spread among five million accounts. Claim yours today!

Getting money into superannuation

People are sometimes confused about how they can put money into superannuation. This may be a function of the government's changing legislation on an already complex system, but the result is that some people simply 'opt out' — that is, they don't put money into superannuation because they simply don't understand how. This section will describe the benefits of superannuation contributions.

Superannuation guarantee

If you earn more than $450 per month and are aged under 75, your employer must put an additional amount of 9 per cent (rising to 9.25 per cent from 1 July 2013) of your salary into a complying superannuation fund within 28 days of the end of each quarter. The age limit is abolished on 1 July 2013. This is the law and penalties apply to employers who do not abide by these regulations. The employer receives a tax deduction for your superannuation contributions, and your super fund must pay 15 per cent tax on your contributions, or 30 per cent tax if you earn more than $300 000 per year.

You can put money into superannuation in a number of ways and a few payment methods are also available, but before you make a contribution, you need to know that there are two types of contribution.

Tip

The superannuation guarantee (SG) will rise from 9 per cent to 12 per cent between 1 July 2013 and 1 July 2019. You can see the rate of superannuation you will receive under these proposed changes in table 7.1, for example income levels of $50 000 per annum and $100 000 per year.

Table 7.1: rates of superannuation guarantee (SG) rise

Year	Rate (%)	Income $50 000 ($)	Income $100 000 ($)
2013–14	9.25	4625	
2014–15	9.50	4750	9500
2015–16	10.00	5000	10000
2016–17	10.50	5250	10500
2017–18	11.00	5500	11000
2018–19	11.50	5750	11500
2019–20	12.00	6000	12000

Concessional contribution

A concessional contribution is a superannuation contribution made before any tax has been deducted from your income. It was previously known as a deductible contribution and is sometimes informally called a pre-tax contribution. If you make a concessional contribution to your super, your fund deducts 15 per cent tax. Concessional contributions include salary-sacrifice contributions and tax-deductible contributions for self-employed people who earn 10 per cent or more (the 10 per cent rule) of their earnings from self-employed activities. The difference is that employees cannot make lump-sum concessional contributions, unless they earn a bonus — they have to make their contributions as they earn their income.

If you earn more than $277 778 per year (lucky you!), then your super guarantee contributions will be capped: that is, your employer doesn't have to pay you any more than $25 000.

Self-employed people have the benefit of leaving their superannuation contributions until the end of the year to manage their tax better.

If your highest marginal tax rate is more than 15 per cent, then it would be beneficial to put money into superannuation if you have spare cash.

How to reduce your CGT

If you are over the age of 55 and under the age of 65, and retired, you are considered to be self-employed as 10 per cent or more of your income will come from self-employment activities (simply because you will receive no income from employment sources). If you are selling a property or shares to move money into superannuation, you can reduce your capital gains tax (CGT) by contributing up to a $25 000 of the capital gain to superannuation.

If you are employed, you can make salary sacrifice contributions throughout the year to reduce the amount of CGT payable on the sale of an asset by maximising your concessional contributions and paying just 15 per cent tax on your income instead of 19 per cent, 32.5 per cent, 37 per cent or 45 per cent tax: a saving of up to 67 per cent!

Contribution tax

For the vast majority of taxpayers, super contribution tax is levied at 15 per cent of your concessional contributions. For example, if you put $25 000 into your super fund, as an employer superannuation guarantee amount or salary sacrifice, or both, you will pay 15 per cent tax on that $25 000 contribution: $25 000 × 15 per cent = $3750. If you earn $80 000 per year and do not salary sacrifice anything, your employer will have to pay $7200 into your super fund, and it would attract a 15 per cent tax or $1080. The tax is deducted inside the fund.

However, if you earn more than $300000, that 15 per cent contribution tax will be doubled to 30 per cent. Income will be defined as including your taxable income, concessional superannuation contributions, adjusted fringe benefits, total net investment loss, target foreign income, and tax-free government pensions and benefits, less child support.

The government even gives an example for a person earning $285000, who made $20000 in concessional superannuation contributions. That $20000 would be included as income, making the earnings exceed $300000 ($285000 plus $20000 = $305000), so the contribution would be subject to the additional 30 per cent tax. The first $15000 would be taxed at 15 per cent and the $5000 excess above $300000 would attract 30 per cent tax.

The government has previously introduced similar programs for higher income earners that ended up costing more for all super funds and thus all account holders by increasing administration costs, just to calculate these higher levels of tax. New systems and more staff means more resources are needed to administer super funds and so costs increase for all superannuation account holders. Certainly this is not a desired outcome for the government, but I don't think this strategy was well thought through and previous models also failed, but it is nonetheless the current law.

Non-concessional contribution

Previously known as undeductible contributions, and known informally as after-tax contributions, non-concessional contributions are made from your after-tax salary. They are tax-free contributions, because the theory is that you have probably already been taxed on that money, unless the money came from an inheritance, windfall or compensation payment that is not taxable. When this money goes into the super fund it is not taxed.

Non-concessional contributions are limited to $150000 per year; however, they can be averaged over three years, as shown in table 7.2 (overleaf).

Table 7.2: superannuation contributions limits

Age	Concessional limit ($)	Non-concessional limit ($)
Under 65	25 000	150 000 per year or 450 000 (three-year average)
Over 65 but under 75*	25 000	150 000
Over 75†	25 000	Nil

* Over-65s must meet the work test to make a contribution to super; that is, they need to work at least 40 hours in any 30 consecutive days in the financial year to be eligible to make a contribution to super.

† Over-75s will be allowed to receive mandated superannuation guarantee contributions after 1 July 2013.

Government co-contribution

The government co-contribution scheme is designed to boost retirement savings for lower income workers. If you make a non-concessional (after-tax, not salary sacrifice) contribution to super, and you satisfy the eligibility rules, the government will pay up to $500 into your super fund when you complete your tax return (so the co-contribution goes into your super fund in the year after you make the contribution). To be eligible for the full $500 from the government, you must earn less than $31 920. If you earn between $31 920 and $46 920 you will receive part of the additional $500; once your income exceeds $46 920, you are no longer eligible for the co-contribution. Details are provided in table 7.3.

Table 7.3: co-contribution limits

Date	Lower income threshold ($)	Higher income threshold ($)	What will I get for every $1 of eligible personal super contributions?	What is my maximum entitlement?
From 1 July 2009 until 30 June 2012	31 920	46 920	$1, up to a maximum super co-contribution of $500 a year	Your maximum entitlement is $500. However, you must reduce this by 3.333 cents for every dollar your total income, less allowable business deductions, is over $31 920, up to $46 920

Source: www.ato.gov.au.

For part-timers, casuals and those working for part of the year, making a concessional contribution to get the co-contribution is a no-brainer, assuming you can afford to put $20 per week aside from your after-tax income or have your partner put the $1000 in for you. You can even have your employer set up the $20 per week after-tax contribution so you don't have to think about it. This is a popular way of building super for families where one partner is full time and the other partner is part time or on a lower wage (below $46 920).

This is also great for young adults and students with casual jobs. Parents can even consider helping out reluctant young adults, by contributing $1000, or part thereof, to get them interested in superannuation. Remember, superannuation must be paid to all employees who earn more than $450 per month (and work more than 30 hours a week if aged less than 18), so why not teach your kids to learn about super as early as possible by helping them out with a few extra dollars for the co-contribution.

The co-contribution has been reduced in past budgets and table 7.4 (overleaf) shows the reductions.

Table 7.4: co-contribution rates

Year	Amount ($)
2011–2012	1000
2012–2013+	500

Eligibility for co-contribution

The ATO states that to be eligible for the co-contribution scheme, you must meet the following conditions:

- you must make an eligible personal super contribution by 30 June each year into a complying super fund and not claim a deduction for all of it

- your total income (minus any allowable business deductions) must be less than the higher income threshold

- 10 per cent or more of your total income must come from eligible employment-related activities, carrying on a business or a combination of both

- you must be less than 71 years old at the end of the year of income

- you must not be the holder of a temporary visa at any time during the income year, unless you are a New Zealand citizen or holder of a prescribed visa

- you must lodge your income tax return for the relevant income year.

Co-contribution case study

Margaret earns $36 000 per year, before tax, working three days per week in a bookshop. Margaret has no allowable deductions. She has organised to put $20 per week ($1040 per year) from her pay into her super fund as a non-concessional contribution (no tax is deducted). As Margaret's salary is less than $61 920, she is eligible for some, but not all, of the superannuation co-contribution.

Margaret visits the ATO website (www.ato.gov.au) and types 'superannuation co-contribution calculator' into the search engine on the top right-hand side of the page and follows the prompts through the calculator process. She discovers that in 2012–13 she is eligible for $382 as a co-contribution.

When the government reduced the co-contribution scheme at the end of the 2011–12 tax year on 30 June 2012, it also introduced a low-income super tax rebate for people who earned less than $37 000 per year. So Margaret will also receive an additional tax rebate from the government of $486 (calculation: $36 000 salary × 9% employer super guarantee amount × 15% super tax). This is designed to compensate people for the removal of the higher co-contribution of $1000 on 30 June 2012, although it a smaller benefit.

The co-contribution is money for nothing and everyone who works and earns less than $46 920 should be taking advantage of the opportunity to get something for nothing.

Super tax rebate for low-income earners

The government has introduced a superannuation tax rebate for those earning less than $37 000 per year. This legislation was initiated on 1 July 2012 to compensate for the reduction in the co-contribution payment from $1000 to $500. This is called the low-income super contribution (LISC). The government rebates the 15 per cent superannuation contribution tax your super fund pays on mandated super guarantee contributions, salary sacrifice contributions or contributions made by self-employed people earning less than $37 000 per year.

The government promised, back in 2010, that they would not penalise those earning less than $37 000 per year under the changing tax and superannuation laws. The LISC is therefore designed to ensure that lower income earners are no worse off. Under this scheme, 3.6 million Australians will receive a contribution of up to $500 into their superannuation funds.

Salary sacrifice

Salary sacrifice directs some of your gross (before-tax) salary into superannuation, and rather than paying your normal marginal rate on that money, your super fund will pay 15 per cent tax on your contributions. Your employer makes the deduction from your pay and sends the money direct to your super fund.

The reason why it is a 'sacrifice' is because your money is placed into superannuation, where you can't get access to it until you meet a condition of release, such as retiring permanently from the workforce. You will reduce the amount of cash you receive from your pay, but benefit from increasing your retirement savings and reducing your personal tax rate on the sacrificed amount.

How to set up salary sacrifice

Speak to your human resources manager or paymaster at your place of employment to set up a salary sacrifice arrangement. It is a simple process and, as you can see in the following case study, a very profitable activity.

If you are self-employed, you can simply write a cheque out to your super fund before 30 June each year or make regular additional monthly or quarterly payments to your super fund by your current method. Speak to your super fund, accountant or bookkeeper about how to do this.

Salary sacrifice case study

James is 40 years of age and earns $75 000 per year. James needs $48 000 per year to live on, although he spends more than that if he has it in his pocket and doesn't really notice the additional spending.

Recommendation: James to salary sacrifice $15 000 per year.

If James does nothing, he will pay $15 921 in tax on his salary each year and have a net income of $59 079. He will also receive $5738 from his employer superannuation guarantee, which is 9 per cent of his $75 000 salary (after contributions tax).

As shown in table 7.5, if James salary sacrifices $15 000 per year from his $75 000 salary, he will have $17 340 in his super fund (after contributions tax) and save $2250 in income tax. Couple this with the power of compound interest, and he will have a very comfortable retirement.

Table 7.5: salary sacrifice comparison for James*

Description	Without salary sacrifice ($)	With salary sacrifice ($)
Gross salary	75 000	75 000
Salary sacrifice amount	0	15 000
Taxable income	75 000	60 000
Income tax payable	15 921	11 046
Superannuation contributions tax payable	861	810 on 60 000 2250 on 15 000
Total tax payable	16 782	14 106
Net income	59 079	48 954
Amount that goes into his superannuation account	5 730†	4590 + 12 750 = 17 340‡
Tax savings	**Nil**	2 676

* Based on tax rates in the 2012–13 and 2013–14 tax years.
† 9 per cent employer super guarantee contribution on a wage of $75 000 per year (less 15 per cent contributions tax). This figure will rise to 9.5 per cent as of 1 July 2013.
‡ Includes the 9 per cent SG contribution from his employer on $60 000 wage as required by law.

To illustrate the recommendation further, if James earns $75 000 per year and salary sacrifices $15 000 per year, assuming an investment return of 8 per cent for 20 years and an existing superannuation account balance of $100 000, then James will retire with $1 379 802, as you can see in table 7.6 (overleaf).

This excludes any increases in salary or any increases in the legislated superannuation guarantee amount of 9 per cent, both of which will certainly increase. So if this simple and very conservative example can produce a $1.4 million retirement benefit then imagine what you can do by integrating a number of other superannuation strategies to augment your retirement savings.

Table 7.6: superannuation balance with salary sacrifice

Year	Opening balance ($)	Super guarantee ($)	Salary sacrifice ($)	Total ($)	8% return ($)	End of year balance ($)
1	100 000	5738	12750	118488	9479	127967
2	127967	5738	12750	146454	11716	158170
3	158170	5738	12750	176658	14133	190790
4	190790	5738	12750	209278	16742	226020
5	226020	5738	12750	244508	19561	264068
6	264068	5738	12750	282556	22604	305160
7	305160	5738	12750	323648	25892	349540
8	349540	5738	12750	368027	29442	397469
9	397469	5738	12750	415957	33277	449233
10	449233	5738	12750	467721	37418	505138
11	505138	5738	12750	523626	41890	565516
12	565516	5738	12750	584004	46720	630724
13	630724	5738	12750	649211	51937	701148
14	701148	5738	12750	719636	57571	777207
15	777207	5738	12750	795694	63656	859350
16	859350	5738	12750	877837	70227	948064
17	948064	5738	12750	966552	77324	1043876
18	1043876	5738	12750	1062363	84989	1147352
19	1147352	5738	12750	1165840	93267	1259107
20	1259107	5738	12750	1277594	102208	1379802

Getting money out of super

You can only withdraw money from superannuation if you meet a condition of release. Conditions of release include:

- being over age 65 (working or not)
- being aged 55 to 64 (preservation age), if you are retired (working less than 10 hours a week)

- transition to retirement (limited to a maximum of 10 per cent of super balance for over 55s)
- financial hardship (very strict rules and regulations)
- death
- disablement (permanent or temporary)
- if your benefits are less than $200
- terminal medical condition
- compassionate grounds.

Preservation age

Your preservation age is the age at which you can retire and legally gain access to your superannuation funds. Naturally, you can retire before that — in fact, whenever you want — but you will not have access to your superannuation, so you will need to live on funds held outside of the superannuation environment.

Depending on the year you were born, your preservation age will vary. For those born before 1 July 1960 your preservation age will be 55. For those born after 1 July 1960, your preservation is listed in table 7.7.

Table 7.7: preservation ages

Date of birth	Preservation age
Before 1 July 1960	55
1 July 1960–30 June 1961	56
1 July 1961–30 June 1962	57
1 July 1962–30 June 1963	58
1 July 1963–30 June 1964	59
From 1 July 1964	60

Source: www.ato.gov.au.

For your information

The ATO website (www.ato.gov.au/super) provides information about all of the other conditions of release and how to access your super.

Superannuation is tax-free for over 60s

If you are over the age of 60 and you have met a condition of release, you can cash money out of super and pay no tax.

Account-based pension

Formerly known as an allocated pension, an account-based pension is simply a retirement income stream commenced with money from superannuation. It is not a product and you pay no additional tax when you change from accumulation mode to pension mode in your super fund.

In order to be eligible to commence an account-based pension, you must meet a condition of release. This includes being retired over the age of 55, or being over the age of 65, whether you are working or not.

You must withdraw a minimum amount from your pension account each year in order to maintain the tax benefits, which include no income tax if you are over the age of 60, no capital gains tax and no tax on earnings, no matter what your age. There is currently no maximum draw down, although there used to be.

The minimum draw down, or withdrawal, is calculated according to your age and a percentage minimum multiplied by your account balance at the commencement of the pension or at 1 July each year, as shown in table 7.8.

Table 7.8: minimum draw downs from an account-based pension

Age	Minimum payment as a percentage of account balance
55–64	4
65–74	5
75–79	6
80–84	7
85–89	9
90–94	11
95+	14

The government has allowed a 25 per cent reduction in the minimum percentages in the past few years in light of the GFC and its effect on superannuation balances. The theory is that they were hoping that sharemarkets would pick up and people could draw less from their funds, allowing them to grow in value. You will need to check to see if that benefit has been extended at the beginning of each financial year.

You do not have to have all of your superannuation in pension mode and you may split your superannuation into more than one account-based pension. If you leave some of your super in accumulation mode you may be eligible to contribute into it after you retire, for example, if you get part-time work or if you sell an asset and make a contribution before you turn 65.

An account-based pension is very flexible, allowing superannuants to make lump-sum withdrawals if they want to, in addition to receiving their regular income payments. If you are retired and you want to take a lump sum out of your superannuation fund, say to buy a caravan or renovate the bathroom, you can do so.

If an account-based pension recipient dies, a surviving dependant can continue to take the tax-free pension and enjoy the tax-free status of the pension until they die. Non-dependants may receive some of the account free of tax, but pay 16.5 per cent tax on other parts of the account (there's more about this in chapter 13 and a worked example in chapter 14).

Account-based pension case study

David has $800 000 in his super fund and he wants to draw an account-based pension at age 60. David will need to declare retirement so he can meet a condition of release and therefore begin his account-based pension. The minimum David can draw from his super pension account will be 4 per cent of his account balance ($32 000). There is no maximum withdrawal amount.

On the $800 000 invested in his account-based pension, David will pay no earnings tax and no capital gains tax (CGT), no matter where the funds are invested so long as they stay in the superannuation environment. David can access lump sums in his super when he wants to and he can even cease his account-based pension and put his super back into accumulation mode, and recommence a pension at a later stage. This pension has a very flexible structure.

David will not pay any income tax on the income he draws once he is over 60 years of age. In summary, David pays no CGT, no earnings tax (so he receives 100 per cent of his franking credits back on shares) and no income tax.

On David's death, his dependants will be paid the remainder of David's account as a lump sum or an income stream free of tax. Non-dependants, such as adult children, will receive a lump sum, though some tax may be deducted.

Transition-to-retirement income stream

A transition-to-retirement income stream (TRIS) allows you to withdraw between 4 per cent (3 per cent in the 2012–13 financial year) and 10 per cent of your total TRIS account each year to subsidise your normally earned income if you want to work part time or so you can salary sacrifice up to $25 000 into your super fund. This can be a smart strategy for boosting your super in the years immediately before retirement. You need to be aged over 55 and less than 65. Once you are age 65 or over, you have reached a full condition of release and you can have full access to your super investments, so you don't need a TRIS. TRIS is a non-commutable income stream, meaning you cannot make lump sum withdrawals from the fund, as you are limited to withdrawing 10 per cent of the fund balance each year, but most people choose to take it monthly.

When you set up a TRIS, your superannuation money is split into a pension account and an accumulation account. Further contributions go into the accumulation account; you cannot make contributions to your pension account. However, you can stop a TRIS, consolidate your accounts, and then re-establish a TRIS to combine funds as your superannuation savings grow.

If you are a member of an SMSF, before setting up a TRIS you must ensure that your SMSF trust deed allows for such an income stream. If not, you will need to update the trust deed (for a cost of about $500).

If your spouse has a low super balance, it may also be possible to establish a TRIS and re-contribute the TRIS income as a non-concessional contribution to their account and also salary sacrifice the maximum concessional contributions into their account too. This may be a major benefit to avoid the $500 000 benchmark, whereby your concessional contributions will be limited to $25 000 if your balance exceeds $500 000.

A TRIS can be useful if you want to sell an asset inside your SMSF that may attract CGT. Not only do you not pay the 15 per cent earnings tax in a TRIS but there is also no CGT, so if you want to sell an asset free of CGT, then a TRIS offers a tax-free method.

A TRIS offers the same benefits as an account-based pension: income paid from it is tax-free for over 60s or concessionally taxed for those aged 55 to 59; there is no CGT; and no earnings tax for assets held inside your TRIS account. Even if you don't need the income and may still be able to afford to salary sacrifice up to the full $25 000 per year, establishing a TRIS can offer benefits.

For those aged 55–59 the non-taxable portion of their income is tax-free and the taxable portion is taxed at their normal marginal tax rate. However, it also attracts a 15 per cent rebate, ensuring maximum tax paid is just 31.5 per cent (including Medicare).

Here's an example. Let's say you have $400 000 in your pension account and $350 000 is taxable and $50 000 is non-taxable (check your member statement in your tax return if you're not sure). The portion of income that relates to the taxable component ($350 000) will be taxed at your normal marginal tax rate, but you will also receive a rebate of 15 per cent to reduce that tax (to nil for many people). Your non-taxable portion ($50 000) remains tax-free.

If you withdraw the minimum of 4 per cent of the account balance at 1 July, you would be drawing $16 000 per year. Since $50 000 of the $400 000 balance is tax-free, that equates to 12.5 per cent of $16 000, or $2000. The remaining $14 000 is fully taxable. If you earn less than $80 000 but more than $37 000, you would pay $5200 (32.5 per cent) in income tax. However, you would receive a 15 per cent tax rebate that would reduce your tax by $2400 to $2800.

Transition-to-retirement case study

Anna has $350 000 in her super fund: $100 000 is an untaxed portion and she commences a TRIS while salary sacrificing $25 000 per year and drawing enough from her TRIS to ensure her cash flow is exactly the same. So she feels no pain — this is an important point because the moment you mention savings to people they immediately think of having to give up their comforts and inertia sets in. So, Anna would be drawing $13 867 per year, or about 3.8 per cent of her account balance, remembering the minimum she can withdraw will be $10 500 (4 per cent) and the maximum, $35 000 (10 per cent). See table 7.9.

Table 7.9: the effect of Anna salary sacrificing $25 000 per year and supplementing her income with a TRIS of $13 867 per year to help build super*

Item	Do nothing ($)	Implement strategy ($)
Gross income	76 000	71 707
Tax payable	17 387	13 094
Net income	58 613	58 613
Super balance	377 046	22 737
Pension balance	—	360 632
Net super balance end of year 1	377 046	383 370
Balance at 65	720 247	822 840

*Assume investment return of 7 per cent, salary increasing at 4 per cent per year and excess income not reinvested.

Graphically, the benefit of this strategy versus doing nothing over 10 years will look like figure 7.1.

Figure 7.1: a comparison of doing nothing with using a TRIS to boost super

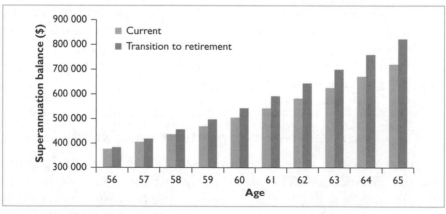

Source: © BT Financial Group.

In this modest example, Anna will be $102592 better off at retirement. With her humble $102592 bonus she would still be better off at age 65 by $100 per week, assuming she drew 5 per cent of her balance as an account-based pension and she feels no pain in terms of cash flow as it remains the same. Her fund pays no earnings tax and no capital gains tax. A TRIS is a no brainer!

Divorce and superannuation

Superannuation forms part of your total assets in the event of a relationship breakdown under the *Family Law Act*. If you divorce, your super will form part of the separation agreement.

Five sample strategies

- Set up a self managed super fund (SMSF).

- Start salary sacrificing.

- Set up a TRIS (transition-to-retirement income stream) if you have reached your preservation age or met a condition of release.

- Set up an account-based pension if you are over age 60 and retired.

- Make non-concessional contributions to super to get the government's co-contribution.

Five sample tactics

- Talk to your accountant or a super specialist about setting up an SMSF for you.

- Talk to your adviser, employer or super fund about how to start salary sacrificing now.

- Call your super fund, accountant or adviser about setting up a TRIS if you're aged over 55.

(continued)

Five sample tactics *(cont'd)*

- Talk to your super fund, accountant or adviser about setting up an account-based pension if you are over 60 and retired.

- Start putting $20 per week of after-tax money (non-concessional contribution) into your super fund if you earn less than $46 920 so you can receive the co-contribution.

KEY POINTS

- Super is a structure, not an investment product, so if you hear someone say they don't like super, then what they are saying is that they don't understand it.

- You can manage your own super using a self managed superannuation fund (SMSF) or you can have someone else manage it for you through a retail or industry fund. The ATO suggests you need around $200 000 to start an SMSF.

- You can't access your superannuation until you are over age 55, if you are born before 30 June 1960. If you were born after 1 July 1964, then you can't touch your super until you are 60. There is a range of preservation ages between these two dates.

- Superannuation, in accumulation mode (in the savings stage, not the income stream stage), attracts just 15 per cent earnings tax and 15 per cent capital gains tax (CGT) for assets owned for less than 12 months, and just 10 per cent CGT for assets held for more than 12 months.

- Salary sacrifice involves transferring some of your gross (before-tax) salary into your super fund; you will pay only 15 per cent tax on the contribution instead of 19 per cent, 32.5 per cent, 37 per cent or 45 per cent income tax if you received it in your normal pay. You can save up to 67 per cent of your tax bill and boost your retirement savings.

- If you earn less than $31 920 per year and you make a voluntary, non-concessional, contribution to super the government will contribute up to $500 to your super account. You will receive a part payment for income levels up to $46 920. It's money for nothing and is specifically designed to provide an incentive to save for your retirement and boost your retirement savings.

- You can buy shares or property (negative or positive gearing) inside your super fund if you have a self managed super fund (SMSF) much like you can in your own name, although most banks will lend only up to 72 per cent of the value of a property. Your tax-effective super contributions can reduce the debt on your investment property faster. The result can be far more attractive than negative gearing in your own name.

- A TRIS, or transition-to-retirement income stream, is designed for people aged 55 to 64 to draw down on their super while not paying much (or any) tax, and offering the opportunity to salary sacrifice up to $25 000 of their salary, saving up to 66 per cent in tax and boosting their super balance.

- An account-based pension is simply a retirement income stream commenced with superannuation money. You need to have enough cash in your account to pay you an income each year. People over the age of 60 drawing an income stream pay no tax: no income tax, no earnings tax and no capital gains tax on the sale of the fund's investments.

- There are two types of contributions to super: concessional (15 per cent tax as it goes into the fund) and non-concessional (zero per cent tax on entry). Salary sacrifice is a concessional contribution and is limited to $25 000 per year. Non-concessional contributions are limited to $150 000 per year or, if you are under age 65, you can make a lump-sum contribution of $450 000 and no further contributions for the subsequent two years (averaging provision over three years). Over 65s are limited to contributing $150 000 per year, and they must meet the work test to make a contribution to super.

CHAPTER 8

SELF MANAGED
SUPER FUNDS (SMSFs)

As technology advances, it reverses the characteristics of every situation again and again. The age of automation is going to be the age of 'do it yourself'.

Marshall McLuhan, Canadian philosopher

A self managed super fund (SMSF) is a superannuation fund that has four or fewer members and is controlled by the members with the sole purpose of providing retirement planning benefits to members or their beneficiaries. The members are the trustees (the two words 'members' and 'trustees' are virtually interchangeable when talking about self managed superannuation funds).

Self managed superannuation funds are regulated by the Australian Taxation Office (ATO) and not by the Australian Prudential Regulation Authority (APRA), which regulates, for example, retail and industry funds. The ATO will send you questionnaires to test your knowledge of your SMSF trustee duties, undertake audits on SMSFs and issue penalties for non-compliance.

The members as trustees make the investment decisions and manage the fund's compliance responsibilities, including preparing the annual accounts and tax returns, having the audit completed, organising actuarial certificates, managing superannuation contributions and paying pensions.

The ATO produces a number of booklets about setting up and running SMSFs and I highly recommend that you obtain copies from the ATO website (www.ato.gov.au) or a local office of the ATO to get a better understanding of how to run an SMSF.

Tip

For a thorough overview of SMSFs, you can obtain my book *SMSF DIY Guide*, published in 2012 by Wiley, from your regular bookshop or online.

Why set up an SMSF?

People who set up SMSFs are usually seeking more flexibility in, and control of, their superannuation investments. Many are seeking independence from large institutions; some may have lost faith in the superannuation system because of poor investment management, poor advice or lack of genuine investment options. Some people are seeking a better range of investments than is available through a public-offer super fund, such as direct shares, direct property, instalment warrants, contracts for difference (CFDs) or even physical assets such as gold.

SMSFs allow members to combine superannuation assets so they have a larger pool of funds to invest, which may be handy if you want to buy a property or seek economies of scale for your investment funds. While you can combine the assets for investment purposes, it's important to point out that each member will always have a member balance, which needs to be identified and separated for accounting purposes and to meet the requirements of the laws governing superannuation. You will see a section in the end of year SMSF tax return called Member Statement, where you have to show the breakdown of your superannuation components and the total superannuation in each trustee's name. If the balances are combined, and not segregated, when invested, you may need to hire an actuary to determine which portion of the asset is owned by each member and this has to be shown in their account balance. This sounds complex, but it is very straightforward as you simply hire someone to work it out for you for a couple of hundred dollars.

Keep in mind that superannuation is not a managed fund or a specific investment; it is a structure under which you invest (see chapter 3 for information about investment structures), so do not get disheartened with superannuation if you have lost money in the past; it's more likely that your investment strategy needs attention, not the superannuation structure. Many SMSF members invest directly into term deposits, direct shares or direct residential or commercial property to improve their investment strategy. Many small and medium-sized business owners establish an SMSF so they can buy their commercial property and operate their business from the property. The property becomes their retirement fund. Incidentally, if they sell their business (goodwill and physical assets of the business), there is a chance that the sale of the premises will be free of capital gains tax (CGT) under the small business CGT exemptions and rollovers. This gives many small business owners significant advantages in establishing and running an SMSF, and since they are used to doing things for themselves, they feel reasonably comfortable with the compliance obligations.

How popular are SMSFs?

There are about 500 000 SMSFs in Australia, representing about 950 000 members. SMSFs hold more superannuation funds than both industry and retail super funds. They represent the largest level of funds invested in the superannuation environment: while about 4 per cent of the population is a member of an SMSF, the funds invested equate to more than one-third of all funds inside Australia's superannuation system and the SMSF sector is growing faster than all other superannuation sectors. Of the $1.4 trillion invested in superannuation, around $500 billion is invested through an SMSF.

As I mentioned in the previous chapter, the average SMSF has an account balance of $900 000, with an average member balance of $450 000; however, the average balance for members across all superannuation funds and across all Australians is around $71 000 for all age groups, according to the Australian Bureau of Statistics. These figures are also growing as the number of new funds grows. It is forecast that the average SMSF balance will be more than $2 million in just five years.

The global financial crisis (GFC) only accelerated the number of new funds being set up. In addition, a number of changes to superannuation made before the GFC, such as the ability to put up to $1 million into super, also catapulted the number of funds to record levels.

When sharemarkets across the globe crashed during the GFC, some superannuants lost faith in the industry and retail systems, and many took control of their superannuation by establishing an SMSF to minimise their tax and boost their retirement savings.

How to set up an SMSF

Setting up a self managed super fund is simple. First of all you will need to work out who will be a member of the fund. You may have up to four members in an SMSF, and it may include children if they are eligible to contribute to super. If you have more than two children, however, it is probably best to just have mum and dad as members. Despite the fact that an SMSF can be a great estate-planning tool, until the children have significant retirement savings it may not be worth having them as members as your costs may rise with the additional work for a disproportionate benefit early on.

An SMSF may have a single member. The tax office notes that a single-member fund will need an additional family member or any other person who does not employ the member to act as a trustee of the fund or, better still, they will need the additional layer of a corporate trustee.

You can create a corporate trustee by establishing a company to act as the trustee of the SMSF. The single member is the director of the company. For example, your corporate trustee will be known as 'Smith Pty Ltd' and it will be the trustee of the 'Smith Super Fund'. This additional layer enables a single member to act without consultation and signatures from other trustees, and the power of the corporate trustee can be delegated via estate-planning tools such as powers of attorney.

When there is more than one member in an SMSF, the members can also set up a corporate trustee in the same way. Many accountants and SMSF administrators recommend setting up a corporate trustee because a company has a perpetual life and can change directors more easily than a trust can change trustees. A trust also has a finite life of 80 years. In a trust structure, if a member dies, they have to be replaced as a trustee. This is an important reason for having a corporate trustee, so you don't have to replace trustees. You can replace or reduce the number of directors of the corporate trustee if one of them dies.

In my opinion most funds don't need corporate trustees (for example, simple mum and dad SMSFs), but it's important to seek advice on the appropriateness of the best structure for you.

You will need a name for the fund. Keep it short and simple. You will probably be writing the name many times so it is best that you keep it short. It does not have to be a unique name. You can call it the 'Smith Super Fund'. The fund will identified by its unique tax file number (TFN) and Australian Business Number (ABN), so it is quite possible to have thousands of Smith Super Funds, and yours will still be easily identifiable through the ATO.

Once you have thought of a name, then set up the fund with your SMSF administrator or accountant. They will have a service to establish a fund and will be able to provide ongoing services to satisfy most of the compliance requirements. Expect to pay between a few hundred dollars and $1500 for the establishment of a fund and another $800 to $1000 for a corporate trustee.

You will also need to provide all the details of the members to the person or company setting up the fund so they can record the members'/trustees' details, including name, address, TFN and other personal details so the ATO knows who the members/trustees are.

Once all the details are established in the application, a trust deed can be prepared and a TFN and ABN can be applied for. Expect to wait at least 28 days for your ABN and TFN. Once the trust deed has been prepared and you have received your ABN and TFN, you will need to set up a bank account in the name of the fund into which your existing superannuation can be rolled over.

Rolling over super to an SMSF

Once your fund is set up, you have received the fund's ABN and TFN, and your bank account is ready to operate, you can then roll over (or transfer) your existing superannuation accounts and consolidate them into the SMSF. Each new member of the SMSF follows the same procedures.

Your SMSF will need to send a letter of compliance to your existing superannuation fund accompanied by a standard rollover form (often supplied by your existing super fund). Your existing fund will then send the funds to your SMSF via cheque or EFT. Each transfer will be accompanied by a member statement from the original fund. Your member statement will have a breakdown of your account balance, taxable and non-taxable funds portions, contributions and other account details that are to be carried forward into your SMSF. It's very important to ensure that whoever receives your member statements (an accountant or SMSF administrator, for instance) checks the accuracy of your member details.

Tip

Please note that your trust deed must be updated regularly as legislation changes to incorporate the new legislation. You don't have to update it each year, but approximately every three to five years is prudent, or at least have it reviewed by your accountant, administrator or adviser to ensure that it is up to date. For example, I've seen many people wanting to establish (or already established in) a transition-to-retirement income stream, but the trust deed does not specifically allow it because they have an old trust deed compiled before the TRIS legislation was introduced.

Nomination of beneficiaries

Before the trust deed is finalised, one important section must be completed. The trust deed must set the rules for how members can direct their super to be paid on their death. I strongly recommend that your trust deed allows for both binding and non-binding nomination of beneficiaries, but specifically recommend that you make a binding nomination of beneficiaries.

It's also important that the trustee can pay reversionary pensions in the event of death, which means that dependants can continue to receive tax-free incomes from superannuation that were previously received by their deceased partners. For example, when a husband dies and leaves behind his wife who continues to need income, she can receive his account-based pension tax-free rather than having to cash the money out of the tax-effective superannuation system.

Each SMSF member needs to plan for what will happen with their super when they die by filling out a nomination of beneficiaries form. If the member completes a binding nomination of beneficiaries, the fund's trustees will be bound, without discretion, to distribute your super funds on your death as you direct in your nomination; they are not bound by non-binding nominations, and can use them simply as a guide for distributing your super. There are special rules to be followed for a binding nomination, but these nominations are worth the extra effort because they give greater certainty for paying out your super after your death.

This is your chance to name a financial dependant to receive your funds in the event of your death. For example, '100 per cent to wife' is how a binding nomination may distribute your account balance. There will most likely also be an option for dependants to receive your account balance tax-free or, if you are drawing a pension at the time of death, for dependants to continue to receive a pension after your death.

Non-dependants cannot receive pensions that were being paid to the deceased member; instead they will be paid lump sums, minus 16.5 per cent tax on the taxable portion of the fund. This is a bit like a death tax because, if you are over 60 and cash out money from super, you don't pay any tax, but if you die with money in your taxable portion, your non-dependants will pay tax on the money they receive. Dependants, however, pay no tax on death benefits. The trick is to die slowly, cash out your money, distribute it to family and exit the planet — I'm just kidding of course, but that is the implication of the tax law governing this little piece of legislation.

The investment strategy

Your SMSF needs a written investment strategy to detail the purpose, circumstances and objectives of the fund. The strategy also has to be reviewed regularly to ensure it remains appropriate to all members. The investment strategy must consider the following:

- investing in such a way as to maximise returns based upon the risk profile of members
- diversifying investments to minimise risk through setting a long-term strategy
- funding costs, benefits and pensions to members
- considering personal insurance for all members
- considering the different needs of members based on age, sex, life expectancy, employment and retirement needs, to name a few.

> ## Tip
>
> See the resources section at www.samhenderson.com.au for a sample investment strategy.

Rules for investing in an SMSF

Given the many tax advantages of investing inside an SMSF, it's important to be aware of your investment restrictions and understand what you can and can't do with your fund.

Some of the rules surrounding self managed super are more or less common sense, although the ATO is careful to point these out in case there is any doubt. These rules are simple and straightforward and include the following:

- You must act honestly in all matters concerning your fund.
- You must exercise skill and diligence in managing your fund.
- You must act in the best interest of members.
- You must keep the money and assets of your fund separate from your other money and assets, for example, your personal assets.
- You must retain control over the fund.
- You must develop and implement an investment strategy.
- You can't enter into contracts or behave in a way that hinders you or other trustees from performing or exercising functions or powers.
- You must allow members access to certain information.
- You cannot allow members to access funds before a condition of release is met (see chapter 7 for a discussion of conditions of release).

You may appoint advisers to help you manage your fund; however, the ultimate responsibility lies with you as a member/trustee of the fund. The ATO will be asking questions of you if an audit shows an irregularity, so it is very important that you understand your role and responsibilities as a member/trustee of your fund.

Other essential matters you must be aware of in managing your fund include:

- the sole purpose test
- in-house assets
- related-party transactions
- arm's length transactions
- no borrowing allowed except under particular circumstances.

The sole purpose test

The sole purpose of your SMSF is to provide retirement benefits to members or distributions to beneficiaries in the event of death — this rule actually applies to every super fund in Australia. This means that you cannot set up an SMSF with the intention of accessing your funds early. Such schemes are likely to receive the full attention of the ATO, and strict penalties apply to trustees who break the law. The sole purpose test is the most important of all the rules relating to SMSFs.

You cannot seek to run a business with your super fund: you cannot trade your assets in a business-like manner and take the risks associated with running a business. As you can probably work out, the risks of running a business jeopardise your retirement savings. Given that the fund is set up to manage your retirement savings and ensure that you can be self-funded in retirement, the government does not want you taking such risks: otherwise you may end up on the Age Pension and supported by the government — exactly what it is trying to avoid and the reason that it provides these wonderful tax breaks to superannuation.

In-house assets

An in-house asset is an investment or a loan to a related party of your SMSF. You may only provide a loan to a member of the fund for personal purposes for up to 5 per cent of the member's account balance, and you may only have up to 5 per cent of your fund invested in the assets of members of the fund.

The biggest exception to the in-house asset rule is what's called 'business real property'. That means a business owner may purchase a property inside the SMSF and then lease the property from the fund to run their business. This is one reason many small and medium-sized businesses start an SMSF. It is a terrific way to purchase the business property, pay it down with tax-efficient superannuation contributions (15 per cent tax instead of 19 per cent, 32.5 per cent, 37 per cent or 45 per cent marginal tax rates) and, at retirement, dispose of the property as well as the business free of capital gains tax!

Related-party transactions

Your fund may not buy assets, such as a residential investment property, from yourself or any other associates of the fund, such as family members or business partners. I've had many clients wanting their fund to buy investment properties from them personally so they could boost their super and reduce their capital gains tax at retirement. This is not possible. However, it is possible to purchase a *new* residential investment property within an SMSF structure and sell it at retirement free of capital gains tax, under the current legislation. Under the right structure, you may also borrow money to do this.

However, there are circumstances where you may transfer an asset into the fund. For example, you may transfer listed securities (shares) into your fund because they are priced daily by an external exchange with no means of manipulation by fund members. You may also transfer commercial property (business real property) into the fund from a related party.

Arm's length transactions

Any transactions made by an SMSF need to be made on a commercial basis. You cannot sell an asset to the fund at a discounted rate to save yourself stamp duty or capital gains tax — this is strictly forbidden. Sale prices and purchase prices must always reflect their true market value — this is called an arm's-length transaction.

The same can be said for income received by your fund. All income received on your investments must be received under commercial terms. For example, all income received from commercial rental property tenanted by your own business must be at a commercial rental rate.

No borrowing — but there are ways

You may not take money out of your fund to lend to members or associates or anyone else under any circumstances until a condition of release is met that fulfils the legal requirements. Nor can you use the fund's assets as security against lending facilities for yourself, your relatives or associates, or anyone else.

That being said, there are some exceptions to the borrowing rules that may provide an opportunity for you and your fund to boost members' retirement benefits. Under these following circumstances you can:

- borrow up to 10 per cent of the fund's assets for a maximum of 90 days to meet benefit payments to members

- borrow up to 10 per cent of the fund's total assets to settle share transactions for a total of up to seven days

- enter into limited recourse borrowing arrangements, such as instalment warrants or similar structures, that meet the requirements of the ATO.

For investment purposes, the last of these provides the greatest opportunity for borrowing to buy shares or property inside your fund. While borrowing in general is not allowed, since 24 September 2007 investment through instalment warrants have been allowed. An instalment warrant, also known as a limited-recourse borrowing arrangement (the terms are interchangeable), allows the borrower to borrow money from a lender to purchase a new asset. The lender is only able to have recourse, in the event of default by the borrower, on the actual asset for which the loan was intended. That is, it cannot take security over the other assets inside your SMSF. As a result, lenders generally won't lend to the same extent as they would if they had your house and other investments as security for the loan.

For example, if I wanted to buy a property inside my super fund, a bank would lend me a maximum of 72 per cent of the value of the property (although banks are slowly raising their loan-to-value ratios as they realise the risk of SMSF loans is lower than first expected). Furthermore, the bank may ask for personal guarantees, as it can't have further security on any of the fund's other assets (try to resist such requests by the bank). The interest rate is likely to be a bit higher and the costs of establishing the loan may also be higher, as legal fees are higher and risks are greater for the bank. A document outlining the nature of the instalment warrant or limited recourse loan must also be provided, and there will be further costs for this.

Despite the additional costs for setting up this structure and additional ongoing costs, it can be an attractive strategy for those who are five or more years away from retirement because the debt is repaid with tax-effective super contributions, and the property can be sold free of capital gains tax in retirement. So, too, income from the property will be tax-free for retired people over the age of 60.

Who can give you advice?

Despite the name 'self managed', you will definitely need assistance from one or more advisers, who may include an accountant, a specialist SMSF administrator, a financial adviser, an auditor, an actuary or even a lawyer. At the very least you will need someone to do your annual accounts and tax return; that will also include your annual audit, which should be conducted by an external party other than your accountant (though your accountant is likely to recommend the auditor). Accountants and SMSF administrators are well placed to take care of your basic needs.

As the owner and operator of both an SMSF specialist administration firm and a financial planning firm, I can assure you that it is virtually impossible to avoid employing the services of an SMSF administrator or accountant.

Despite hiring an SMSF administrator, accountant, financial adviser or any other service provider, the responsibility for running the fund rests solely in the hands of the members/trustees, so if the ATO comes knocking on your door, you will be the one called upon to answer questions and you will have to pay any fines or penalties for a non-compliant fund. So choose your advisers carefully and don't always go for the cheapest options. Remember what Warren Buffett says: 'Price is what you pay, value is what you get'. The simple approach is to find someone you can trust.

Accountants and SMSF specialist administrators will do the annual accounts, tax returns and assist with your annual ATO compliance of \$259 (this figure is correct for 2013–14 but is subject to change). If an actuarial certificate is required, they can organise that as well. You may need further services from these providers for organising the payment of pensions and managing contributions or withdrawals. For this type of service you can expect to pay upwards of \$2000 per year, including the preparation of annual tax returns and member statements. You will pay more for additional products, services, once-off advice or further complexities such as multiple members or administrative-heavy investments.

Many people set up SMSFs so they can manage their investments by themselves. About to 40 per cent of SMSF members employ a financial adviser to assist them with the strategic decisions and tactical portfolio management decisions. So you are never alone in managing your portfolio, and there is someone to assist you with every part of managing an SMSF.

Many financial advisers, including my own firm, now specialise in SMSF administration and advice. These specialist firms are well placed to provide you with advice for your investment strategy and portfolio management. This may include strategic advice regarding tax minimisation, super contributions, pensions, estate planning and other structural advice, and most advisers will offer tactical advice specific to your portfolio management.

What fees will you pay?

Portfolio managers will mainly be interested in investing in shares or managed funds; however, many fee-for-service firms can also offer advice on property structures and investment strategies, including gearing strategies. While fee-for-service advisers have been hard to come by in the past, the financial planning industry is undergoing a renaissance and sweeping legislative changes are aimed at moving all advisers to a fee-for-service environment. This is aimed at steering advice away from product distribution (selling of managed funds) and into quality strategic advice. Time will tell, but the importance of finding someone you can trust and relate to is paramount.

A financial adviser may charge a fee for written advice in the form of a statement of advice (SoA) and this may vary from a few hundred to many thousands of dollars, depending on the nature of advice that you are seeking. Typically an independent adviser will charge more than a large financial institution, such as a bank, because the banks recommend their own products and focus more on selling products than providing strategic advice. Many institutions will not charge for a statement of advice or they will charge a nominal advice fee of less than $1000; however, they may have entry or establishment fees, so be aware that every company will charge a different fee.

Independent advisers will typically charge upwards of $2000 for a statement of advice, in addition to further fees for implementing the advice and an ongoing fee for managing the strategy and portfolio for you.

You may be charged either a percentage-based fee or a fixed monthly or annual fee for assistance with your portfolio management and the strategic direction of the fund. If you are assessing a fee from a financial adviser, then you will need to understand how they charge. A percentage-based fee will include an adviser fee, a product fee (for a managed fund if they are used) and a platform fee. There may also be brokerage fees for trading shares and performance fees to provide a better incentive for your fund manager. The total of these will be your total annual fee. A reasonable fee for such a service is between 1.5 per cent and 2 per cent per year of the fund value so it's important that you receive good service and feel comfortable with your adviser.

More information

You can purchase my book on self managed super funds, *SMSF DIY Guide* (also published by Wiley) from any good book store or online. The book discusses in more detail many of the topics discussed in this chapter. Significantly more detail is often required before undertaking some transactions, particularly in the case of property investment purchases and transfers to, or from within, the superannuation environment.

Five sample strategies

- Establish an SMSF: choose the name; obtain the trust deed; sign binding nominations of beneficiaries; obtain a tax file number (TFN) and Australian Business Number (ABN).

- Open a bank account for your SMSF.

- Write your investment strategy.

- Open a share trading account or see an adviser about getting advice as to where and how to invest for your SMSF.

- Buy a property in your SMSF.

Five sample tactics

- Contact your adviser, accountant or an administrator to establish your SMSF, sign your binding death nominations and obtain your TFN and ABN (takes about 28 days).

- Visit your regular bank and establish a transactional bank account in the name of the fund and obtain a cheque and deposit book.

- If you are an employee, inform your employer of the new bank account details for the SMSF so they can pay your superannuation guarantee and salary sacrifice contributions into the SMSF (you may need a certificate of compliance to prove that your SMSF is a complying superannuation fund under Australian law — your adviser, administrator or accountant can assist).

- Contact E*TRADE, CommSec or a broker of your choice to establish an account to manage shares in the name of your SMSF.

- Obtain finance through a broker or directly with the bank before you start looking for a property and ensure the property is in the correct name before signing any sales transaction documentation.

KEY POINTS

- People wanting to set up an SMSF should have more than $200 000 to put into the fund (this can be the combined balances of members).

- Most SMSF members have set up an SMSF to get better control of and flexibility for their superannuation.

- Investments held inside SMSFs now account for more than one-third of all superannuation money in Australia.

- Expect to pay between $200 and $1500 to establish your fund.

- Your annual expenses will be $1500 to $2500 for administration, including preparing:

  - annual accounts

  - tax return

  - audit.

- The sole purpose of your fund is to provide retirement benefits to members or distributions to beneficiaries in the event of death.

- Other key rules affect the areas of:

  - in-house assets

  - related-party transactions

  - arm's length transactions

  - no borrowing allowed, except under particular circumstances.

- Most accountants and some financial planning specialists provide help with SMSFs, but make sure you choose a specialist.

CHAPTER 9

BORROWING MONEY TO MAKE MONEY

> When a man spends his own money to buy something for himself, he is very careful about how much he spends and how he spends it … when a man spends someone else's money on someone else, he doesn't care how much he spends or what he spends it on.
>
> *Milton Friedman, US economist*

The concept of someone else's money is simply based on the premise that you can borrow money to make money. Many people borrow money from a variety of places to put into investments, such as home loans, investment loans, margin loans, credit cards, solicitors' loans and a variety of other miscellaneous lending structures. The more desperate the circumstances of the borrower, the higher the risk and the higher the interest rate paid.

Why borrow to make money?

Many investors firmly believe that if you do not borrow money to make money, then you are not efficiently using your own assets to an optimal level. That is, you can borrow against your existing assets. But finding the right balance of debt versus equity is the key. Too much debt increases risk significantly and too little may result in an inefficient use of assets.

Many companies listed on the sharemarket borrow money to expand and increase their operations to produce more income and profits. Borrowing does, however, increase the risk for those companies, particularly if the deployment of the borrowed money does not produce the expected output needed to repay the debt and, of course, the interest. So there is risk associated with borrowing money and understanding that risk is really important. There is no shortage of countries, states, companies and individuals that have overindulged in debt.

A consistent theme throughout this book is to do your homework and create a methodology for investing. Remember, you are investing for the bad times not the good. The good times take care of themselves, but skilful management is required in challenging economic times. The reason for making this point is that if you borrow money you have two obligations to the lender:

- to repay the debt
- to pay the interest.

If you cannot do either of these two things, then you risk having your assets repossessed and being sold by the lender. In effect, the lender owns your assets until you repay them. Further ramifications of defaulting on a loan include bankruptcy, which is something you never want to experience. Defaulting is a very serious event that may have far-reaching consequences for you and your family, so it's important to read your loan contracts carefully and understand what events trigger a default or breach of your contract. For example, just because you repay your loan, you may still be in default (or breach a covenant) because the value of the asset may have dropped, increasing your loan-to-value ratio, or your profitability or cash flow may affect the bank's methodology for calculating its risk on you or your company (profitability ratios). There are many downsides to bankruptcy, including travel restrictions, and not being allowed to be a company director or trustee of an SMSF.

> ## Tip
>
> If you or someone you know is experiencing financial hardship or crisis or are considering bankruptcy, perhaps tell them to call Wesley Mission's Creditline on 1800 007 007 Monday to Friday, 9.30 am to 4.30 pm, for free financial counselling from experts in the *Bankruptcy Act*. Bankruptcy should not be taken lightly and other alternatives do often exist and should be exhausted before bankruptcy is considered. For more details, visit www.wesleymission.org.au/centres/creditline.

Investment guru Warren Buffett sums up economic slowdowns as follows: 'It's not until the tide goes out that we see who's been swimming naked'. Throughout the global financial crisis (GFC) entire nations, states and industries were caught 'swimming naked'. Some banks, through collateralised debt obligations (CDOs) and the commercial property industry, were hammered beyond recognition by the GFC and risk became the biggest talking point, as investors cashed out their money and put it under the mattress. Many banks around the globe simply went bust and others called in their loans at a time when refinancing was difficult, sending many borrowers to the wall and, because they couldn't repay the bank's loans, the banks soon followed.

When to borrow and invest

While we have seen some of the worst press commenting on how bad borrowed money is, the GFC created some of the best conditions in recent years for borrowing money: low interest rates, more stringent lending criteria and the opportunity to borrow in property and sharemarkets that were still rising. Borrowing money is still considered a common practice for assets such as shares, property and businesses.

In chapter 6 we saw how you can borrow money via a margin loan to buy shares or even use a line of credit secured by your property. In chapter 5 we saw how you can borrow money to invest in property. We also saw that the best time to buy assets is at the bottom of the economic cycle (see figure 4.2 on p. 54). When the market bottoms is also the time when people are at their most fearful, so you need to be strong in your decision-making abilities and understand how to value assets at a time when few investors are investing to take advantage of the low prices. Acting in a counter-cyclical manner can make you a lot of money, but it's not without risk, so make sure you can afford it.

I've seen in my own business that clients often cash out and sell their investments right at the worst time in the economic cycle, only to see massive increases in values within a short period of time. This is what happened in March 2009. People cashed out when share prices were low, only to see many share prices rise more than 100 per cent in the following 12 months. This is not a constructive way to invest. Cashing out at the worst time is like saying: 'We want to exit the market when assets are cheap and we will wait for asset values to rise and then reinvest when they are more expensive'. This is decision making based purely on emotion (fear) and is a certain recipe for disaster.

I remind investors that the night is always darkest before dawn. When the economic conditions appear to be at their worst and the media is going wild stirring up fear to sell more newspapers, it is often the single most opportune time to invest in the right companies. This is the time when you will see when the world's smartest investors come alive. In 2008, at the height of the banking crisis in the GFC, Warren Buffett embarked on a large preference share deal with Goldman Sachs to effectively save Goldmans — preference shares are shares in a company that offer a special deal for certain shareholders and, in Buffett's case, he negotiated a dividend of 10 per cent on his $5 billion investment, with the opportunity to buy more stock at a discount. Within 12 months he had received more than 110 per cent return on his investment, and had an option to buy $5 billion more stock at a huge reduction of market value. No doubt Mr Buffett had done his homework, but he invested good money into a good company that had short-term problems that he could solve by investing $5 billion cash into their ailing balance sheet. This is a great example of how to invest when others are running for cover.

The economic clock is a handy benchmark by which to work, although it does not always act in perfect synchronicity, and the time between each stage can vary. Having a grasp of these economic progressions gives you some insight into the best times to borrow money and invest.

I started investing straight after the 1991 recession — the one 'we had to have' — after I had left school and saved enough money to buy a property.

Actually, I had a hotted-up car that was stolen and I used the insurance money to make up a large percentage of the deposit. I used a deposit of around $15 000, to buy my first property in Newtown, a suburb of Sydney (3 kilometres from the CBD) for $155 000 and borrowed the balance. As the property increased in value, I borrowed again to purchase a house in Neutral Bay, and again to buy a property in Rozelle, and then another property in Erskineville, followed by one in Darlington (apart from Neutral Bay, they were all inner west suburbs of Sydney).

Effectively I used someone else's money to purchase all of these properties and I started with just $15 000 (plus stamp duty and legal fees) of my own money. One thing remained constant over that period: rising house prices. I used the growing equity in my properties to borrow more money, even though I wasn't necessarily making more money in my job. Rents also rose significantly, so my power to repay the interest remained strong.

Unfortunately, house prices in Sydney are now higher and a standard house in an inner-city suburb will cost you well over half a million dollars or even more than $1 million. That being said, opportunities still abound in all suburbs, in all cities and all price ranges because you can do some work yourself to renovate and improve the properties, as I did so many years ago.

House prices in Sydney remained stagnant from 2003 to 2009 and many areas, even the top areas, such as Bondi and Paddington, saw a huge drop of 25 per cent to 30 per cent or more in 2009. Then in 2010 we saw a further drop and the next up cycle didn't occur until 2013. But, over the long term, house prices and share prices have continued to rise, albeit with some fluctuation. The key for a borrower is to understand and allow for risk.

Why cash is not an investment

Putting regular amounts of money into a savings account is a handy way to accumulate cash, but it is not a sound investment for the long term, because it has no potential for capital growth. The only benefit cash offers is interest and, allowed to accumulate, that will grow your bank balance. But because cash has no means of growth beyond interest, it offers no means of leverage. Cash is therefore not an investment but simply a savings program.

While cash is considered an asset class because you have a choice to park your money in cash, many professional investors do not see cash as an investment because it will usually track inflation and therefore offers no potential for real growth beyond inflation. You need to invest into growth assets, such as shares and property, if you want to increase your wealth beyond inflation. The following case study shows the benefit of saving. The subsequent property and shares case studies will clearly illustrate the benefits of investing in growth assets. The case studies illustrate how to make money through borrowing with an investment of $50 000, and compares cash, property and shares over a 10-year period. While we assume constant growth and income levels, it's important to point out that consistency rarely reigns in any investment market, including cash interest rates, so it's easier to work with averages over a 10-year period, which are reflected in the examples.

Case study 1: cash — turn $50 000 into $81 445 in 10 years

If you put $50 000 in the bank at 5 per cent interest calculated annually for 10 years your 'investment' would look like that shown in table 9.1.

Table 9.1: growth in cash over 10 years

Year	Start of year ($)	Interest ($)	End of year ($)
1	50 000	2500	52 500
2	52 500	2625	55 125
3	55 125	2756	57 881
4	57 881	2894	60 775
5	60 775	3039	63 814
6	63 814	3191	67 005
7	67 005	3350	70 355
8	70 355	3518	73 873
9	73 873	3694	77 566
10	77 566	3878	81 445

In this example, the initial investment of $50 000 increased to $81 455, which represents a 62 per cent increase in value on the initial investment over 10 years, but it probably barely kept up with inflation.

Borrowing to invest in property

Property is a great asset class for investing using someone else's money. It has tax benefits for negative gearing, depreciation and deductible expenses, and it is a secure asset class that is appreciated by banks, which therefore provide the lowest interest rates for borrowing money for property. This means that your after-tax, after-expenses profit will be high.

Now I'm not necessarily pro-property, because there are many other great ways to make money, but property is simple and easy to understand. The following case studies are modelled on my own experience, and such opportunities are still abundant around Australia.

Case study 2: property—turn $50 000 into $373 504 in 10 years

If I buy an investment property worth $350 000 and put down just $35 000 of the $50 000 available (initial loan $315 000) as a deposit (the remaining $15 000 is used for legal fees and stamp duty), and that investment property rises by 7 per cent per year, my return on investment, assuming interest only, is shown in table 9.2. (Note: I am using a rate of 7 per cent as the growth rate, which, in the interests of conservatism, is 1.5 per cent less than the long-term average according to the Russell Investments report of 2012 noted in chapter 5.)

The outcome in this example is an investment return of 647 per cent over the 10-year period. In fact, we would have to calculate any income losses or gains and the after-tax effect of such an investment to establish the real return, but on a simple basis, the return in case study 2 is far greater than that in case study 1.

Table 9.2: growth in property over 10 years

Year	Loan ($)	Value ($)	7% increase ($)	Total value ($)	Equity ($)
1	315000	350000	24500	374500	59500
2	315000	374500	26215	400715	85715
3	315000	400715	28050	428765	113765
4	315000	428765	30013	458779	143779
5	315000	458779	31114	490894	175894
6	315000	490894	34363	525257	210257
7	315000	525257	36768	562024	247024
8	315000	562024	39342	601366	286366
9	315000	601366	42096	643462	319462
10	315000	643462	45042	688504	373504

Case study 3: property — turn $50000 into $879758 in 10 years

Taking the previous example to a more extreme level, case study 3 illustrates the effect of investing $50000 into an investment property with $35000 as a deposit and the remaining $15000 to cover legal costs and stamp duty. Further, every three years, as equity grows, we are going to buy a $400000 property with a 20 per cent deposit taken from the equity of the existing property; stamp duty and legal fees (around $20000) are paid by cash saved, for the sake of simplicity in the example. The results are shown in table 9.3 (overleaf).

Even if we deduct the cost of stamp duty and legal fees at $20000 per property, we have a 1759 per cent return over the 10-year period. In fact, in many cases when I was buying these properties, I also borrowed the cost of the legal fees and stamp duty into the loan so I didn't have to put any money into the new properties except the created equity.

Table 9.3: growth in property over 10 years when buying another property every three years

Year	Loan ($)	Value ($)	7% increase ($)	Total value ($)	Equity ($)
1	315000	350000	24500	374500	59500
2	315000	374500	26215	400715	85715
3	715000	800715	56050	856765	141765
4	715000	856765	59974	916739	201739
5	715000	916739	64172	980910	265910
6	1115000	1380910	96664	1477574	362574
7	1115000	1477574	103430	1581004	466004
8	1115000	1581004	110670	1691675	576675
9	1515000	2091675	146417	2238092	723092
10	1515000	2238092	156666	2394758	879758

Case study 3 is a fairly common way that people make money in property. In fact, shares work in much the same way. So long as you can afford to repay the loan, the strategy of using someone else's money to make money has worked for generations. The same strategy can be used in businesses, which generally have a much higher return (and risk) than property or shares, and a host of successful entrepreneurs in the *BRW* Rich 200 each year would employ this strategy to their advantage.

Just remember, you are investing for the bad times not the good, so have a look at historical data to see how your chosen asset class has performed in tough economic times. This will give you an understanding of what the pressures on you will be if the economy heads south.

Other ways to add value and leverage property

One of the best things about property is the ability to renovate and profit. If you think you are handy at painting, tiling, landscaping, polishing floorboards or simply organising tradespeople, then property may be a good investment choice for you.

All of the properties I have bought were unrenovated 1880s terraces or colonial cottages because they were finite in supply and always in high demand by tenants. They also needed updating, which added value to my rents and ultimately increased the property value within a very short time, because I often did all the work, saving on building costs.

Borrowing to buy shares

If you are looking for a more passive means of investment then share investment may be the best way forward. You can invest in shares without the headaches of property ownership, such as regular maintenance, problems with tenants, chasing rents, strata fees, neighbours and real estate agents.

Borrowing money to buy shares is simple and effective so long as you understand the attributes of the sharemarket (see chapter 6). Like property, leveraging into shares has implicit risks. Sharemarket risks include economic risk, market risk, country risk, company risk, management risk, industry risk, and legislative and political risk, to name a few. Borrowing money adds interest rate risk and the chance the shares could be sold if they drop in value or you cannot make a repayment. There are ways to alleviate these risks, but let's have a look at some of the ways to invest into shares with borrowed money:

- margin loans
- lines of credit against property
- self-funding instalment warrants.

Margin loans

A margin loan is a loan provided by an institution to buy shares. The idea of having a margin loan is to buy shares that you believe will increase in value over time and provide an income to repay the interest. The interest is 100 per cent tax deductible and, like property, shares can be negatively or positively geared. The institution lending the money will use the shares as collateral against the loan.

Institutions will lend money only against certain stocks listed on the ASX. They will not lend money on speculative stocks.

Margin loans generally attract an interest rate about 1.5 per cent to 2.5 per cent higher than home loans. The lender will have a certain margin, a debt-to-equity ratio, that cannot be breached; if it is breached, the bank will sell the shares or you will have to contribute more money to increase your equity. Different shares attract different levels of loan-to-value ratios (LVR) that relate to the volatility and security of each stock. For example, lenders will lend up to 75 per cent on the value of a Commonwealth Bank share, but only 50 per cent on a smaller company such as Webjet Ltd. Each bank will have its own lending criteria and it's important that you do your homework and research the various pros and cons with each loan provider.

What's a margin call?

A margin call occurs when the bank seeks to recover its debt because the margin between its debt and your equity has breached a particular pre-determined level. For example, if you buy a Commonwealth Bank share for $70 with a debt-to-equity ratio of 75 per cent, then your debt to the bank would be $52.50 and your equity would be just $17.50. However, if the share price fell to $58, then your equity would be just $5.50 and it's likely that the bank would consider this a breach of their margin of safety (the chance of getting their money back in the event of further share price falls), so they would sell the share for $58 and you would get your $5.50 less brokerage, interest or penalties and the bank would get their full $52.50. Banks don't like losing money—it's bad for shareholders, who sit on the other side of your equation in the event of default. It's always prudent to borrow less than 50 per cent, where possible, but 40 per cent or less is more comfortable.

Case study 4: shares (margin lending)—turn $50000 into $285319 in 10 years

The following margin loan example shows how you could turn $50000 into $285000 over 10 years. Assuming you have equity or savings of $50000 and borrow another $50000 from a margin lending institution at an interest rate of 9 per cent and have a share price growth of 7 per cent plus income of about 5.9 per cent fully franked, then your investment over 10 years would look like the example in table 9.4. This example was built using CBA shares and actual figures as at February 2013 (taken from E*TRADE), so it is a realistic example.

Table 9.4: growth in shares over 10 years with a margin loan

Item	Amount
Equity	$50 000
Loan	$50 000
Total share holding	$100 000
Interest rate	9%
Share price growth	7%
Dividend grossed up (including franking credits)	8.70%

Year	Opening value ($)	Growth ($)	Income ($)	Loan ($)	Interest ($)	Closing value ($)	Closing equity ($)
1	100 000	7 000	8 700	50 000	4500	111 200	61 200
2	111 200	7 784	9 674	50 000	4500	124 158	74 158
3	124 158	8 691	10 802	50 000	4500	139 151	89 151
4	139 151	9 741	12 106	50 000	4500	156 498	106 498
5	156 498	10 955	13 615	50 000	4500	176 568	126 568
6	176 568	12 360	15 361	50 000	4500	199 789	149 789
7	199 789	13 985	17 382	50 000	4500	226 656	176 656
8	226 656	15 866	19 719	50 000	4500	257 741	207 741
9	257 741	18 042	22 424	50 000	4500	293 707	243 707
10	293 707	20 559	25 552	50 000	4500	335 319	285 319

As you work your way through this example, keep in mind that the variables will change over time. Share prices are volatile; interest rates change; company profits and dividends change; and economics vary from time to time. As they always say, past performance is no indication of future performance, but it certainly helps in your decision-making process to see what a share price has done over time: it's often a reflection of how a company is run.

Lines of credit against property

A line of credit (LOC) is a loan against a property, just like a mortgage, up to a certain loan-to-value ratio. While you do not have to draw the full amount you have applied for, a line of credit gives you access to borrowed money when you need it without having to go through the full credit assessment process each time. For example, if you own a property, you can usually obtain finance for up to 80 per cent of the value of that property without having to pay lenders' mortgage insurance. If your current loan is 40 per cent of the value of your property, you may borrow an additional 40 per cent of your property value for investment purposes.

So if you own a $500 000 property with a current loan of $300 000, you can obtain an LOC facility for up to $400 000 (80 per cent × $500 000), giving you access to another $100 000, which can be used for investment purposes (or any other purpose in theory). The interest on borrowed money used for the purpose of investment is 100 per cent tax deductible, so an LOC can be tax effective.

Like all loans, you have to assess your risk and make sure you have a plan to repay the loan and its interest over time, otherwise the process is not worth considering. Only borrow money to invest into blue-chip assets and always remember to reduce your risk by diversifying your investments: invest in a variety of assets, and in shares for instance, across a number of companies across different industries.

An LOC has two key advantages over a margin loan:

- an LOC loan will never get a margin call (having your shares sold if they drop in value) because the security for the loan is property, not shares

- an LOC attracts a lower rate of interest (by around 2 per cent per year).

So if you own property and can obtain a line of credit, you will never need a margin loan and will benefit from a lower interest rate. You will also be able to invest without the fear of having a margin call.

Case study 5: shares (line of credit) — how to turn $50000 into $306329 in 10 years

This case study is similar to the previous one in that we are looking at a $50000 investment with a line of credit loan of another $50000 over 10 years. With a 7 per cent share price growth and an 8.7 per cent dividend (grossed up) we can see in table 9.5 that the investment has risen from just $50000 to $306329 over the 10-year period. The key difference between this example and the margin loan example is that the interest rate in this case is 2 per cent less, providing a net benefit of some $20000 over 10 years. The other difference is qualitative and that is that you would not get a margin call in this case study.

Table 9.5: growth in shares over 10 years with an LOC

Item	Amount
Equity	$50000
Loan	$50000
Total share holding	$100000
Interest rate	7%
Share price growth	7%
Dividend grossed up (including franking credits)	8.70%

Year	Opening value ($)	Growth ($)	Income ($)	Loan ($)	Interest ($)	Closing value ($)	Closing equity ($)
1	100000	7000	8700	50000	3500	112200	62200
2	112200	7854	9761	50000	3500	126315	76315
3	126315	8842	10989	50000	3500	142647	92647
4	142647	9985	12410	50000	3500	161542	111542
5	161542	11308	14054	50000	3500	183405	133405
6	183405	12838	15956	50000	3500	208699	158699
7	208699	14609	18157	50000	3500	237965	187965
8	237965	16658	20703	50000	3500	271825	221825
9	271825	19028	23649	50000	3500	311002	261002
10	311002	21770	27057	50000	3500	356329	306329

Self-funding instalment warrants

A self-funding instalment (SFI) warrant is where you can buy a portion of a share (for example, a 50 per cent share) and allow the dividends to repay the other half of the value over time, or in instalments, as the name suggests. If done correctly over the right company's shares, it can be a very profitable method of using someone else's money. At the end of the period, you will most likely own the shares and have paid off the debt or most of the debt.

The beauty of using SFIs is that they are a passive means of gearing into quality shares over a set period of time, and the dividends will repay a large portion of the loan over the time of the investment.

The interest rate is about the same as a margin loan (so not as low as a line of credit) and there is no possibility of a margin call. However, issuers of SFIs put a stop-loss in place, which means that if the underlying share price falls to a certain point, the SFIs will be sold. Unlike margin loans, though, the only security the lender has is the shares themselves and they have no recourse over your other assets.

Another key difference is that the franking credits (tax paid by the company whose shares you own) are passed on to you and can't be used to reduce the loan amount. They can, however, be used to reduce your tax so the benefit is not lost. In the next case study, $42 000 worth of franking credits are paid, which can be used to reduce tax payable on other income.

Case study 6: shares (self-funding instalment warrants) — how to turn $50 000 into $203 977 in 10 years

In this case study, I illustrate how you can turn $50 000 into more than $203 977 over 10 years using SFIs over CBA shares. This particular example is actually a product by RBS (Royal Bank of Scotland, formerly ABN Amro) for a 10-year SFI over CBA shares with the stock code CBASZU (ASX:CBASZU).

As you can see in table 9.6, if we assume the dividend was 5.9 per cent and average growth of the shares was around 7 per cent (as it was at the time of writing) and the franking credits (approximately

$43 000) were added back after the calculations, over 10 years the $50 000 investment grows to $203 000-odd. One of the key differences is that there is no chance of your assets being repossessed if the product fails, as opposed to a margin loan or even a line of credit. There is, however, a stop-loss that would be triggered if the stock price fell by more than about 30 per cent, which could erode your capital. The stop-loss level reduces with time, as does the loan, as the dividends are used to reduce the debt and so your equity increases over time, reducing risk.

Table 9.6: growth in shares over 10 years with SFI warrants

Item	Amount
Equity	$50 000
Loan	$50 000
Total share holding	$100 000
Interest rate	9%
Share price growth	7%
Dividend grossed up (including franking credits)	5.90%

Year	Opening value ($)	Growth ($)	Income ($)	Loan ($)	Interest ($)	Closing value ($)	Closing equity ($)
1	100 000	7000	5900	50 000	4500	108 400	58 400
2	108 400	7588	6396	50 000	4500	117 884	67 884
3	117 884	8252	6955	50 000	4500	128 591	78 591
4	128 591	9001	7587	50 000	4500	140 679	90 679
5	140 679	9848	8300	50 000	4500	154 326	104 326
6	154 326	10 803	9105	50 000	4500	169 734	119 734
7	169 734	11 881	10 014	50 000	4500	187 130	137 130
8	187 130	13 099	11 041	50 000	4500	206 770	156 770
9	206 770	14 474	12 199	50 000	4500	228 943	178 943
10	228 943	16 026	13 508	50 000	4500	253 977	203 977

The key with SFIs is to use them only over good-value stocks that offer solid dividends and growing return on assets (ROA) so you know that earnings have a better chance of increasing, thus decreasing your risk over time. SFIs can also be tax effective as the interest is 100 per cent tax deductible and the franking credits can be used in your tax return to reduce your income tax.

There are several providers of SFIs including RBS, NAB, Macquarie, UBS and others. For more information, I suggest you download the information booklets from the ASX website (www.asx.com.au) and speak to one of the providers listed in the booklet to obtain a better understanding of the products they provide and the risks associated with those products. The leverage will vary from product to product and the risk will vary from share to share.

Managing the risks of borrowing

If you borrow someone else's money, they're going to want it back, and rightly so. Given the fact that you have interest to pay on a loan, the key to borrowing money is being able to pay the interest and, in the foreseeable future, the principal. It is therefore sensible to borrow money to invest only into assets that create an income to help repay that debt. The other key objective is for the asset to go up in value, so it's important to invest in blue-chip, quality assets, and not speculative assets.

There have been times when asset values have fallen and people ended up owing more than they owned because they borrowed money and geared into investments. During the GFC, Americans who invested in properties using easy credit just before the GFC found themselves owing more than they owned. In the United States, they were able to simply walk away from the asset and the loan, leaving it to the bank to clean up. In Australia, our banks will not provide finance on such terms, and they need an asset to repossess if something goes wrong, and they will send you into bankruptcy if they need to.

Share values can be volatile so the research techniques we used in chapter 6 should be employed to find shares that offer good dividends, solid growing earnings, high return on equity and good return on assets compared with their peers. These types of assets may still be subject to volatility, but they will usually rebound quickly with the market.

Diversification can help to reduce risk. By diversifying your assets across a number of companies or asset classes, it is possible to reduce portfolio risk. For example, if you always keep some funds in cash or fixed interest that you can use in case of a rainy day you will have a fall-back position. A company with growing dividends, steady profit margins and steady income growth may be a good start for people beginning to invest in shares.

Ensuring you and your partner, if you have one, have consistent and safe income is paramount when it comes to investing. If you work in an unstable industry exposed to the whims of economic volatility, you should keep more cash and ensure you don't borrow too much in case you lose your job. Your ability to earn is your greatest asset, and your whole investment strategy will be severely affected if you lose your job and can't replace it quickly.

Similarly, if you don't have personal insurance and you are injured, disabled or die, your assets will be threatened and your family could be in severe financial difficulty. Life, trauma and income protection insurance are important if you own debt of any kind. Make sure you are covered, and if you can't afford the insurance, then perhaps you can't afford the investment (look at chapter 10 for more information or visit www.samhenderson.com.au).

Other ways to mitigate risk are to make sure you read all the documentation and research the loan products that you use so that you clearly understand what happens in the event of default. Many margin loans are simply sold out from underneath you by the provider, as the provider has the right to sell your assets if you default on your loan. A home or investment loan secured by property will be more flexible, and arrangements can be entered into to repay the debt over time or to give you a 'holiday' if your loan cannot be repaid for a short period of time. Contact your lender to find out what happens in such an event.

Five sample strategies

- Obtain a quote for financing a line of credit (LOC) to buy a property or shares and to determine if you can afford it.

- Set up a self-funding instalment warrant (SFI) over CBA shares.

- Research property and possibly renovating to see if it suits your personal style of investing.

- Consider a margin loan of up to 50 per cent of the value of a blue-chip stock with a long history of growth and high dividends, such as the Commonwealth Bank (CBA).

- Obtain life, total and permanent disablement, income protection and trauma insurance *before* taking on debt.

Five sample tactics

- Call your bank or a broker to obtain a quote for finance and determine how much you can borrow and how much you can comfortably afford.

- Check the Canstar or RateCity websites for the best interest rates available for all types of loans and bank deposits.

- Have a look at the RP Data, Residex or Australian Property Monitors websites for research about areas, suburbs or specific properties to assess affordability.

- Check the Morningstar website or a broker's website, such as E*TRADE or CommSec, to look at shares that may be appropriate to buy with borrowed money.

- Contact a personal insurance broker or financial planner about obtaining insurance before you borrow money.

KEY POINTS

- Borrowing can be a great way to supercharge your investments, but it is not without risk.

- You are investing for the bad times, not the good, so make sure you mitigate as many risks as you can.

- Invest in blue-chip assets that offer good income and growth prospects. You can ensure this by undertaking thorough research and writing down your risks and how you will reduce them.

- Not every asset goes up in value and there are never any guarantees when it comes to investing, so ensure you are well versed in all the possible outcomes and always leave some cash up your sleeve for a rainy day.

- Sometimes we don't know how long it will be until it rains, but it *will* rain. It's just the same in investment.

CHAPTER 10

RISK MANAGEMENT AND INSURANCE

Hope for the best and prepare for the worst.

Proverb

Risk is the chance of danger or loss. In the context of investment, it's the potential to lose money. In my experience, people are happy to take a risk, but they aren't happy to take a loss. It sounds like a paradox, and in effect it is. The difference exists only in the mind of the investor. If an investment involves risk (and virtually all investments do), you can potentially lose money on it, but most people don't think it will happen. Naturally, we are optimistic, and we don't want to think that investing money into something will create a loss. Investing into a loss-making situation doesn't make sense.

It's for the same reason that people hang onto bad investments for far too long, even though the opportunity cost of keeping a bad investment is so high — in other words, if you sold the bad investment, even at a loss, and bought a good investment, you would be back on the road to recovery faster.

The main types of risk

Investments are subject to many different types of risk, any or all of which can significantly affect your net wealth. Table 10.1 lists the main types of risk to which investments are exposed.

Table 10.1: the main types of investment risk

Type of risk	Description
Economic risk	Slowdown in economic growth will affect investments.
Country or political risk	Politics can affect investments: for example, Papua New Guinea and African nations have high political risk.
Industry risk	Some industries have negative reactions to certain events: for example, the tobacco industry is very risky in Australia.
Company risk	Certain companies are run better than others. For example, ABC Learning had high borrowings in 2008, when the GFC hit, and so did Babcock and Brown: neither company exists any more.
Legislative risk	Legislation and regulation can affect share and house prices: for example, land tax, mining tax or financial services reform,
Management risk	Poor decisions by management will affect a company's share price: for example, NAB management has made a number of poor decisions in its strategy to expand overseas.
Interest rate risk	Rising interest rates will affect companies that have a lot of debt or clients that are affected by such conditions.
Key-person risk	Some companies rely heavily on their key management figures, such as Harvey Norman (Gerry Harvey), News Corp (Rupert Murdoch) and Consolidated Media and Crown (formerly Publishing and Broadcasting, James Packer).
Market risk	When the sharemarket goes down as a whole, it takes share prices with it for no specific local reason: for example, when the US markets go down, our market usually follows the next day.

How to reduce risk

As discussed in the chapters on shares, property and borrowing money, there are ways to reduce the risks—for example, by choosing investments that have good management; investing into areas that are not affected by interest-rate movements; or investing in companies that have sound business models and strong demand for their products, even in times of low economic growth.

Another way of mitigating risk is to diversify your assets, as we saw in the chapter on portfolio construction. If you have your assets spread across a variety of asset classes, you will find that some assets are negatively correlated, which means that when some assets are going down in value, others are going up in value. This diversification protects your overall wealth and ensures that your ultimate investment goals are being met.

The ultimate goal of investing is to enable you to meet your lifestyle goals and objectives. The style of investments that you have in your portfolio should be sympathetic to these lifestyle goals. Diversifying your investments across a variety of assets can reduce risk and therefore help you to reach your goals sooner. But there are other types of risk, too; in particular, there are risks to your health and your ability to earn money and therefore accumulate further assets and investments. This type of risk is quite different from specific investment risks, and the ways of managing it are also quite different.

Insurance and risk management

What would happen to your family financially if you or your partner were to die? What would happen if one of you were disabled or fell ill with a debilitating disease, and you could no longer work? You need to consider these questions carefully and put measures in place to ensure that your assets are not at risk of being sold to repay debt or interest owed if something happens to you or your partner.

Question: What is your biggest asset?

Answer: Your ability to earn income.

Consider these facts from the Lifewise website (www.lifewise.org.au) run by the Financial Services Council:

- 50 000 Australians have heart attacks every year.

- One-third of women and a quarter of all men will suffer cancer at some stage in their life — more than 60 per cent of whom will live for longer than five years after diagnosis.

- More than 43 000 people are expected to die from cancer in 2013.

- Half of all men and a third of women will be diagnosed with cancer before the age of 85.

- More than 1600 people die on Australian roads every year, most aged 26 to 59 years.

- One stroke event occurs in Australia every 12 minutes.

- Just under half the population with an arthritis-associated disability are aged 15 to 64 years.

- With symptoms generally developing between the ages of 20 and 40, multiple sclerosis is the most common chronic central nervous system condition among young Australian adults.

Most people have some life insurance through their super fund, but according to the Lifewise website, actuaries Rice Warner estimate that the level of life insurance cover within superannuation in Australia is, on average, just 20 per cent of what is needed. In addition, the Financial Services Council reckons that just 4 per cent of Australian families with dependent children have adequate levels of insurance.

The fact is that Australians are massively underinsured. An acceptable level of insurance is said to be around 10 times your annual earnings for life insurance, and on that basis we are underinsured by more than a trillion dollars, according to Rice Warner.

At some point in life, up to one-third of Australians will need to take some time off work to convalesce from an illness. And at some point we are all going to die, but you need to make allowances for an early death or illness events in your life to ensure your family's needs can continue to be met and your goals can still be achieved. You need to put mechanisms in place to make sure that your goals can still be met under most *controllable* circumstances. Not all risks can be mitigated, but it's wise to reduce the number that can't be mitigated by taking the necessary precautions.

Any of the reasons for needing insurance will place a great deal of stress on your family, and the last thing they will want on their minds will be the financial mess that they have to clean up while they are caring or grieving. Some of the companies that specialise in insurance include One Path (formerly ING Life), AMP, MLC, TAL (formerly Tower), Zurich, AIA, Macquarie and just about all of the industry super funds and most corporate super funds.

If you think you don't need insurance, you are either underinsured, meaning you need it but don't have it, or you are self-insured. Being self-insured means that you have the assets or income to pay for your needs no matter what your circumstances, including death, disablement and illness. For example, many retirees are self-insured because if anything happens to them, they can take care of themselves or the government will assist them. Moreover, many retirees can't obtain certain forms of insurance, so they have to self-insure.

The terrible three

The terrible three are illness, disability and death.

They can all affect your financial plans and your lifestyle. Insurance offers a way of protecting yourself, and your family, against the consequences of the terrible three.

Life insurance

We are all going to die — we just don't know when. We need to allow for premature death, and ensure our family, despite their emotional heartache, is in a strong financial position to cope. If finances are not in order and life insurance does not exist for a family, houses or businesses may have to be sold to extinguish debt, children may have to move schools, and your family's whole lifestyle will be at risk.

Life insurance is simply the ability to take out insurance on someone's life. The life insurance company pays out life insurance on death or the diagnosis of a terminal illness of the insured. The amount you pay in premiums will depend on a number of factors, including your age, sex, smoking status, health history, job, family history and pastimes, to name a few. Life insurance is generally difficult to obtain once you have reached the age of 59 and may become cost prohibitive. As you'd imagine, the premiums go up with age if you want to maintain a certain level of cover; however, you can also choose for the cover to decrease over time so your premiums stay reasonably level. Premiums are tax deductible to a super fund, but not tax deductible if held in your own name or outside super.

It's very important to read the product disclosure statements (PDS) for the insurance products you are considering to ensure you understand how the product works, how the premiums are calculated and what the exclusions are.

How much life insurance do you need?

The following is a simple method of calculating the level of life insurance you need:

- Add together your total amount of debt, including mortgages, investment loans and credit cards.
- Add together the total cost of all future schooling costs for your children.
- Add together the lump sum that your partner would need to fill the income gap if you were no longer working and create an income to meet the family's normal expenses.
- Deduct the value of any assets that you are *willing* to sell (you may want to exclude the family home, for instance).
- Deduct the value of any existing insurance.

If you don't want to do the maths, you can use the calculator on the Lifewise website (www.lifewise.org.au) to work out how much insurance you need. The following case study gives an example of the calculation.

Life insurance case study

James and Amanda are 44 and 39 respectively and they have two children (Jack and Isabelle) who are aged nine and 11, and attending state schools. There is a mortgage of $300 000 owing on the family home, and they have a car loan of $8000 and credit card debts of $3000. James's and Amanda's life insurance requirements are shown in table 10.2 (overleaf).

Table 10.2: life insurance requirements

Description	James ($)	Amanda ($)
Income	80 000	55 000
Mortgage	300 000	300 000
Car loan	8 000	8 000
Credit card debt	3 000	3 000
Schooling costs until Year 12	50 000	50 000
Lump sum to provide income to surviving partner (income × 10)	800 000 *	550 000*
Life insurance required	1 161 000	911 000

* Lump sum for income coverage is 10 times current income.

In summary, James's life needs to be covered for $1 161 000 and Amanda's life needs to be covered for $911 000. There may be other considerations, such as the lump sum for income replacement not being so large to cover Amanda, but you would need to consider how the children will be looked after and you would probably assume that the surviving partner would need help around the house and may have to work less, necessitating a larger lump-sum payout, especially if they had to change jobs or industries or pay for help.

Total and permanent disability

Total and permanent disability (TPD) insurance is a lump sum paid when the insured is diagnosed with a total and permanent disability. Like life insurance, the premiums are paid over time; they are tax deductible to a super fund but not tax deductible if held in your own name or outside super. TPD is often coupled with life or trauma insurance, but it can be taken as a stand-alone product.

At One Path, for example, TPD insurance is available up until the age of 75 and payable to an amount of up to $2.5 million, but the details of each product will change from one product provider to another. Like other insurances, a small amount of life insurance is included and if you make a claim you may choose to take the payment in instalments.

Tip

Ensure you disclose all medical ailments when you fill in the forms, because insurance companies will check your detailed medical records in the event of a claim.

Like all insurance, the details are important: make sure you read all documentation and compare products to arrive at the best result for you or speak to a financial adviser who specialises in insurance, as most will provide an insurance service. Always make sure your policies are kept up to date and never let them lapse. The following is a true story that shows why.

A true story

The other day I was talking to a client who had had insurance coverage with the same company for many years and his brother was in fact the insurance broker. He had taken out life, TPD and income protection insurance.

Each year the insurance was updated and each year the client paid the insurance premiums without claim. One year when the insurance was due, a form had to be filled out to renew the insurance, so the client promptly made a time to meet with the insurance broker. However, his brother was away on holidays, so he sent a junior. The junior brought the wrong forms on a Friday afternoon (the final date of the policy) and therefore couldn't complete the documentation and effectively the cover lapsed but by no fault of the client.

On the Saturday night the client had a massive heart attack and nearly died. One of his arteries was 95 per cent blocked and he needed bypass surgery immediately; he was consequently rushed into emergency surgery. It was some months before the client could work again.

The insurance company denied the claim, stating that he was outside the coverage period. Fortunately for this client, his brother put in an appeal and it was upheld by the insurance company and he was paid his income protection insurance.

This anecdote should serve as a reminder to keep your insurances updated and always read the terms contained in the PDS.

Income protection insurance

Income protection insurance provides you with a taxable income in the event that you are incapacitated and cannot work. It usually provides 75 per cent of your normal income, paid until you are ready to go back to work or for an agreed length of time; for example, until age 65, for just one year, for two years (as in most super funds) or to an agreed age. Make sure you understand how long your policy is paid for.

You will be required to provide proof of your income when you apply for income protection insurance. Key to the calculation of your insurance premiums will be your age, sex, smoking status, job position, education level, industry, physical activity at work, and your hobbies and pastimes, to name a few items. The provider may also check your current health status via a medical test and check your health history and records to see if you pose a significant risk. Finding any risks or history will mean that either your premiums will be raised or the insurance company will provide an exclusion: that is, they won't cover you for certain illnesses or events.

You will also have a choice as to how the premiums are structured. They can be stepped, which means they go up each year, or stable, which means they stay the same but the cover decreases with your age. You will also be able to reduce your premiums by increasing the waiting period before payments start in the event of a claim. You will have the choice of a 30-, 90- or 180-day waiting period, and the longer the wait, the cheaper the premiums. If you have enough spare cash to live on for a time, you may choose to use it up before you rely on the income from the insurance company in order to reduce your premiums.

Income protection can be quite complex to understand, and it's important that you shop around and read each PDS to understand the products and how they differ in features, benefits and costs. The difference in cost doesn't necessarily mean you get more features or benefits.

Trauma insurance

Trauma insurance is paid to you in the form of a lump sum in the event of experiencing a traumatic event, such as certain types of cancer, a heart attack, transplant surgery, or lung or kidney disease. Trauma insurance is designed to cover the costs of treatment and rehabilitation for the insured. As you know, medical expenses can add up and the extra help at times like these can be essential.

One of the companies I was recently looking at will cover you from age 15 to age 65; the minimum amount of coverage is $50 000 and it will cover you for up to $2 million if necessary. If you recover from an illness, it will reinsure you for the same type of certain illnesses. It will also pay a small amount ($10 000) in the event of death. It also has the option of receiving your payment in instalments over a lifetime or pre-determined periods.

Each policy will be different and what is most important with this type of insurance is the exclusions. Make sure you read what you are *not* covered for in the PDS. In fact, make sure you read the entire PDS and undertake a thorough product comparison with this type of product.

Out of the three types of insurances, I'd classify this one as the least important, but don't exclude it just because of that comment. It can be expensive but it can also be very helpful.

Key-person insurance

Key-person insurance is life insurance over a key person in a business. It provides a lump sum payment on the death of a business owner or key person to the business. The business is the owner of the policy and is the recipient of the payment. The payment is designed to ensure the business is not starved of cash in the event of the death of a significant person in the business. The business can use the money to repay debts or can find a replacement for the key person without too much damage to the business.

Key-person insurance typically offers a payment of $500 000 to $10 000 000 but depends on the business's requirements. The calculation for key-person insurance is similar to that for life insurance whereby a business owner or key person needs to calculate the debts of the business that would need to be retired in the event of death and what lump sum would be required to maintain cash flow for a certain period.

The tax deductibility of key-person insurance depends on whether the payout is for revenue purposes or capital purposes. That is, it depends on whether the payment is to pay regular ongoing expenses, in which case the premiums may be tax deductible and the payments taxable. If it is a lump-sum payment then it is unlikely the premiums will be tax deductible and the payout will not be taxable.

It is very important to document the process and reasoning for your key-person insurance as your tax deductibility will rely on those notes or minutes if the ATO audits you. You may also have to consider capital gains tax consequences, so seek advice if this is an area of interest for you.

Tax deductibility of insurance

In some cases it is possible to receive a tax deduction for your personal insurance premiums, so knowing the ideal investment structure under which to insure yourself may save you quite a few dollars over your lifetime. The added benefit may also be used to increase your cover or to obtain additional cover you thought you couldn't afford.

Inside superannuation

Life, TPD and income protection is tax deductible inside your super fund. Before 2007, income protection was only tax deductible if it was payable for two years or less. Now it is tax deductible if payable to age 65. It is often best to have these types of insurance inside your super fund so your super fund pays the premiums, which means that your cash flow is not affected by having to pay for insurance. In addition, many large super funds can obtain cheap insurance for their members — often much cheaper than can be obtained individually outside of superannuation.

Tip

You cannot have income protection insurance by itself in a fund because income protection is considered an ancillary benefit and thus does not meet the sole purpose test — the sole purpose of a super fund is to provide retirement benefits to its members. In this case, income protection is not a retirement benefit so it must be accompanied by life or TPD insurance, or both.

Insurance and SMSFs

If you have a self managed super fund (SMSF), from 1 July 2013 the law requires you to consider insurance for every member of the fund as part of the fund's written investment strategy. Consideration must be documented in the investment strategy from the establishment of the fund and as you regularly review the investment strategy. Although you must consider insurance, there is no obligation to actually obtain insurance. Of course, it would be negligent to consider insurance necessary and then not to obtain insurance.

In a report commissioned by the government in 2012, it was suggested that just 12.7 per cent of SMSFs carried insurance. Australia has a huge under-insurance problem and this is carried through into superannuation, even though your fund can pay your insurance premiums for you and claim a tax deduction for doing so.

> ## Tip
>
> Self managed super funds must now consider insurance as part of their written investment strategy. You must make notes and also be able to show the calculations made in deciding why or why not you do or do not need insurance, the types you may need and how much insurance you need for each insurance type and for each trustee/member of the fund. This is now law.

Insurance inside super has the following key benefits:

- It is tax deductible to your super fund — speak to your adviser about which insurances are tax deductible and what the exceptions are.

- The expense is borne by the super fund so paying premiums does not impinge upon your cash flow.

There is no excuse for not having insurance.

Outside superannuation

Only income protection insurance is tax deductible outside of superannuation. Life insurance, TPD and trauma insurance are not tax deductible if held outside of super. Income protection is tax deductible because if you make a claim the income received from the insurance company is considered normal income and is therefore fully taxable at your marginal tax rates, depending on what your taxable income is for that year. Payments from life insurance and trauma claims are not taxed. Life or TPD claims within super are taxed as a death benefit payment and the calculations are extremely complex. You should seek advice from your fund or adviser, or see the detailed example given in my book *SMSF DIY Guide* (Wiley, 2012).

General insurance and health insurance

General insurance includes general property insurances, such as insurance cover for the home (fire and theft), contents, motor vehicle, mobile phone and other individual items such as jewellery, cameras or sporting equipment that may need to be individually identified for the insurance company. These types of insurances are essential to the smooth operation of your lifestyle. If you can't afford insurance, then perhaps you can't afford the items or you can afford to simply replace them. Always keep your insurances up to date and never let them lapse.

If there is one thing you can never compromise on, it's your health. Apart from anything else, one of your biggest motivations for having money should be the ability to source the best health services for you and your loved ones. Maintaining health insurance at the highest affordable level is so important for the continuity of your health, given your health can fluctuate faster than global sharemarkets, so you need to be prepared for anything. Accidents happen; diseases are contracted; and illness is all around us so, without wanting to paint a frightening picture, it's best to make sure your health insurance is always up to date and you get yourself into a financial position to assist your loved ones if they cannot help themselves.

Five sample strategies

- Determine an insurance plan considering life, TPD, income protection and trauma insurance—what insurances you (and your partner) need to ensure you, your family and your business will not be affected by unforeseen events.

- Calculate how much of each type of insurance you need and what you are willing to pay for each one.

- Obtain life and TPD insurance quotes in your personal name, and through your super fund, and then decide the best structure to hold the insurance.

- If you have an SMSF, make sure you consider personal insurance in your written investment strategy from fund establishment and at each regular review of your investment strategy (you do regularly review it, don't you?).

- Review insurance every year or when your circumstances change.

Five sample tactics

- Call a broker or an insurance company and obtain a PDS and application for life, TPD and income protection insurance.

- Contact your super fund and ask if you have insurance inside your fund. Clarify what types of insurance you have. Calculate your insurance needs versus what is currently covered to ensure that you have adequate coverage for you and your family in the event of 'the terrible threes'.

- Obtain income protection insurance quotes—possibly in your own name for higher income earners (because it's tax deductible) and possibly in super for lower income earners (so premiums don't affect cash flow).

(continued)

Five sample tactics *(cont'd)*

- Contact an industry super fund and compare their rates for insurance as they are often very cheap. You will need at least $5000 in your account if you transfer the balance out of your industry fund to maintain insurance if you already have it. (This is a popular tactic if one fund has cheaper insurance than another.)

- Review your insurances by undertaking a calculation of how much insurance you need each year and if your types of insurance are still appropriate for your needs. If your assets are increasing, your need for insurance may reduce.

KEY POINTS

- Risk is all around us, and insurance is a fundamentally important aspect of wealth protection.

- Your biggest asset is your ability to earn money — so insure it.

- If you can't afford insurance, then you probably can't afford to do what you plan on doing.

- Insurance is an implicit cost of doing business, and when things go wrong, you will want the peace of mind of knowing that you have insured not only your physical assets but also your physical wellbeing.

- If you have dependants or debt, then make sure you obtain quotes for life and TPD insurance, income-protection insurance and trauma insurance.

- SMSFs have to document evidence of considering insurance for every member from fund establishment and at each review.

- Never lose sight of your general insurance and health insurance obligations.

- Always obtain the maximum amount of insurance that you can afford or that is practical for you.

CHAPTER 11

CENTRELINK AND SOCIAL SECURITY

There's a lot of talk about the federal deficit. But I think we should talk more about our empathy deficit...when you choose to broaden your ambit of concern and empathise with the plight of others...it becomes harder not to act; harder not to help.

Barack Obama, President of the United States of America

The key objectives of our Australian social services are to enable people to become self-sufficient and to care for those in need. There are so many people in need in Australia, for so many reasons, and a number of important government programs are administered by Centrelink, our federal government social services organisation, to assist people in need. Centrelink is now part of the federal government's Department of Human Services (www.humanservices.gov.au).

There is only one method through which the government can raise money — tax. In order for the government to be able to afford social services, our economy needs to be in good order with plenty of workers who are paying tax, which in turn assists those who are unable to work because of illness or disability, who are studying or who are actively looking for work.

The dependency ratio

There about 10 workers for each person on social security payments, but by 2050 that number is forecast to drop down to three workers for each person on social security. Fewer workers means less tax revenue, and less tax revenue means that the government will have fewer financial resources to support social services and welfare. The result will be that more people will need to be self-funded for retirement, in particular, and a huge shift will need to take place to ensure people have enough money to look after themselves. Taxpayers directly pay for the welfare system.

The good news is that the trend can be reversed if people increase their savings and superannuation. That's why the government is raising the superannuation guarantee — the super contributions paid by your employer on all salary earned over $450 per month — to 12 per cent by 2019. From 1 July 2013 the first rise will be made, from 9 to 9.25 per cent. The economic elements of immigration (to ensure there are enough workers in the country) and general economic stability (to ensure our country grows with plenty of jobs and a good standard of living) are also important in ensuring the government can continue to raise enough tax to fund social security payments. Maintaining a healthy and growing economy is essential to a healthy social services and welfare regime.

The number of people reaching the age of 80 will quadruple by 2030 as the baby boomers mature. An ageing population combined with falling government revenue will put massive pressures on social security, medical services, and accommodation and care for the elderly. Given that most people want to maintain their standard of living in retirement, the need to become fully self-funded will be of paramount importance. Make sure that you and the people around you become financially independent, because at some time in the not-too-distant future your life, or that of a close family member or friend, may depend on it.

Types of social security assistance

Centrelink runs a multitude of programs to assist people throughout their life-stages. The key programs include the following:

- *Youth Allowance:* allowance for youths who are studying, training or looking for work from age 16 to 24
- *Austudy/ABSTUDY:* study and training assistance for those aged over 25
- *Newstart Allowance:* assistance while looking for work
- *Baby Bonus:* assistance for having a baby and a vaccination program to encourage population growth
- *Family Tax Benefit:* help with work and family responsibilities

- *Child Care Benefit and Child Care Rebate:* assistance with paying for child care

- *Carer Payment and Carer Allowance:* payment or allowance, or both, for people caring for loved ones

- *Age Pension:* income assistance in retirement

- *Disability Support Pension:* income assistance for people unable to work due to a disability.

The amount people receive for any of the allowances will depend on age, marital status, assets, other income, disability, whether there are children and the person's capacity to work or look for work. Centrelink assesses eligibility and payment or allowance amounts. Allowances are generally paid by Centrelink fortnightly and the amounts received for the allowances increase twice a year, in March and September, as the payment levels are indexed to maintain pace with wages growth.

The best source of information for any of the social security allowances, cards and benefits is the local Centrelink office (phone 13 24 90 or visit www.centrelink.gov.au or www.humanservices.gov.au). A great deal of information can be downloaded from the website, in all languages, and the local branches are willing to assist you.

It's a good idea to do some research on Centrelink payments and allowances if you believe you are entitled to a payment of any kind; if you don't get the right answers the first time, go back and make sure the person you speak to is experienced and well-versed in all payments. Like any large organisation, service levels will differ so if you have any reservations, ask to speak to a manager.

For retirement information, it is best to see a Financial Information Service Officer (FISO). To book an appointment, call Centrelink on 13 23 00 or book into one of its regular seminars at fis.seminar. bookings@centrelink.gov.au.

Tip

Many allowances and payments from Centrelink are indexed up each six months on 20 March and 20 September. For the latest figures, check the Department of Human Services website (www.humanservices.gov.au), where you will find updated versions of the tables in this chapter.

Youth Allowance

Youth Allowance is for people aged 16 to 24 who are studying full time or undertaking an apprenticeship. It is also available to those who haven't finished school or are considered independent and above the minimum school age, between the ages of 15 and 20 under particular circumstances. Youth Allowance supports young people as they move into the workforce with studying, training, undertaking an apprenticeship or looking for work. Payment amounts are shown in table 11.1.

Table 11.1: Youth Allowance payments as at 20 March 2013

If you are	The maximum fortnightly payment is ($)
Single, with no children, under 18 years, and living at home	223.00
Single, with no children, under 18 years, and required to live away from home	407.50
Single, with no children, 18 years or more, and living at home	268.20
Single, with no children, 18 years or more, and required to live away from home	407.50
Single, with children	533.80
Partnered, with no children	407.50
Partnered, with children	447.40
A single job seeker, principal carer of a dependent child (granted an exemption for foster caring/relative (non-parent) caring under a court order/home schooling/distance education/large family)	683.50

Austudy

Austudy is paid to people aged 25 or over who are studying full time or undertaking an apprenticeship full time. Courses need to be approved by Centrelink but generally include university, secondary school, TAFE courses, diplomas and some postgraduate courses. Doctorates are not included in the Austudy program. Payment amounts are shown in table 11.2.

Table 11.2: Austudy payments as at 20 March 2013

If you are	The maximum fortnightly payment is ($)
Single	407.50
Single, with children	533.80
Partnered, no children	407.50
Partnered, with children	447.40

Like all payments, the amount received will depend on income and asset levels, and any support you receive from family. Applicants may also be eligible for additional benefits, such as rent assistance, fares allowance, mobility allowance, pharmaceutical allowance or a student start-up scholarship, so it's important to have a chat to Centrelink to ensure the maximum benefit is paid.

ABSTUDY is a similar program for Indigenous Australians who are seeking secondary or tertiary education assistance.

Newstart Allowance

Newstart Allowance is simply another name for what used to be called the dole. It is primarily designed to provide financial assistance for people seeking employment or undertaking activities to increase the chances of employment. It is a fortnightly payment that is paid to people over the age of 21 who meet certain strict criteria, such as the assets and income test, and the activity test, and who are prepared to undertake an Employment Pathway Plan, to name a few requirements for eligibility. Payment rates are shown in table 11.3.

Table 11.3: Newstart Allowance payment rates as at 20 March 2013

If you are	Your maximum fortnightly payment is ($)
Single, no children	492.60
Single, with a dependent child or children	533.00

(continued)

Table 11.3: Newstart Allowance payment rates as at 20 March 2013 *(cont'd)*

If you are	Your maximum fortnightly payment is ($)
Single, aged 60 or over, after nine continuous months on payment	533.00
Partnered (each)	448.70
Single principal carer granted exemption for foster caring/relative (non-parent) caring under a court order/home schooling/distance education/large family	663.70

The activity test ensures the recipient meets these requirements:

- actively look for suitable paid work
- accept suitable job offers
- attend job interviews
- attend Centrelink meetings and interviews
- attend approved training courses
- not leave a job or training program without a valid reason
- enter into and comply with an Employment Pathway Plan.

There are exemptions from the activity test, but the government wants to ensure you are actively looking for work if you are to receive the allowance. If you are 55 years of age or older, or are a principal carer of a child or have been assessed as having only a partial capacity to work, then more flexible conditions may apply to your activity requirements.

The amount of Newstart Allowance will increase if you have four or more children, or are a home foster carer or a distance educator. The amount received will be affected by your assets test, income test, partners' income status and a variety of other methodologies that are applied to test eligibility. You may also be eligible for a Health Care Card or a Pensioner Concession Card.

Payments may also be received under the Parenting Payment for a couple or single who are looking after a child under age 6 for couples or under age 8 for single parents. These payments are subject to income and assets tests as set out on the Department of Human Services website.

Youth Allowance is a similar payment to Newstart Allowance but it is designed to assist those aged 16 to 24 who are looking for work, studying or doing an apprenticeship. The eligibility criteria differ from Newstart Allowance and between individual circumstances but, like all Centrelink payments, a visit to the Department of Human Services website is highly recommended before you traipse down to Centrelink.

Baby Bonus

The Baby Bonus ($5000 for the 2013 tax year) is paid over 13 fortnights to parents who earn a household income of less than $75000 for the six months before the baby is born. The baby bonus rate will be reviewed in June 2015. The first payment is for $846.20 and the 12 subsequent payments equal $346.15 each. It is payable to all new parents of babies and adopted children (under 2 years of age) so long as you submit your claim within 52 weeks of the child being entrusted into your care and you register your baby with Births, Deaths and Marriages. Parents may also be eligible for a Maternity Immunisation Allowance, which is not income tested and is designed to encourage child immunisation in Australia.

The Baby Bonus was designed to encourage population growth because Australia was showing signs of having an ageing population.

Family Tax Benefit

Family Tax Benefit is made up of two parts: Family Tax Benefit A and Family Tax Benefit B. It is an income-tested payment designed to assist with the cost of raising children for parents, grandparents (responsible for children) and foster parents. Rates are shown in table 11.4 (overleaf).

- Family Tax Benefit A is a fortnightly or annual payment designed to help people raise their children. It is income tested and dependent on the ages of the children, the number of children and the family's income.

- Family Tax Benefit B gives extra assistance to single-parent families or families with one main income. It is possible to receive both payments A and B, or just one payment.

The Centrelink website provides the following information about Family Tax Benefit A. It relates to rates as at January 2013:

- If the family's adjusted taxable income for 2013 is $47815 or less, the payment will not be affected by the income test.

- In most cases, the Family Tax Benefit Part A payment is worked out using two income tests. Centrelink applies the test that gives the higher rate of payment.

- The first income test reduces the maximum rate of Family Tax Benefit Part A by 20 cents for each dollar above $47815 until the payment reaches the base rate of Family Tax Benefit Part A.

- The second income test reduces the base rate of Family Tax Benefit Part A by 30 cents for each dollar above $94316 (plus $3796 for each Family Tax Benefit child after the first) until the payment reaches nil.

- If the family income is close to the limit cut-off, people should check their eligibility after the end of the financial year, once actual income is known.

- The income test does not apply if a single person or either partner gets an income support payment, such as a pension, benefit or allowance or a Department of Veterans' Affairs service pension.

Table 11.4: actual annual family income limit beyond which only the base rate is paid ($ per year) as at 20 September 2012

Number of children aged 0–12 years	Number of children of 13–15 years or secondary students of 16–19 years			
	Nil ($)	1 ($)	2 ($)	3 ($)
Nil		69496	91177	n/a
1	62853	84534	n/a	n/a
2	77891	99572	n/a	n/a
3	92929	n/a	n/a	n/a

Notes: Income limits are indicative only; contact Centrelink for a more accurate assessment based on individual circumstances. 'n/a' indicates the base rate does not usually apply for this household combination. This is because the rate calculated under the first income test for this combination is usually higher than the rate calculated under the second income test, which applies the base rate. Income limits will be higher if you are eligible for Rent Assistance. Children aged 16 to 17 who have completed Year 12 are eligible for the base rate only.

Applicants must provide an estimate of their family's income for the financial year in which they will receive the benefit; any payment received over the eligible amount will have to be repaid. Applicants must lodge a tax return within two years of the end of the financial year and they will get a choice as to how to receive their payments. At the end of each year there is a supplement period when all payments are balanced up. Payments for both Family Tax Benefit A and B are complex. Contact Centrelink for more information or visit www.humanservices.gov.au, or call 13 61 50 to speak to someone from the Department of Human Services.

Child Care Benefit

The Child Care Benefit is a subsidy paid to a childcare facility on behalf of parents to reduce the amount they have to pay for childcare. It is an income-tested payment that depends on how many children the applicant has, as shown in table 11.5.

Table 11.5: Child Care Benefit payments as at 20 September 2012

Number of children in care	Income limits before your payment reduces to nil ($)
1	142 426
2	147 594
3 or more	166 656 plus 31 495 for each child after the third

Payments reduce to $0 if income is more than these thresholds.

The amount paid for up to 50 hours of care in an approved facility is $3.90 per hour to a maximum of $184 per week. The Centrelink website has a Child Care Estimator that can be used to calculate the payment parents may be eligible to receive.

Child Care Rebate

The Child Care Rebate is a non–income tested, government lump sum payment that covers 50 per cent of out-of-pocket expenses for childcare to a maximum of $7500 until the end of the 2013–14 financial year. To be eligible you must be an Australian resident; use an approved childcare facility; you, and your partner if you have one, must work, study or train; and you must be registered for the Child Care Benefit (even if you do not receive or are not eligible to receive the benefit).

Carer Allowance

The Carer Allowance is a fortnightly payment of $115.40 (as at 1 January 2013) to someone who is looking after a person who is 16 years or older who is disabled, has a severe medical condition, or is frail or elderly.

The Carer Allowance is not income or assets tested and it is not taxed. Recipients are also eligible for a Carer Supplement, which entitles them to an additional lump sum payment of $600 per year. Recipients who have a child under 16 years of age, are also eligible for a Health Care Card and Child Disability Assistance Payment of up to $1000 per year.

Carer Payment

The Carer Payment is to assist those who are looking after a person who has a severe disability, has a medical condition, or is frail or aged; the situation must be reviewed every two years by Centrelink. The Carer Payment is a fortnightly payment of up to $733.70 for a single and $553.10 each for a couple, as at 20 March 2013. If the carer receives income it must be less than $101 656 per year and their assets cannot exceed $627 000 and these are assessed each January. Other eligibility criteria apply, so people who believe they are eligible should speak to Centrelink.

As with the Carer Allowance, recipients are also eligible for a further Carer Supplement of $600 per year. In addition, there is a Pension Supplement of another $61.20 for singles and $92.20 for couples per fortnight. You will receive this supplement automatically if you are receiving a Carer Payment and it's designed to meet the needs and costs of daily expenses. The rates for Carer Payment are shown in table 11.6; they are updated on 20 March and 20 September each year. If you are looking after someone, make sure you apply for these payments and get yourself down to Centrelink for some financial assistance because caring for an individual is an incredibly difficult and taxing job without having to worry about your finances.

Table 11.6: Carer Payment rates as at 20 March 2013*

Status	Rate per fortnight ($)
Single	733.70
Couple	533.10 each or 1066.20 combined
Couple separated due to ill health	733.70 each

* These amounts exclude the Pension Supplement, a fortnightly payment additional to the base pension. The maximum rates of Pension Supplement for singles and for each member of a couple separated due to ill health is $61.20 a fortnight, and for couples $92.20 a fortnight (combined).

Age Pension

The Age Pension is a fortnightly allowance from the government that is not taxable, but is income and assets tested (unless you are blind, in which case there is no income or assets test). Payment rates are shown in table 11.7 for the full Age Pension, but reduce depending on the effect of the income and assets test.

Table 11.7: Age Pension rates as at 20 March 2013

Family situation	Pension rate per fortnight ($)
Single	733.70
Couple	533.10 each or 1106.20 combined
Couple separated due to ill health	733.70 each

In addition to satisfying the income and assets test, applicants have to meet a number of other eligibility criteria. For a start, you must be of Age Pension age, as specified in table 11.8 (overleaf). The age for accessing the Age Pension is also being increased from age 65 to age 67 between 2017 and 2023.

Table 11.8: Age Pension age

Born	Women eligible for Age Pension at age	Men eligible for Age Pension at age
Before 1 July 1935	60	65
Between 1 July 1935 and 31 December 1936	60 and a half	65
Between 1 January 1937 and 30 June 1938	61	65
Between 1 July 1938 and 31 December 1939	61 and a half	65
Between 1 January 1940 and 30 June 1941	62	65
Between 1 July 1941 and 31 December 1942	62 and a half	65
Between 1 January 1943 and 30 June 1944	63	65
Between 1 July 1944 and 31 December 1945	63 and a half	65
Between 1 January 1946 and 30 June 1947	64	65
Between 1 July 1947 and 31 December 1948	64 and a half	65
Between 1 January 1949 and 30 June 1952	65	65
Between 1 July 1952 and 31 December 1953	65 and a half	65 and a half
Between 1 January 1954 and 30 June 1955	66	66
Between 1 July 1955 and 31 December 1956	66 and a half	66 and a half
After 1 January 1957	67	67

Once you have ascertained your eligibility status based upon your age, you will then need to check your eligibility according to the assets test and the income test. Whichever test results in the lower amount is the test that is applied to your situation. If the lower amount is zero, you are not eligible for an Age Pension.

The income test

As you can see from table 11.9 if your income is under $268 per fortnight as a couple or $152 as a single, you will get the full Age Pension. Once your income is over $1768.80 as a single or $2705.60 as a couple per fortnight, you will no longer be eligible for any Age Pension income. Income from an allocated pension or account-based pension is included in the income test but it is discounted to a point where it is hardly relevant.

Table 11.9: Age Pension income test as at 20 March 2013

If you are	You will receive a full pension if your fortnightly income is less than this amount ($)	Payment reduces to $0 once your fortnightly income reaches this amount ($)
Single	152	1768.80
Couple (combined)	268	2705.60
Illness separated (couple combined)	268	3501.60

The assets test

For most people, the assets test is more relevant than the income test because income from an account-based or allocated pension (from your superannuation) is discounted, but once you start drawing your superannuation pensions, the value of your super will be included in the assets test. Your home is excluded from the calculation of your assets. Your home contents are usually valued at $5000 'fire value' and motor vehicles at wholesale rates to keep the values down.

Table 11.10 shows the assets test for homeowners and non-homeowners.

Table 11.10: assets test limits as at 20 March 2013

Chart A: assets test limits for allowances and full pensions

Family situation	If your assets are less than these amounts, you will receive the full pension ($)	
	For homeowners	For non-homeowners
Single	192 500	332 000
Couple (combined)	273 000	412 500
Illness separated (couple combined)	273 000	412 500
One partner eligible (combined assets)	273 000	412 500

Chart B: assets test limits for part pensions

Family situation	Assets must be less than this amount to receive a part pension ($)	
	For homeowners	For non-homeowners
Single	731 500	871 000
Couple (combined)	1 086 000	1 225 500
Illness separated (couple combined)	1 351 000	1 490 500
One partner eligible (combined assets)	1 086 000	1 225 500

Table 11.10 shows that if your assets are between the two table amounts—$273 000 and $1 086 000 for a homeowning couple, for instance—you could get a part Age Pension (depending on the income tested calculation). The Age Pension will reduce by $1.50 for every $1000 you exceed the lower limit.

For example, if you are married and own your own home, and your assets, excluding your home, are worth less than $1 086 000, then you could be eligible for a part pension (depending on the income tested calculation). If your assets are higher than this, you will not be eligible for an Age Pension at all. If you are single and do not own your own home and your assets are less than $332 000 you could be eligible for the full Age Pension.

Age Pension case study

Allan and Margaret are 65 and 64.5 respectively and retired. Their assets excluding their home are $700 000, including their superannuation, cash investments and some shares. They are keen to obtain an Age Pension. Because they are both of Age Pension age, their full assets are counted except their home. The assets test is the one that could apply to their situation and with the lower limit of $273 000 and the upper limit of $1 086 000, they fall above the lower limit and below the upper limit, so they will receive a part pension.

To calculate the pension they are entitled to we subtract the lower limit from their assets ($700 000 − $273 000 = $427 000). We then divide that amount by $1000, which equals $427. The Age Pension decreases by $1.50 for every thousand dollars you are over the lower limit. So to arrive at the right figure we have to multiply $427 by $1.50 and that is the reduction in Allan and Margaret's fortnightly pension: $427 × $1.50 = $640.50 per fortnight. The full pension for a couple is $1218.80($609.40 × 2 = $1218.80). You subtract the amount of $640.50 from that figure. Allan and Margaret will be eligible for a combined Age Pension of $578.30 per fortnight ($15 035.80 per year). This amount includes both Pension and Clean Energy Supplements. They would also be drawing an account-based pension from their $600 000 superannuation investment to create a total income in the vicinity of 5 per cent of their lump sum or a total figure in excess of $45 000 per year.

Strategy to boost the Age Pension

If you or your partner is below Age Pension age, and if you do not draw your superannuation pension until you are of Age Pension age, then you will be able to have your superannuation assets excluded from the assets test until you reach Age Pension age. This is important if there is an age difference between you and your partner because you can maximise an Age Pension before you or your partner reach Age Pension age. It's an income maximisation strategy. If you draw your superannuation below the age of 65 (for a man, at present) then your superannuation will be included in your assets test.

For example, a couple aged 65 and 59 has assets outside their own home of $1 000 000, including super. Assume there is $500 000 in each of their super funds. If the 59-year-old's superannuation remains undrawn (not drawing a superannuation pension) then the assets will not be included in the assets test until they reach Age Pension age (age 65 in this case). They could withdraw, tax-free, $200,000 from the 65-year-old's superannuation and make a non-concessional contribution to the 59-year-old's superannuation fund, allowing the 65-year-old to receive close to the full Age Pension, maximising the couple's income.

The couple could then draw on the 65-year-old's super to create an income, while the 59-year-old's super remains in accumulation mode (undrawn and accumulating income and growth).

In addition to the base rate Age Pension, recipients may be eligible for a fortnightly Pension Supplement of up to $61.20 for a single and $46.10 for each member of a couple ($92.20 in total) as well as the Clean Energy Supplement of $13.50 (singles) and $20.40 (couples) (as at 20 March 2013), which includes a GST supplement, and a pharmaceutical, telephone and utilities allowance.

So as you can see, the Age Pension calculations can be complex and there is more detail than can be included in this short explanation. Further issues may need expanding for particular individuals, such as couples separated by illness, rent assistance, hardship provisions, aged care and Veterans' Affairs issues. In addition, there is also the interaction of other payments and allowances that affect the Age Pension.

So make sure you speak to a financial information service officer (FISO) at Centrelink for more information on how the Age Pension will work for you or your family members, or speak to your financial adviser about obtaining your maximum possible benefit. Some planning ahead will assist immensely and help you have the fantastic retirement that you deserve.

Concession cards

In addition to the allowances for recipients of the social security payments, a number of related concession cards can be obtained.

Pensioner Concession Card and Health Care Card

Pensioner Concession Cards (PCC) are for Australian residents who have received any of the following payments for more than nine months: Newstart Allowance, the Age Pension (from date of grant), Sickness Allowance, Widow Allowance, Parenting Payment, and special benefit or partner allowance over the age of 60 or over 65 for Age Pensioners. Other job seekers and Youth Allowance recipients or those on disability pensions or Carer Payments are also eligible. The card is issued annually around your birthday and is automatically updated, but you need to contact Centrelink if your circumstances change.

The PCC will allow you to receive concessionally priced pharmaceuticals, bulk-billed doctors' appointments (at the discretion of doctors), an increase in benefits for out-of-pocket medical expenses, out-of-hospital medical expenses and assistance with hearing tests and hearing aids. It will also allow you to receive a discount on mail redirection from Australia Post.

A Health Care Card (HCC) entitles you to cheaper medicines under the Pharmaceutical Benefits Scheme (PBS) and various concessions from the Australian government, which could include:

- bulk billing for doctors' appointments (this is your doctor's decision)
- more refunds for medical expenses through the Medicare Safety Net
- assistance with hearing services through the Office of Hearing Services
- discounted mail redirection through Australia Post.

You may also get some of these Australian government concessions for a dependent child.

The PCC and HCC cards will also allow for some further state-based concessions such as dental services, hearing services, home care, and optical and ambulance services. They will also allow for discounted council rates, electricity services, telephone line rental, some housing costs, education costs and transport costs.

Commonwealth Seniors Health Card

One card is provided specifically to self-funded retirees with an income of less than $80 000 for a couple or $50 000 for a single, and that is the Commonwealth Seniors Health Card (CSHC).

It is not subject to an assets test, just the income test. You need to be of Age Pension age and a resident of Australia to receive the card. There is also a Seniors Supplement to assist with household costs. The Seniors Supplement is an annual lump sum payment of $825.80 per single or $642.20 per member of a couple annually (annual total of $1284.40 per couple), as at 20 March 2013. The supplement is paid quarterly in March, June, September and December.

The CSHC allows for cheaper pharmaceuticals, bulk-billing service by certain doctors and other healthcare concessions through the Medicare safety net specifically for self-funded retirees.

State-based Seniors Cards

The final card that may be available to you is the state-based Seniors Card. That's the one that has seniors boasting about their $2.50 daily travel. This card is not administered by Centrelink and the benefits it offers will vary from state to state. Generally, these cards will give holders discounts to travel, health, clothing, hairdressers, restaurants and other products and services from any businesses that participate in the program.

For your information

Websites to help you include:

- ACT: www.dhcs.act.gov.au or phone 13 34 27

- New South Wales: www.seniorscard.nsw.gov.au or phone the Seniors Hotline on 1300 364 758

- Northern Territory: www.nt.gov.au or phone 1800 777 704

- Queensland: www.communities.qld.gov.au or phone 13 74 68

- South Australia: www.seniors.asn.au or phone (08) 8168 8776

- Tasmania: www.dpac.tas.gov.au 1300 135 513

- Victoria: www.seniorscard.vic.gov.au or phone 1300 797 210

- Western Australia: www.seniorscard.wa.gov.au or phone (08) 6551 8800.

Five sample strategies

- Split your super to take advantage of super assets in accumulation mode not being counted under the assets test when an age difference exists between members of a couple.

- If you are not eligible for an Age Pension but fall below the $50 000 assessable taxable income threshold for singles and $80 000 for couples, apply for a Commonwealth Seniors Health Care Card.

- Once you turn 60, and meet the other eligibility criteria for a Seniors Card, make sure you talk to your state-based Seniors Card providers to obtain a list of the host of discounts for retired over-60s, including cheap travel and other benefits. (Seniors Card is available to those working less than 20 hours per week, which differs from the 'less than 10 hours a week' definition under Commonwealth law for accessing super.)

- Apply for a Carer Allowance or Carer Payment if you are looking after someone who needs full-time care.

- Attend a Centrelink seminar to learn more about the Department of Human Services and what they can do for you to boost your income.

Five sample tactics

- Talk to a financial planner or a licensed accountant about how you can take advantage of super splitting to boost your income in retirement when an age difference exists between partners.

- Call a Centrelink Financial Information Service Officer on 13 23 00 about obtaining the Commonwealth Senior Health Card if you are over Age Pension age. You can do this if you are not receiving the Age Pension and have taxable income less than $50 000 for a single and $80 000 for a couple.

(continued)

Five sample tactics *(cont'd)*

- Have a look at the website for your state-based Seniors Card provider once you turn 60 to ascertain your and your partner's (if you have one) eligibility criteria and possible features, benefits and available discounts.

- Phone Centrelink on 13 24 68 if you are caring for someone full time and see if you may be eligible for a Carer Payment or Carer Allowance.

- Have a look on the Centrelink website or call 13 23 00 to book a seminar or find out what seminars are being held by Centrelink's Financial Information Service. This will help to further your education with respect to eligible payments.

KEY POINTS

- Centrelink administers a great many benefits designed to support people in need. They each have their own eligibility criteria.

- Two key tests apply for eligibility to the Age Pension (Disability Support Pensions and the Carer Payment): the income test and the assets test.

- Make sure you understand how each test works and how it affects your potential benefit in the first instance, and how your benefit may change over time, as you will be continually tested.

- Seek help from Centrelink, but if you are retiring make sure you call 13 23 00 and talk to a Financial Information Service Officer (FISO).

Disclaimer: The text and tables in this chapter are correct at the time of publication and may be amended by the Australian Government Department of Human Services at any time. If seeking to rely and/or make a claim in relation to the text/tables, please consider the most recent version of the relevant text/tables available on the Department of Human Services website at www.humanservices.gov.au

CHAPTER 12

AGED CARE

Old age: the crown of life, our play's last act.

Marcus Tullius Cicero, Roman statesman, born 106 BC

Being able to navigate your way through the aged-care system for a loved one requires some careful steering, as the complexities of aged care can baffle the inexperienced. The time constraints of organisers — you or your family — coupled perhaps with resistance from the person needing care, can compound the problem. You will want to navigate with your loved one's best interests at heart and in a way that maximises their ability to maintain dignity and independence. These are as important in old age as at any other time in life.

Aged care is a difficult and tricky topic to broach because you are often dealing with people who may have impaired mental or physical capacity and who may be determined to maintain their independence. Those who are physically incapacitated often like to think they could recover and rehabilitate themselves to a point of returning to their home. And who can blame them?

When an ageing loved one needs extra care and attention beyond what family members are reasonably able to provide, then the aged-care system needs to be employed. You need to be well equipped to understand home and residential options, the bonds, daily rates, income tests and the assets test to protect pensions and use your family's resources wisely, which often involves selling the family home to accommodate your mum or dad, or grandma or grandpa.

Sometimes the situation may be rushed, and decisions driven by emotions will affect the financial outcome for mum or dad. For example, paying a larger accommodation bond may mean that a resident receives more Age Pension or does not lose their Age Pension (which is important to the elderly). The fact is that the decision process will involve some financial management skills that you or your family may not possess. I strongly recommend seeking an aged-care specialist financial adviser to step you through the process and explain the financial implications. You will want the best care for your loved one, but the financial implications will have significant ramifications.

Let's say your mum has a fall and needs accommodation quickly. The hospital may need to find her accommodation quickly and choice may be limited, as going home may simply not be an option. The situation is desperate, emotional and draining for all involved. The whole process of finding accommodation can become pressured, and decisions may need to be made quickly. Seek advice from a professional as soon as is practically possible. On the next few pages I have listed websites and organisations that will also be able to support your decision-making process.

Statistically, around 11.5 per cent of people over the age of 70 will be accommodated by some sort of aged-care facility. The average length of stay at an aged-care facility differs significantly for men and women. On average, women stay for a little over three years and men for about two years. The vast majority of residents do not return home. The population of people over the age of 70 is currently a little over two million and is increasing by around 5 per cent per year as the baby boomers head towards retirement and beyond. An average 65 year old will live for around 20 years. Again, women will live longer on average (21 years), and men for a little less (19 years). The average stay and the average life expectancy for people over 65 are both increasing in line with health and living standards.

For more information on aged care, visit the website of the Department of Health and Ageing (www.health.gov.au). You may also benefit by looking up the Aged Care Australia website at www.agedcareaustralia.gov.au. Finally, another helpful website is www.agedcare.org.au, which is funded by more than 1400 churches, community groups and not-for-profit organisations that can help with aged care concerns and accommodation.

Given the relative complexities of aged care, I propose a five-step process for finding solutions:

- understanding care options
- understanding upfront fees

- understanding ongoing fees
- selecting suitable accommodation
- managing the Age Pension.

Let's take a look at each in turn.

Step 1: understanding care options

The three types of aged-care options are: home care; low-care facilities known as hostel accommodation; and high-care facilities known as nursing homes.

It's essential that you know what sort of care you are seeking for a loved one before you commence your search for the appropriate accommodation. The decision is not up to you, so don't worry about having to carry that burden: there is a team of people that will assist you through the process from ACAT (Aged Care Assessment Team).

Home care

People usually want to stay at home for as long as possible. Home is familiar and comfortable, and therefore highly preferred by a person requiring some assistance with their basic living requirements. People do not like to give up their independence and they want to maintain control over their own lives rather than having someone they don't know make decisions for them. There are a number of options for home care for the elderly. Assuming a person is in reasonable health, assistance may come in the form of meals or someone coming in to do housework or personal assistance or even social outings, allowing a person to stay at home for longer. Home care is often referred to as community care.

A number of community-care options are provided by programs jointly funded by both the state and federal governments around Australia. Strict government standards apply for all programs, which include the assurance of a recipient's privacy, confidentiality and dignity at all times. Programs include:

- Home and Community Care (HACC)
- Community Aged Care Packages (CACP)

- Extended Aged Care at Home (EACH)
- Extended Aged Care at Home Dementia (EACH D).

To access government-funded programs, assessment by an Aged Care Assessment Team (ACAT, or ACAS in Victoria) may be necessary. Contact Aged Care Australia (www.agedcareaustralia.gov.au) or call the Aged Care Information Line on 1800 200 422 to find out which program is most appropriate for the person's circumstances.

These programs are designed to ensure that they are based on the recipient's needs being met, that the service is satisfactory and the process consultative.

Importantly, a program is also available for carers of the elderly. While caring is an important obligation, it requires a great deal of commitment that can be draining and receives little recognition, especially when care is provided for the mentally ill. Carers may require respite from time to time, regularly or for occasional holidays or other personal commitments. The two programs for carers are Home and Community Care (HACC) and the National Respite for Carers Program (NRCP). The latter also encompasses a host of other programs, including the provision of daily care, counselling and associations of carers of aged people to provide support and other services in metropolitan and rural areas. For respite assistance call the respite information line on 1800 200 422. This is the central point of contact for all consumer aged care enquires; it is run by the Department of Health and Ageing.

Low-level care

Residential care is broken up into low-level care and high-level care services and both can be provided under the same roof. This is known as 'ageing in place' and it allows residents to stay at the same facility when their needs change from low care to high care.

Low care refers to residents who are generally mobile but need assistance with personal-care services such as meals, toileting, bathing, mobility, dressing, continence and rehabilitation services. It also assists with accommodation care matters, such as providing meals, laundry, cleaning and the basics of maintaining a living facility, such as building maintenance.

Low care is really for people who need some assistance without complex personal services or 24-hour nursing facilities. They are typically mobile and can move about on their own. They also have access to other health services, such as doctors and nursing when they need it. Most homes or hostels offer easy access to the services of health professionals.

High-level care

High-level care, as opposed to low-level care, services, are for someone who requires 24-hour nursing care and complete use of all care services. It includes daily living services, such as bathing and toileting, and constant medical monitoring administered by nursing staff, in addition to all of the other services provided for low-level care, including accommodation. High-level care also assists with mobility services, continence aids, rehabilitation, oxygen use, as well as social activities and services.

ACAT assessment

Once you have a general understanding of the types of assistance that exist for the elderly, you need to organise an assessment. Everyone needing aged-care facilities or assistance and wanting to access the government subsidies *must* be assessed by ACAT (Aged Care Assessment Team). Without an ACAT assessment form, an aged-care facility will not consider admitting a person, unless you are willing to pay all the costs. Approval by ACAT will allow a government subsidy of about $60 000 per year for high-level care and $20 000 per year for low-level care to be applied to the prospective resident. Waiting times for ACAT can be more than six months, unless patients are awaiting ACAT to leave the hospital system. You may want to consult your GP to hurry the system along somewhat.

The Aged Care Assessment Teams could be made up of a number of healthcare professionals, including nurses, doctors, psychiatrists, social workers and other healthcare workers, who are required to assess anyone wanting access to care. The ACAT team will provide advice on what sort of care facility is required and any other care options that are possible.

Step 2: understanding upfront fees

Residents of aged-care facilities are required to pay a set of fees that are determined by a number of factors, including a resident's income and possibly their assets. There are both upfront fees and ongoing fees.

Upfront (entry) fees

Upfront (entry) fees are known as *accommodation bonds*. They are fees payable to a facility within the first six months of admittance. Generally, hostels (low-care facilities) charge accommodation bonds, while nursing homes (high-care facilities) have an ongoing accommodation charge, unless they are classified as an 'extra service facility', in which case a bond is payable. Extra service nursing homes tend to provide more conveniences for residents, such as larger rooms, private bathrooms or more high-end facilities.

While a facility will generally prefer to receive a lump sum upfront, it may accept periodic payments (with interest being charged at a pre-determined rate) or a combination of upfront and periodic payments. This could be for a long period or for a short period until, for example, the family home is sold or assets are sold to raise cash for a bond. The bond is refundable, minus a retention charge (a non-indexed monthly deduction for a maximum of five years at a rate set by the government) when the resident leaves the facility.

Accommodation bonds average about $215 000 Australia-wide, but typically they will range from $300 000 to $450 000 in major cities, with some as high as $1 000 000 for a luxury, resort-style facility. Bonds vary from place to place and will also differ according to the quality and services offered. When undertaking your due diligence on suitable residences, it's important to ask how much the bond is to ensure you can afford to pay it.

Anecdotal evidence suggests that — particularly in city areas, but also in some major regional areas — facility owners prefer to seek residents who have sufficient assets to pay bonds in excess of $300 000 to ensure financial viability of their operation. It can therefore be difficult for residents with fewer assets to obtain good-quality care accommodation. Further searching may be required by your family to find the most appropriate place if you are in this situation.

If the elderly person's assets, including their home, are less than $108 266 (as at September 2012), then they will be classified as a supported resident, which may help you find a place in a facility. Every facility must keep a certain quota of beds available for supported residents and the government provides the facility with extra assistance to help meet supported residents' costs.

The amount of a bond may vary from resident to resident depending on a resident's financial situation. Sometimes it makes more sense for a person to pay a higher bond to positively affect their social security (Age Pension) situation. The accommodation bond is excluded from Centrelink's assets test and therefore it can increase the amount of Age Pension a person may receive. There are other ways to 'hide' assets or reduce income that may increase the Age Pension. This is where a financial adviser that specialises in this type of advice can assist you. We'll look at a few later in the chapter.

In addition, accommodation bonds, less the retention amount, are government guaranteed. A retention amount is an amount of the bond that the facility operator is entitled to deduct from the bond on a monthly basis. The government regulates the retention amount and if bonds are over $38 760 in the 2012–13 financial year, the monthly retention amount will be $323. If bonds are below $38 760, the amounts vary according to a scale that you can find on the Department of Health and Ageing website (www.health.gov.au). These amounts change each financial year, but are fixed at the applicable rate when a resident moves in.

Step 3: understanding ongoing fees

Ongoing fees are broken up into a number of separate fees:

- daily fees: basic daily fee and daily income-tested fee
- accommodation charge
- extra service fees.

Daily fees

Both hostels and nursing homes charge daily fees that are to be paid by all residents, but the amounts may vary depending on the income status of the resident.

There are two types of daily fees. The first is a *basic daily fee*. This is a minimum fee payable by all residents. It will vary depending on circumstances, but most people will fall into this lower category. The current daily rate ranges from $43.22 to $49.07 (as at 20 September 2012; the rate is indexed every March and September).

The second daily fee is a *daily income-tested fee* that will be tested against the income of the resident and increase in line with the resident's income from nil to a current maximum of $68.65 (as at 20 September 2012). It is tested against the person's income, including payments received from Centrelink or Veterans' Affairs, and private income calculated using the Age Pension income test rules, regardless of whether the resident is a recipient of the Age Pension or not. The amount set is reviewed each quarter. There are a number of ways to strategically reduce a person's income using certain types of products, including insurance bonds through trusts or annuities.

Accommodation charge

An accommodation charge is not payable by residents who pay an accommodation bond, and it is therefore more relevant to nursing home (high-level care) accommodation. Technically, it is an entry fee, but it is payable monthly for as long as a resident is in the facility.

Accommodation charges are payable monthly, and the government sets a maximum fee payable for residents who have more than $109 640.80 (as at 20 September 2012) in assets. Residents who have assets less than $41 500, will pay no accommodation charge. With assets valued between $41 500 and $109 640.80 a partial amount that is pro-rated will be payable. The amount is set at the time the resident enters the facility and does not rise after that date. The current maximum daily rate is set at $32.76 per day (as at 20 September 2012).

Details of the prospective resident's assets must be provided to Centrelink for an assessment, as the situation can change depending on the nature of the family home and who is remaining in the home; for example, a spouse, dependant or carer, or close relative on income-support payments from Centrelink.

Extra service fees

Extra service fees are charged for aged care facilities that provide a higher level of service or accommodation. They will vary from residence to residence and depend on the type of services provided, such as 'hotel-style' services with better food options and hotel-style facilities and services. You will need to ask each of the facilities that you are considering if there are any extra service fees payable and, if so, how much they will be and what extra services can be provided.

Step 4: selecting suitable accommodation

Now that you understand the types of different accommodation and fees payable, you can start to look around for a suitable facility for your partner, parents or grandparent. You will want to give key consideration to the assessment from ACAT and discuss with them the recommended accommodation type and perhaps even which facilities would be most appropriate in your area. Build a list of the appropriate facilities and perhaps work out a scale for the quality, suitability and appropriateness of each for the resident based on care type, location and cost.

Step 5: managing the Age Pension

Before a final decision is made, an important consideration is the effect of the resident's finances on their ability to optimise their access to an Age Pension. For many residents, maintaining and maximising the Age Pension from Centrelink is very important. Given the importance of the income test and assets test, there are a few ways to reduce income and assets to achieve a more favourable result when Centrelink apply either test.

The effect can be paying lower ongoing fees and charges from the chosen facility and receiving a higher Age Pension — the services remain consistent, no matter the fees. In summary, you can save money and earn more for your family member by having the best strategy. It's well worth seeking advice to optimise your situation.

Be cautious when looking at the strategies, because you need to make sure that the person's total financial situation is improved, and that you don't just focus on an increase in their Age Pension or lower fees.

Insurance bonds to reduce fees

One way of reducing the daily income-tested fee is by establishing a family trust and investing assets through the trust into an insurance bond, which makes it possible to reduce the person's deemed or actual income. This may have the effect of decreasing the daily income-tested fee for someone in the aged care system. It also means their other assets can be invested in growth assets such as shares and have the potential to grow.

> ## Tip
>
> Deeming is a set of social security rules used to assess income from certain financial assets, no matter what the actual income is. For example, as a single person, the first $45 400 of your financial assets is deemed to produce 2.5 per cent returns, and further income is deemed to produce 4 per cent (as at 14 February 2013, when they were reduced). A couple is deemed to earn 2.5 per cent on the first $75 600 then 4 per cent thereafter.

An insurance bond does not distribute income so there is no income to declare or deem. If the trust isn't accessed within the first 10 years, the earnings are reinvested and there is no income assessment. The insurance bond will be assessed under the assets test when determining the Age Pension, but the assets test does not affect the daily income-tested fee, which may be as high as $68.65 per day (as at 20 September 2012). Effectively, the daily fee could fall to as low as zero.

This strategy may be appropriate for people who have money left over from the sale of a house or other assets that will have income deeming applied. The aim is to reduce the daily income-tested fee to as close to zero as possible.

This strategy requires further explanation that is not possible in the confines of the pages of this book, so make sure you seek assistance and advice to ensure the appropriateness of the strategy. It's also important to understand the nature of the product and the effect of locking away money in an insurance bond. You also need to consider the costs of setting up this strategy.

Maximise accommodation bond

Maximising the bond payment can reduce the assets test assessment — the accommodation bond has been exempt from the assets test when calculating Age Pension entitlements since 2005.

Given there is no limit on the size of the bond payable, theoretically you could pay a bond of $1 000 000 and receive the full Age Pension, for which you may have been previously ineligible. If a facility is flexible as to the amount of bond payable, it could be advantageous for a resident to pay a higher amount and maximise their Age Pension.

If a principal residence has to be sold to fund a bond for aged care, the amount left over from the sale, after the bond is deducted, is fully assessable as an asset under the assets test. If the house sale proceeds pushes someone over the assets test limits this could potentially be damaging for a person who has been receiving the Age Pension. By increasing the size of the bond, the assets test can be reduced, potentially producing a higher Age Pension entitlement.

Assets test limits, as at 20 September 2012, are shown in table 12.1.

Table 12:1: assets test limits for accommodation bond payments

Description	Assets test limit for non-homeowners ($)	Assets test limit for homeowners ($)
Single lower limit	332 000	192 500
Single upper limit	847 250	707 750
Couple lower limit	412 500	273 000
Couple upper limit	1 189 500	1 050 000

The family home assessment

The family home, normally excluded from the assets test for calculation and entitlement to the Age Pension, becomes assessable after two years after the aged-care resident leaves the home, and any rent received will be assessed under the income test from the first day after departure. For the first two years of a resident's stay in an aged-care facility, either low or high care, the house remains an exempt asset under the Centrelink rules. However, after the two-year period has expired, the house can become assessable (at market value), with the resident considered to be a non-homeowner.

Fortunately, there are exemptions to the assets test application. If a spouse or dependent child is still living in the home, the home remains exempt. If a spouse stays in the home and then leaves to go into an aged-care facility, then the two-year rule will apply from the departure of the last spouse.

Where a resident pays their accommodation bond (in full or in part) as periodic payments or pays the accommodation charge and the family home is rented, the home remains exempt under the assets test beyond the first two years and the income is exempt from day one under the income test. This is a very favourable strategy to reduce the effect of the assets test and the income test, to increase the Age Pension and to reduce the income-tested daily care fee.

Understanding the operation of the assets test can save you thousands of dollars and add significant benefits that flow from the receipt of an Age Pension over and above the extra cash flow.

Gifting to reduce your assets

Gifting is a genuine strategy that allows a person to achieve a lower level of assessable assets under the Centrelink assets test rules. However, any amounts gifted over the allowable limits will still be considered in the assets test and will increase the Age Pension recipient's assets in the eyes of Centrelink, thus reducing the Age Pension they receive every fortnight.

An Age Pension recipient may gift up to $10 000 per year to a maximum of $30 000 over a five-year period. For more information on gifting visit Centrelink's website (www.centrelink.gov.au).

Granny flats

Centrelink allows for the transfer of significant assets to another person for the right of occupancy in the form of a granny flat. The definition of a granny flat, for social security purposes, is more broad-based than simply a unit attached to a house. The beauty of this allowance is that a person can transfer an entire house or contribute a significant lump sum to a family member in exchange for the rights of lifetime occupancy for the homeowner making the gift. This may help to reduce the assets test and will not be covered by the gifting provisions mentioned earlier.

Apart from the ability to reduce the effect of the assets test, this has some very practical applications and facilitates some smart utilisation of the family's assets. For example, a mother can transfer a property into her daughter's name in exchange for the right to permanently reside with the daughter. Another example may be where a daughter builds a new house with her husband and the mother contributes $200 000 to add a granny flat or an outbuilding to the property in exchange for life tenancy. The $200 000 is used to build a better house and the mother solves her residency and assets issues.

Certain requirements must be met to accommodate the requirements of the granny flat provisions. To quote the Centrelink fact sheet directly:

'Whether you live alone, with the owner, or in a separate self-contained dwelling on someone else's property, your home will meet the granny flat requirements and can be assessed under special rules if:

- it is all or part of any private residence

- it is not owned by you, your partner, or an entity (trust or company) that you control, and

- you have established a granny flat interest.'

A granny flat interest is where your arrangement allows you to have a lifetime interest in the property in the form of a lifetime tenancy (the right to occupy the property) or a lifetime interest (the right to use and benefit from the property). There should be a written legal agreement that remains with the property, even when it's sold (in theory), and the agreement recognises the life interest and if any rent or property upkeep fees are to be paid by the occupant of the granny flat.

If you transfer your home into someone else's name, if you contribute an amount to the building of a granny flat on someone else's property or if you buy a property in someone else's name and establish a lifetime right to accommodation, then no gifting amount is applied (known as 'deprivation of your assets' by Centrelink) to your asset test. However, if you contribute more than the amount of the cost of the home or the cost of the above situations, then a formula is applied to calculate a possible deprivation amount. Download the Centrelink fact sheet for more information on granny flats and the deprivation rules from www.centrelink.gov.au.

Strategies and tactics for aged care

It's difficult to set strategies for an aged care plan as each situation is different and the circumstances are often challenging. My advice is to call 1800 200 422 or visit the www.agedcareaustralia.gov.au website for information, keep up to date with the latest rates and figures, and educate yourself on the topic of aged care before an event gives rise to an immediate need.

Finally, make sure you use my five-step aged care checklist available to download from www.samhenderson.com.au. It will help you summarise and compile all the information you need to know about aged care.

Another handy website and service is provided by some friends of mine at Aged Care Steps (www.agedcaresteps.com.au). I often invite the directors to talk on my show on Sky News Business, *Your Money, Your Call* (retirement segment) on Friday nights to discuss technical matters about aged care and financial planning. They are the experts.

KEY POINTS

- Understanding aged care is complex and time consuming, but help is on hand from numerous government and private bodies.

- The complexities of aged care can be magnified by the emotional burden of finding suitable accommodation, particularly if the need suddenly becomes urgent.

- Understand the difference between low-level care and high-level care facilities.

- Not many financial advisers specialise in aged care, but if you do need advice, seek a specialist.

- The Department of Health and Ageing and Centrelink should be your first ports of call.

- Remember, people on the Age Pension detest the idea of losing it because they've worked hard all their lives, so make sure you do what you can to keep it in place for the person you're caring for.

- Download the five-step aged-care checklist from www.samhenderson.com.au.

CHAPTER 13

ESTATE PLANNING

Animals have these advantages over man: they never hear the clock strike, they die without any idea of death ... their funerals cost them nothing, and no-one starts lawsuits over their wills.

Voltaire, philosopher

Estate planning is a very important part of the financial planning process, but it is often neglected. Often people don't care what happens to their assets when they are gone, but estate planning is so much more than dealing with your assets when you are no longer on the planet. Estate planning is about how you structure your assets while you are still alive and about gaining an understanding of what happens in the event that you are unable to make decisions, sign documents or act of your own accord. It can also instruct trusted individuals on how to take care of your children.

True, estate planning does address how your assets are distributed at the time of your demise and beyond, but if you have built significant assets, or simply own a house in Australia, then you will want to protect those assets and ensure your loved ones and beneficiaries receive their share, as you would intend if you were here to distribute the assets yourself.

There are many examples of deserving beneficiaries who have had their share of an estate significantly depleted because of the lack of a valid will. Understanding the process of estate planning and how assets are distributed from various structures plays an important role in the financial planning process. Many myths surround estate planning and dispelling those myths forms the basis of a few salient points in this chapter. It's important to have a factual reference and to avoid 'barbecue advice' (when friends give you advice that's straight off the grapevine and without any factual basis).

Wills

A will is a legal document that sets out your intentions for the distribution of your assets after your death. More than 40 per cent of Australians do not have a will, so the first thing to deal with is constructing a legally valid and up-to-date will, and ensure it remains up to date in the face of life's major changes, such as marriage, divorce, the birth of additional children or the death of possible beneficiaries or executors.

If you do not have a will, then it is said that you have died intestate (without a will). In that case the state government will apply a formula to your estate to distribute your assets to the beneficiaries prescribed under the laws of intestacy. The process will be open to dispute, and the people that you wanted to benefit from your estate may be disadvantaged and the people you wanted to exclude may benefit. Having a valid and up-to-date will is essential, and it's a simple process if you speak to your solicitor or estate-planning specialist. A good financial adviser should also be able to help you.

Wills are dealt with at a state level, not federal, so each state may have slightly different rules for the operations of estate planning and how they deal with the issues surrounding wills and the distribution of assets.

Tip

For some free information on managing a will or an estate, have a look at the Law Society website at www.lawsociety.com.au. There are FAQs for the community on wills and estates. Click on the Community tab on the home page to see the list of FAQs.

Preparing a will generally costs $600 to $3000 depending on what is required and how specific the instructions and documentation need to be. The upper level of costs will normally involve your beneficiaries receiving their inheritances via testamentary trusts, which provide asset protection and tax advantages, along with including powers of attorney, powers of enduring guardian and some specific instructions around estate equalisation (making sure everyone gets their fair share). For example, if you lent money to son number one, you may wish to make sure son number two receives a similar benefit in the will and that the loan reduces the inheritance received by son number one. You can buy will kits for around $25, but I strongly recommend that you seek the advice of a good estate-planning specialist and invest in good advice, as without such advice your directions may be in breach of your legal obligations to your family.

Also make sure your beneficiaries know where the will is located, otherwise you may die intestate. As an adviser, I always make sure I have a copy of my clients' wills and keep them on file. Many clients leave the wills on the kitchen table before they go away in case something happens; that's extra cautious, although not a bad idea.

What is a valid will?

For a will to be accepted by a court of law, the will-maker (testator or testatrix) must be of sound mind and not under any duress (undue pressure). There are three basic common elements to the construction of a will, required in all states:

- The will must be in writing.
- The will-maker must sign the bottom of the will.
- Two witnesses must also sign the bottom of the will:
  - Witnesses have to be over 18 years of age.
  - Witnesses cannot be beneficiaries, or married to beneficiaries, or the de facto partners of beneficiaries.
  - Witnesses must be physically present with the testator or testatrix when he or she signs the will.

Certain parts of a will become invalid in the case of divorce in New South Wales, Queensland and Tasmania. In the other states and territories, the will remains in force after divorce unless a new will is prepared. Marriage also invalidates a will, and it is recommended that a new will replace your existing will to allow for your spouse when you marry. So, too, minors who reach the age of 18 are granted certain rights in courts in Australia. It's important to mention all children, ex-partner's shared children and spouses in your will to alleviate the possibility of a legal challenge to your estate.

Who are the parties to a will?

There are a number of parties involved in the administration of an estate and each has an important role. The parties are as follows:

- *Testator* or *testatrix* (*female*) — the will-maker and original owner of the estate; the deceased.

- *Executor* — the person(s) or entity appointed under the will to be the trustee and administrator of the testator's/testatrix's estate. The executor plays a very important role, being responsible for identifying, administering and distributing the assets in accordance with the law and the will.

- *Beneficiary* — a person or entity that receives assets or benefits from the distribution of the estate on the death of the testator.

- *Administrator* — if a person dies without appointing an executor, an administrator is appointed to administer the estate and to act as an executor. In the case of someone dying intestate, the administrator will have to apply for a grant of letters of administration to provide him or her with the power to act for the estate.

Probate — administration of an estate

Probate is simply a process of identifying that a valid will exists and that the executor has the authority to act on behalf of the estate. It is an application to the Supreme Court (in your state) and the legal document that you apply for is called a grant of probate. The court reviews the will and verifies its validity before granting probate. Once granted, the executor can gain access to bank accounts and set about assembling the deceased's assets and liabilities, pay any duties and taxes, and then distribute the remaining assets of the estate to the beneficiaries. Depending on the state of the will, and the complexity of the instructions and assets, the probate process may take anything from a couple of months to a couple of years.

For example, if the will allows for cash to be distributed to a number of beneficiaries then a property may have to be sold before there is any cash available to distribute. So, too, the land titles office may need to be involved to transfer a property to a beneficiary if the will allowed for a particular property to be passed to a specific beneficiary.

The role of the executor is an important one and carries with it a great legal responsibility to act in the best interests of beneficiaries and the testator or testatrix. The role is time-consuming and it can require some considerable effort, including the assistance of a solicitor, which can be costly. The estate meets the costs of the administration, legal advice and assistance, as well as the immediate costs of the funeral arrangements. The job can be quite challenging so be prepared to do some work if someone appoints you as an executor.

What assets form part of the will assets?

Not all assets seemingly held by an individual automatically form the assets of the will. The name or structure in which you purchase assets will affect how the assets are passed to beneficiaries in the event of your death (see chapter 3). Generally, assets held in individual names or as tenants in common form part of the estate assets and can be distributed.

Jointly held assets are not part of the estate. Jointly held assets are owned jointly and severally by owners and on the death of one owner, the assets automatically move to the surviving owner. Jointly held assets skip the probate process entirely and pass immediately to the other joint owner. For example, if a family home is held in joint names, and one partner passes away, the home is not part of the estate and will automatically pass to the surviving owner.

So, too, trust money falls outside the will and assets within the trust do not fall directly into the will because the trust will continue (for up to 80 years) without the deceased. The beneficiaries of the trust do not necessarily own the assets, the trust does, although the beneficiary may control them (by acting as the trustee(s) who really control(s) the assets).

Privately held company assets also fall outside the will; however, shares in the company can be left in the will and there should be a company shareholders' agreement to deal with the instance of death of a director or shareholder. A business succession plan is needed if you own a business or you are a major shareholder in a business. Further, a buy/sell agreement would be recommended in concert with key person insurance to allow beneficiaries to be paid out in the case of the death of a director or major shareholder. You will need to seek advice if you are the owner of private company shares as the area requires specific tools to navigate through estate-planning and business-succession issues.

Superannuation, because it is administered under Commonwealth law, does not immediately fall into the will either. Superannuation is a trust structure and is therefore dealt with under trust law and superannuation law. That being said, there is a simple solution to managing superannuation assets, by completing a binding nomination of beneficiaries form; it should be allowed for in your superannuation trust deed for SMSFs, or you can easily obtain one from your superannuation provider. A binding nomination form binds the trustee of your super fund to distribute the assets outside of the will to financial dependants, or you can even nominate the estate as the recipient of your superannuation assets. The binding nomination must be updated every three years, although many lawyers are now providing perpetual binding death nominations that do not require the update.

In the absence of a binding nomination form, and if there is no spouse or child classified as a financial dependant, then your super death benefits will be paid to your estate. So your super will not be lost, but as part of the estate it has to go through the probate process, which can take many months if not years. Surviving spouses will probably need the income from the superannuation to live on and pay household expenses, so to avoid any financial heartache and disappointment, make sure your binding nomination form is up to date.

If you are being paid a superannuation pension at the time of your death (allocated pension, TRIS or account-based pension), then your surviving tax dependants can continue to receive your pension tax-free, if you ensure your binding nomination form is up to date and your trust deed or the trustee of a public offer fund allows for it. This is called a reversionary pension as it reverts to your dependants. Public offer funds will offer this readily, and SMSFs can use the same functionality.

Non–tax dependants have to receive your superannuation as a lump sum and they also pay 16.5 per cent tax on the taxable portion of your superannuation. Non-taxable portions of super remain tax-free to beneficiaries. These two portions relate to the two kinds of contribution you made to super when it was in the accumulation phase. Concessional contributions were made from your pre-tax salary, and 15 per cent tax was deducted from them when they entered the fund. They include superannuation guarantee amounts, salary sacrifice contributions and any earnings from the fund — these form part of your taxable portion, which is taxed at 16.5 per cent to non–tax dependants (such as adult children) on your death. The non-concessional contributions (after-tax contributions) are not taxed going in or coming out to anyone (so they form the non-taxable portion of a super payout).

One way of ensuring your superannuation is not taxed when paid to non-dependants is to ensure that your power of attorney allows for your super to be cashed out if you are unconscious or incapable of acting for yourself in the event of disability, illness or incapacity of any kind. Speak to your solicitor about adding this simple but effective clause to your power of attorney documentation whether it's a general or enduring power of attorney — enduring is more comprehensive.

Tip

Make sure you regularly update your binding nomination form and your trust deed for your superannuation fund(s). Call your super fund today, or check your trust deed for your SMSF, to ensure that it allows for reversionary pensions and the latest legislative superannuation changes.

Capital gains tax for estates

How your assets have been purchased will determine whether capital gains tax (CGT) is payable, when it is payable and by whom. Any asset purchased after 11 am on 20 September 1985 is subject to CGT. But CGT is only payable on the occurrence of a CGT event, such as the disposal of an asset (sale or transfer).

The family home is exempt from CGT for a period of two years after the death of the owner, so provided it's sold within the two-year period the sale will not attract CGT to the estate or the beneficiary. After two years it will be subject to CGT. I suggest that you obtain a valuation at the date of transfer (or up to two years from the date of death) to determine the cost base of the asset as it will be subject to CGT from then onwards.

Transferring a property from the deceased to a beneficiary is not a CGT event. Essentially, if a beneficiary moves into an inherited house that was not previously subject to CGT, then the CGT exemption for principal residences applies. However, if a beneficiary moves into a house that was purchased after 20 September 1985 and it was rented for investment purposes, then a portion of the gain may be subject to CGT on the eventual sale of the asset.

However, if an asset (other than the family home) has to be sold to pay beneficiaries, and if the asset was purchased after September 1985, then it will be subject to CGT, but the CGT will be payable by the estate, not the beneficiary.

Assets bought before September 1985 are free of CGT to the estate. If a pre-CGT asset is transferred to a beneficiary, then the date of death becomes the registered date of purchase of the asset for the beneficiary, and therefore the cost base is valued from that date onwards, so you should obtain a valuation for property. For shares, it is easy to obtain a valuation from the sharemarket for the date of death.

In summary, when pre-CGT (pre-September 1985) assets are sold, the cost base becomes the value of the asset at the date of death. It is therefore prudent to obtain a valuation on the date of death to establish a cost base for an eventual sale.

Testamentary trusts

A testamentary trust, also known as a will trust, is established on the death of a person to protect the assets of the estate. A testamentary trust is designed to protect the family assets.

One of the key reasons for establishing a testamentary trust is to distribute tax-effective income to minors: this prevents minors having to pay the highest marginal tax rate on the income, as they would normally do. Rather, minors are taxed under the normal marginal tax rates for adults with a tax-free threshold of $18 200. While adults can control the money held in the trust, it can be tax-effectively distributed to minors to reduce tax across the portfolio of assets.

Another reason for establishing a testamentary trust is to protect the assets from adversarial former spouses or de facto partners of beneficiaries. The assets in a testamentary trust can be controlled by the intended beneficiaries and be accessible for the use of beneficiaries, but the assets can be protected in the event of dispute or family breakdown.

This is particularly effective when a father, for example, doesn't like the de facto partner of a daughter and thinks that the relationship will not last. In the event of a relationship breakdown and after the father has died, the father's assets can be held in trust for the daughter, and the de facto partner will have no right to the assets that are held in the trust. Importantly, testamentary trusts also provide protection from bankruptcy, providing security for intergenerational wealth transfer.

In the example above, if there is no testamentary trust and if the assets were passed to the daughter on the father's death and, say, the daughter paid down the mortgage on a jointly owned property with her de facto partner, the de facto partner would have a good argument to claim half of the value of the property in the event of a relationship breakdown. This would be strongly against the wishes of the deceased father, and the father's assets would be lost to an adversary of the family.

A testamentary trust can also be established to look after disabled (disability trust) or other beneficiaries who are not able to look after themselves. This is also a good method of looking after adults who are not capable of managing money, such as drug addicts, alcoholics or other adults who display forms of addiction combined with poor money-management skills. The estate can, for example, be instructed to pay rent and an account at a supermarket rather than giving these people cash that can be misused.

Power of attorney

A power of attorney is a document that, when presented, allows someone to act on your behalf subject to any conditions contained in the document. A power of attorney is particularly handy if you are unable to attend to an important matter because of incapacity, travel (inability to attend) or disability. The person granting the power of attorney to another person is called the donor, and the person who is the grantee is called the attorney. A power of attorney is revoked on death, bankruptcy or insolvency, or when the time that it is set for has expired. The two types of power of attorney are general and enduring.

A general power of attorney allows the attorney to act on behalf of the donor to sign documents, attend meetings and basically act as the donor except in financial, lifestyle or medical situations. The general power of attorney is not applicable if the donor becomes of unsound mind.

An enduring power of attorney allows the attorney to make financial decisions and will continue if the donor becomes of unsound mind. In fact, this is often the intention of an enduring power of attorney and it is ideal for elderly people suffering from Alzheimer's disease or who are incapacitated because of physical or mental illness. However, the power of attorney must be in place before the person is classified as 'of unsound mind', as a signatory must have legal capacity. Without legal capacity, they cannot legally provide a power of attorney and so you will need to make an application to the state. The difference between a general power of attorney and an enduring power of attorney is the functionality for attorney in the event that the person becomes 'of unsound mind' or otherwise incapacitated.

In the event that an enduring power of attorney has not been drawn up and a person becomes of unsound mind, then an administrator or guardian may need to be appointed by making an application to the state. All wills and powers of attorney are managed by state governments.

It is wise to have an enduring power of attorney drawn up as early as possible so that you can choose the people who will be making decisions about your welfare if necessary in the future.

Guardianship — the young and elderly

Each state has a guardianship board or tribunal that has the ability to appoint a guardian in the event that an individual does not have the capacity to act for themselves. This is often the case if children are left without parents or a legal guardian, or for elderly people who have lost their ability to make financial and lifestyle decisions for themselves.

Appointments of enduring guardianship are ideal when, for example, real estate needs to be sold to pay for a room in a nursing home and an elderly person does not have the capacity to act for themselves. A real estate agent would have to be engaged, contracts signed, conveyancing undertaken and a host of other processes carried out that an incapacitated elderly person could not undertake for themselves.

Ideally, you can appoint guardians in the context of your will for your children; however, while your registered desire is contained in your will, your choice is not legally binding and therefore it is subject to dispute. A court will attempt to act in the best interests of the child.

Before you appoint a guardian for your children, it is important to speak to the potential guardian first and make sure that they are up to the task. It is also prudent to have an alternative guardian. It is also a good idea to detail a list of intentions for the way you would like your children brought up and note some of the essential things that you want to be done to make you feel as though the children have the best possible life and upbringing.

A guardian may fall under the dependency definition inside superannuation and therefore have a claim to your superannuation. Dependants have a claim to your superannuation as they may be reliant on income from your superannuation pension — more so than financially independent children (for example). The guardian will need money to look after your children so it's important to outline how this occurs based upon your intentions set out in your will. A testamentary trust is a good way of providing the benefits received by guardians to look after your kids. Make sure the guardian you choose is good with money.

Divorce and family provisions

Family breakdown is common these days: around 50 per cent of marriage partners and more than 50 per cent of de facto partners split up. Financially, this can be a disaster and a good way to halve the assets that you have spent so much time and effort to grow. This is often a heartache that can be avoided through the initiation of a mature discussion and the implementation of a written agreement.

Break-ups are emotional enough, but people truly go crazy when money is involved because money can become an emotional plaything to mess with the other person when the relationship breaks down. A written agreement in the form of a pre-nuptial agreement for marriage or a financial agreement for de facto partners will help to alleviate the financial pain.

A pre-nuptial agreement is a document setting out how the assets of a married couple will be distributed in the event of a marriage breakdown. In the absence of such an agreement it is an expensive and drawn-out process to drag a divorce through the courts, divesting both parties of their life savings. The lawyers are usually the only winners, and the family suffers more than it needs to. Furthermore, it's hardly impressive to have the kids watch the parents thrash it out in court.

A pre-nup is a handy document to have if one partner brings more wealth to the partnership and therefore has more to protect in the event of family breakdown. It is common in very wealthy families who are keen to protect the family's wealth. The reason most couples don't have pre-nups, besides the fact that many don't have any assets to protect, is because they feel embarrassed and that the mere discussion of a pre-nup may signify a negative feeling about the relationship.

Under the Commonwealth's *Family Law Act* superannuation is now also split between the couple and makes up a significant asset. De facto partners and same-sex partners are also covered for superannuation splitting following a relationship breakdown (Western Australians are excluded).

A cohabitation agreement, or a financial agreement as it is legally known, is a written legal agreement between two consenting adults who live together in a de facto relationship. It details what happens in the event that the couple split up. It will cover how the assets will be distributed and what happens to the children of that relationship, if there are any. Recent changes have affected the effectiveness of financial agreements and so getting specialist legal advice is essential.

I strongly recommend you include pets in any of the documentation, as people will fight over pets as much as they will fight over children and money. There have been some changes to the way courts deal with financial agreements so I strongly recommend seeking professional advice on this topic.

In summary, if you have assets that you want to protect in the event of a relationship breakdown, I recommend that you go into your relationship with the right documentation and ensure that you have a partner with whom you can participate in a sensible discussion about your asset-protection strategy. It is a good idea to highlight how hard you worked to acquire your assets and what you had to go through to build your assets to their current level.

Family breakdown is a touchy subject, but don't be afraid to seek legal advice if there is anything you are unsure about. You should hope for the best and prepare for the worst.

Five sample strategies

- Obtain a will as a matter of urgency.

- If you already have a will, ensure it is up to date and continues to reflect your objectives.

- Update your binding nomination of beneficiaries in your super fund.

- Establish an enduring power of attorney for you and your partner, if you have one.

- Appoint enduring guardians for your children.

Five sample tactics

- Read and review your existing will and powers of attorney to make sure they are valid, up to date and continue to meet your ongoing and future objectives.

- Call a specialist solicitor immediately and book an appointment to discuss establishing a will and powers of attorney if you don't have both already.

- Call your super fund (or accountant or administrator if you have an SMSF) and make sure your binding nomination of beneficiaries is up to date and signed—get them to send a copy to you for your records or sign a new one if necessary.

- Talk to your solicitor about obtaining enduring guardianship for your children or elderly parents.

- If you are in a de facto relationship and you have assets that you would like to protect, call a solicitor to discuss the best approach to protecting those assets via financial agreement or pre-nuptial agreement if you are planning to get married.

KEY POINTS

- A will is a legal document that sets out the distribution of your assets in the event of your death.

- Enduring powers of attorney allow a trusted person to act on your behalf in the event that you are unable to do so for yourself. For example, if you are overseas, incapacitated or of unsound mind.

- Not all assets are dealt with under the will. For example, trust, company, jointly held and superannuation assets do not form assets for the purposes of the will unless otherwise directed to do so via trust deed, nomination or shareholders' agreement.

- Binding nominations for super funds bind the trustee(s) to distribute your assets to your financial dependants upon your death, or to your estate.

- Guardianship allows for children, the disabled or the elderly to be looked after in the event of your demise.

- Separation for de facto or same-sex couples can be a financial disaster, with both members of the couple having access to the other's assets (and depending on the circumstances, possibly super as well). Be cautious and protect what you have via a pre-nuptial or financial agreement.

CHAPTER 14

TWELVE STRATEGIES TO INSTANTLY BOOST YOUR WEALTH

> You see, in life, lots of people know what to do, but few
> people actually do what they know. Knowing is not enough!
> You must take action.
>
> *Tony Robbins, motivational speaker*

Strategic action is all about saving tax and boosting your investments and superannuation. It encompasses financial structures, such as trusts, superannuation, companies and ownership entity choices, and how to maximise your contributions to superannuation and distribute income to the most tax-effective sources. Importantly, it also encompasses protecting what you have and ensuring that your assets stay within your family to benefit those you love most so their needs, goals and objectives can be met for the greatest length of time possible. It's all about boosting your total investment assets, no matter what investments you choose.

Tactical advice is about asset allocation and where to direct your savings to boost your investment return. A lot of what you hear about tactical advice is self-serving to fund managers and property spruikers. It's important to find the asset class or asset allocation that makes the most sense to you, feels comfortable to you, and passes the 'eat well, sleep well' test — in other words, gives you a sufficient return for your needs without making you lose sleep from worrying about the risk you have taken.

This chapter gives you an insight into financial planning secrets. It is a description of some specific strategies that I have been using for years to put my clients in a better financial position, no matter what their investment choice is. Most strategies are not related to a particular financial product: they are simply methods of reducing tax and increasing the amount of money you have in your pocket at the end of the day. Some strategies are basic and others are more complex, but the basic ones are a good place to start and provide a foundation for the more complex strategies.

Videos are available on my website (www.samhenderson.com.au) if you'd like some more information on each concept.

Strategy 1: eliminate non-deductible debt first

You may have heard people suggest that you should eliminate non-deductible debt first, but many can't explain why. Non-deductible debt includes your mortgage on your principal residence, credit cards and personal loans.

Here is a simple sum to illustrate the effect of not paying off your non-deductible debt first. The basic principle is that non-deductible debt is repaid from your own salary *after* you pay tax, and, if you don't repay the debt, additional interest will accrue and increase the debt. Some debts, such as a mortgage, can take thirty years or more to repay, and I want you to get off the money-go-round as quickly as possible.

Try answering a few simple questions and then apply the ensuing formula.

A. What interest rate do you pay on your non-deductible debt? _____ per cent

B. What return do you think you can achieve from your investments? _____ per cent

C. What is the highest rate of tax that you pay on your income? _____ per cent

Now we are going to apply the formula that will allow you to make your decision:

$A \div (1 - C) = D$, where D is the guaranteed rate of return you must achieve in order to justify *not* repaying your non-deductible debt first.

For your information

To do these calculations, I often enter the percentages into the calculator as decimals rather than trying to enter them as percentages. For example, 7 per cent is 0.07, 10 per cent is 0.10, and so on. To match the rates of tax, table 14.1 may help.

Table 14.1: using decimals in calculations

Income ($)	Tax rate ($)	Decimal to enter on calculator
0–18200	0.0	0.00
18201–37000	19.0	0.19
37001–80000	32.5	0.325
80001–180000	37.0	0.37
180001+	45.0	0.45

In respect to the second part of the equation (1 − C) I know that 1 − 32.5 per cent = 0.675 (or 67.5 per cent). This will allow you to enter the data into any basic calculator in seconds.

For example, if your rate of interest on your non-deductible debt, such as your home mortgage, is 7 per cent and your highest marginal tax rate is 32.5 per cent, then the formula would look like this:

7% ÷ (1 − 32.5%) = 10.37% (rounded to two decimal places)
On the calculator the calculation is: 0.07 ÷ 0.675 = 10.37%.

In the example above, you would have to be able to *guarantee* a higher rate of return on your investment than 10.37 per cent to justify investing before repaying your debt. While that may be achievable, it probably can't be guaranteed. In fact, if you have credit card debt at say 18 per cent, which is common, the formula will look like this:

18% ÷ (1 − 32.5%) = 26.66%

While 10 per cent *may* be achievable, a *guaranteed* rate of return of 26.66 per cent would be very difficult indeed and the aim of this exercise is to illustrate why you should repay your non-deductible debt first with any spare cash flow that you may have.

Tip

Always pay off your non-deductible debt as quickly as possible, starting with the debt that attracts the highest rate of interest. For example, start with the credit card bill at 18 per cent, followed by the personal loan at 10 per cent, the car loan at 9 per cent and your mortgage at 6 per cent, and then your education (HECS/HELP) debts. Start high; finish low.

People starting out in the investment process often ask me: what should I do first? My answer is to check if they have any store cards, credit cards, personal loans or any other sort of high-interest-bearing loans. They will need to be repaid first as illustrated in the above examples. A mortgage is not so bad, because you need a house to live in, although we still want it repaid as soon as possible. But given the internal rate of return that can be achieved through gearing (use of deductible debt), it is often helpful to focus on repaying the mortgage *and* establishing some investments through shares or property. This is because a mortgage may take 10 to 30 years to repay: time is a precious and valuable commodity in the investment process so it is best to spread the risk and commence your investment strategy as soon as possible.

Strategy 2: salary sacrifice

You can save up to 66 per cent in tax if you salary sacrifice. This is simply the process of contributing your pre-tax dollars straight into your superannuation account rather than accepting the cash as after-tax paid salary.

You are limited in how much you can salary sacrifice, as shown in table 14.2. Salary sacrifice falls under the concessional superannuation contribution structure (as opposed to non-concessional limits) and you are currently limited to contributing $25 000 per year.

Table 14.2: superannuation contribution limits

Age	Concessional limit (e.g. salary sacrifice) ($)	Non-concessional limit (after-tax money) ($)
Under 65	25 000	150 000 or 450 000 (3-year average)
Over 65 but under 75	25 000	150 000
Over 75	0	0

For example, if you earn $90 000 per year, then you will pay 37 per cent on the last $10 000 in tax, as the 37 per cent tax threshold kicks in at $80 001 (see table 14.3 for tax rates for the 2012–2015 tax years). If you salary sacrifice that $10 000 into superannuation, you will pay only 15 per cent tax on that $10 000. That will reduce your tax payable from $3700 to $1500, a saving of $2200 per year, or a tax saving of almost 60 per cent. You can't touch the money until you are of retirement age as it is locked up in super until you meet a condition of release, but then it's better in your hands than with the tax office, and you have plenty of choices as to how you invest it.

If you are on the highest marginal tax rate earning $210 000 per year, the upper tax bracket kicks in at $180 001 (2012–2015 tax years). While your superannuation guarantee amount will be $18 900, you will still be able to put $6100 to salary sacrifice, reducing your tax rate from 45 per cent to 15 per cent on the $6100, a saving of 66 per cent in tax. In this example, on the additional $6100 contribution, by salary sacrificing the $6100, you would save $1830 in tax.

Table 14.3: tax rates for 2012–2015 tax years*

Income ($)	Tax rate (%)
0–18 200	0
18 201–37 000	19
37 001–80 000	32.5
80 001–180 000	37
180 001+	45

* Excludes Medicare levy of 1.5%.

Strategy 3: co-contributions and LISC

Both the co-contribution and the low income superannuation contribution (LISC) can be described as getting money for nothing.

The co-contribution is really simple. If you earn less than $31 920 and you put $1000 of after-tax money into super (non-concessional contribution) then the government will put an additional 50 cents for each dollar (up to $500) into your super fund shortly after you submit your tax return. It's money for nothing, and where else are you going to receive a 50 per cent guaranteed return?

The co-contribution originally offered $1000 for your $1000 after-tax super contribution but it was reduced to $500 in 2012. However, 2012 also saw the introduction of a super tax rebate for those people earning less than $37 000 per year. So from 2012 your superannuation contributions tax will be rebated back to your super fund if you earn less than $37 000 per year. That could be the equivalent of another $499.50, bringing you close to the full $1000 benefit previously received — less for those earning more than $37 000, of course. The rebate was to be funded by the introduction of the Mineral Resources Rent Tax (MRRT), so if future governments make changes to the MRRT, then expect further alterations to the super system, which is really inevitable in any case. See table 14.4 for co-contribution amounts.

Table 14.4: superannuation co-contribution rates for $1000 non-concessional contribution

Year	Amount ($)
2011–2012	1000
2012–2013 onwards	500

If you earn more than $31 920 but less than $46 920, then you will receive a lesser amount for your $1000 contribution: the amount you receive reduces by 3.33c for every dollar you earn over $31 920 per year, up to $46 920, when the co-contribution cuts out.

Strategy 4: using a trust for the self-employed

Use a trust to distribute income and reduce income tax.

As you learned in chapter 3, trusts are a business structure that the self-employed can use to distribute income and reduce income tax. The beauty of running a trust is that you can distribute your income to other entities or family members via the trust, taking advantage of two or more tax-free thresholds and marginal tax rates. Trust law is very complex and it's important to seek advice from your tax professional to assess whether a trust will benefit you. Many consultants operating their own business are not eligible to distribute their earnings under the personal services income laws, so be careful.

If you are eligible, the following examples will illustrate how you can save tax using a trust to distribute your income.

- *Example 1:* If you have a single-director private company without a family trust to distribute to, and your company earns a net profit of $250 000 per year, then your company will pay 30 per cent tax on those profits, or $75 000. If the single-director attracts a tax rate above 30 per cent, then the additional tax burden is paid by the individual, as the income is distributed to them from the company. The remaining amount is taxed in the hands of the single-director at normal marginal tax rates, less the amount already paid by the company (a franking credit). If the single-director's tax rate is below 30 per cent, then they receive a rebate. For example, if the company earns a profit of $250 000 and is taxed $75 000 (30 per cent), and then the remaining profits are distributed to the single-director, the tax payable on $250 000 as a single-director is $86 046, but $75 000 has already been paid by the company so the single-director is burdened with the remaining $11 046 ($86 046 − $75 000 = $11 046) tax liability.

- *Example 2:* Rather than distribute the income to the single-director, a family trust will be established below the company to distribute the income. The family trust can have two beneficiaries (or more) to distribute the income to. In this case, rather than a single-director, a spouse will also join the mix and allow for two beneficiaries and therefore two options to whom to distribute income: a husband and a wife. The beauty of having the spouse to share the distribution of income is to take advantage of two personal tax-free thresholds of $18 200 instead of one. The tax savings are significant, as you can see from table 14.5 (overleaf).

Table 14.5: tax paid

Tax thresholds (tax rates for 2010–11)* ($)	Example 1	Example 2	
	Husband only ($)	a. Husband ($)	b. Wife ($)
0–18200 = 0%	0	0	0
18201–37000 = 19%	3572	3572	3572
37001–80000 = 32.5%	13975	13975	13975
80001–180000 = 37%	37000	16650	16650
180001+ = 45%	31500	0	0
Total tax paid	86050	68394 (husband and wife)	
Total net income	163950	181606	

* Excludes Medicare levy of 1.5 per cent.

As you can see from this example, a tax saving of $17656 can be made by using a trust that can be set up from about $200. If you combine this strategy with superannuation contributions, or any of the other strategies in this chapter, then the savings can be magnified significantly.

For example, if both the husband and the wife were eligible to contribute $25000 each to their super fund, reducing their personal taxable incomes from $125000 each to $100000 each, they would pay just $24947 in income tax each (a total tax payment of $49894). They would also pay $3750 each in superannuation contributions tax ($25000 × 15 per cent) to arrive at a total of $7500 for the two of them. Their total tax paid would drop again from an original, pre-trust amount of $86050 to just $57394. This represents a tax saving of $28656 per year.

I'm sure you will agree an additional $30000, or so, per year would be more than welcomed into an investment portfolio, to reduce debt or buy a new car.

The point I am trying to make is that by seeking a little of the right sort of advice, you could save tens of thousands of dollars per year: money that goes straight into your pocket and will make a big impact on your lifestyle and your life savings.

Strategy 5: buy property in your SMSF

Since September 2007 it has been possible to borrow money to purchase property inside of your self managed superannuation fund

(SMSF) — you can't use this strategy in any other kind of super fund. The ability to borrow money inside super and buy property compares very favourably with the negative-gearing option outside your super.

The initial costs for implementing this strategy may be a little higher than they would be outside super, but you will be able to pay off the loan faster using both rent from the property and tax-effective superannuation contributions (taxed only at 15 per cent). As a benchmark, if your *taxable* income (that's income left after deductions) is more than $18 200 per year, then your average rate of tax will be greater than 15 per cent, so this strategy may be worth consideration.

Table 14.6 illustrates an example of purchasing a $400 000 property with 30 per cent down, assuming a 7 per cent growth rate, 8 per cent interest rate (banks will charge more on super fund loans than home mortgages) and 4 per cent rental growth rate with $25 000 per year super contributions ($21 250 after 15 per cent contributions tax is paid) reducing the debt in concert with the rent. The property is paid off after just nine years with a substantial value inside your super fund of $687 274. This compares with the value of $191 250 ($21 250 × 9) plus the original contribution of $120 000 (deposit), which equates to $311 250: a value-add of $376 024!

Table 14.6: boost your super by buying property

Year	Property value ($)	Beginning debt ($)	Interest ($)	Rent ($)	Super contribution (after tax) ($)	Year-end debt ($)	Equity ($)
1	400 000	280 000	22 400	20 800	21 250	260 350	139 650
2	428 000	260 350	20 828	21 632	21 250	238 296	189 704
3	457 960	238 296	19 064	22 497	21 250	213 612	244 348
4	490 017	213 612	17 089	23 397	21 250	186 054	303 963
5	524 318	186 054	14 884	24 333	21 250	155 356	368 963
6	561 021	155 356	12 428	25 306	21 250	121 228	439 793
7	600 292	121 228	9 698	26 319	21 250	83 357	516 935
8	642 313	83 357	6 669	27 371	21 250	41 404	600 908
9	687 274	41 404	3 312	28 466	21 250	0	687 274

The benefit of the property strategy can be illustrated by figure 14.1, where you can see the debt decrease over time and the equity value increase with time, assuming the property increases at 7 per cent in value.

Figure 14.1: boost your super by buying property

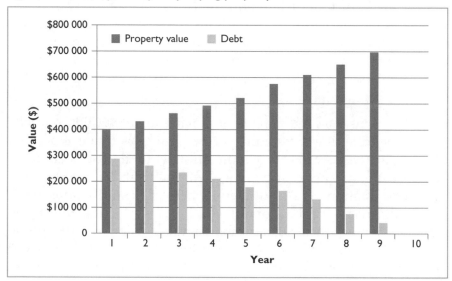

Strategy 6: self-funding instalment warrants

Self-funding instalment warrants (SFIs) can help boost your super and allow you to retire earlier.

SFIs allow you to purchase a share with two payments: the first payment is like a deposit and the second payment is a non-recourse loan (a limited-security loan). It's a bit like buying a share on lay-by for a period of up to 10 years, but the second loan payment can be paid off over that time using the dividends provided by the shares. The higher the dividends, the faster the loan is paid off. SFIs are traded on the sharemarket, like normal shares, but they have six-letter codes: for example, a CBA 10-year SFI issued by RBS (Royal Bank of Scotland) may have the code CBASZZ. The first three letters are the ASX code of the company in which the shares are bought, and the last three letters indicate the issuer, the type and the series of SFI.

Table 14.7 illustrates how the payment mechanisms work with a share price of $50: the first instalment is $25 and the loan amount is $25.

Table 14.7: a schedule of payments for self-funding instalment warrants

Description	Initial purchase ($)	If share price increases from $60 to $70 ($)	If share price falls from $60 to $50 ($)
Share price of CBA	60	70	50
First instalment (equity)	30	35	25
Loan amount	60	30	30

Figure 14.2 illustrates the cash-flow effect of owning an SFI. The interest is capitalised (that means the loan increases without interest having to be repaid) until the dividends are used to repay the loan every six months. The higher the dividends, the faster the loan can be repaid, so finding a share with high dividends will be an advantage. The opposite is also true, where a low-dividend share may have an outstanding loan balance after the 10-year period (you can buy SFIs with a variety of terms).

So the beauty of SFIs is that they are self-funding: that is, the dividends repay the loan and you don't have to outlay any more of your own money until the term of the SFI has expired. On expiry you may also have the option to pay out the loan and convert your SFIs to normal shares or roll over into another SFI. You can also pay out the loan at any time during the term of the SFI and convert your holding to normal shares.

Figure 14.2: cash-flow effect of investing in self-funding instalment warrants

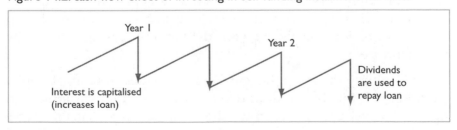

Each SFI is covered by a stop-loss, which means that if the price of the underlying share drops to a certain value, then the SFI will be sold automatically to protect the lender's position.

Table 14.8 illustrates the benefit of owning a CBA 10-year instalment on a conservative 50 per cent initial gearing, with a loan interest rate of 9 per cent, a share price of $60, annual share price growth of 7 per cent per year and a dividend of 5.5 per cent (franking credits are distributed to the owner but can't be used to repay the debt in instalments).

Table 14.8: CBA 10-year instalment warrant

Year	Share price ($)	Loan amount ($)	Interest ($)	Dividend ($)	Equity ($)
1	60.00	30.00	2.70	3.30	29.40
2	64.20	29.40	2.65	3.53	33.92
3	68.69	28.52	2.57	3.78	38.97
4	73.50	27.30	2.46	4.04	44.61
5	78.65	25.72	2.31	4.33	50.92
6	84.15	23.71	2.13	4.63	57.95
7	90.04	21.21	1.91	4.95	65.79
8	96.35	18.17	1.64	5.30	74.51
9	103.09	14.50	1.31	5.67	84.22
10	110.31	10.14	0.91	6.07	95.01

As you can see, the equity grows over time and the debt reduces. Think about this strategy operating within your self managed super fund: unlike a normal loan, where you need to be constantly paying interest, an SFI strategy can tick along using the benefits of gearing inside your superannuation fund — you can't touch your super until you meet a condition of release anyway, so just let it bubble along growing in value, with dividends reducing your debt and increasing your equity until retirement.

If you multiply the above benefit by 1000 shares, your final equity would be $95 010, but you put down only $30 000! You didn't even have an interest repayment because the dividends covered it. Of course, CBA has maintained and grown their dividends despite the GFC, and not many companies are as fortunate, so you need to choose your investments wisely and make sure you are confident of the future of the company's dividend policy.

Tip

I wouldn't invest in any company that I didn't truly think was a blue-chip company that had the potential to both maintain and grow dividends under all economic conditions. Investing and borrowing money outside of these parameters can be risking your capital and gambling with your money.

Strategy 7: depreciation for your investment property

A tax depreciation schedule is a document that lists all of the items in your investment property that can be written down in value over time and can therefore be claimed as an expense each year, even though you have not actually incurred the expense. In simple terms, it is a record of the cost of wear and tear on your property. At some stage, items will need to be repaired, replaced or rebuilt. The document is prepared by a quantity surveyor who inspects the property and allocates a value to each of the items that can be depreciated. Make sure you obtain a genuine tax depreciation schedule from a quantity surveyor. If you don't already have a depreciation schedule on your investment property make sure you obtain one now.

Both buildings and assets can be depreciated and it's important that the tax depreciation schedule accurately identifies each item in the right category. For example, kitchen cupboards are often seen as an asset, but the ATO classifies them as part of a building. Assets include carpets, curtains, furniture, fittings and air-conditioning units. Building items to be depreciated include doors, windows, driveways, electrical wiring and fencing, to name a few. So there is a whole household of items that you can depreciate and claim as an expense each year.

If you've had an investment property for a few years and haven't made a claim, you can still effectively back date your claims: ask your accountant to do an amended tax return to claim back your lost depreciation for two years. Legally, you can go back up to four years! This could give you a lump sum immediately, far in excess of the $700-odd cost of the depreciation schedule.

One of the key benefits of a depreciation schedule from a quantity surveyor is that it gives you the ability to claim a tax deduction on an expense that you have not actually had to pay out in the tax year in which it is applicable. For example, if the depreciation on your new two-bedroom unit is $5592 in year 4 and you have to pay interest of $25 000 and strata fees of $2500, and receive rent of $20 000 per year, then your cash flow would look like that shown in table 14.9.

Table 14.9: depreciation schedule and cash flow

Description	Without a depreciation schedule ($)	With a depreciation schedule ($)
Income (rent)	20 000	20 000
Expenses: Interest	25 000	25 000
Strata fees	2 500	2 500
Depreciation	0	5 592
Net income (loss)	(7 500)	(13 093)

The net income amount is the dollar amount that you can claim as a tax deduction and, as you can see from table 14.9, the effect of the depreciation schedule allows you another $5592 as a tax deduction, giving you more money in your pocket at the end of the tax year.

You can have depreciation schedules completed for any property, including commercial properties. Make sure you speak to the quantity surveyor first to make sure they think it's worth having a depreciation schedule done. Newer buildings have more to depreciate, especially when you have to take into account common areas such as lifts, swimming pools and gyms. Renovated houses also depreciate well. Remember, land appreciates; buildings depreciate. Make sure you get your slice of the non–cash cash flow and get a depreciation schedule completed on your investment property.

Figure 14.3 is an example of a summary from a tax depreciation schedule and illustrates the differences between the prime cost method and the diminishing value method for a two-bedroom unit, and how much you can claim as a tax deduction for each of the next five years in your tax return.

Figure 14.3: sample tax depreciation schedule

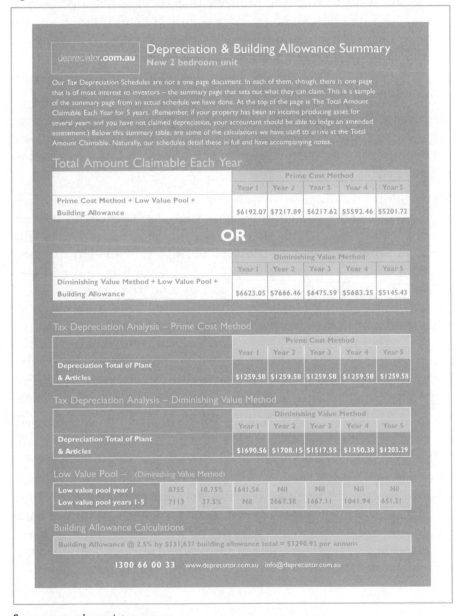

Source: www.depreciator.com.au.

Strategy 8: positive versus negative gearing

Negative gearing is where you borrow money to invest and the net cash flow is negative, allowing you to claim a tax deduction on the difference. If you are negative gearing, there is only *one* reason that you would want to own the property that you are negative gearing and that is if it's going to go up in value over time. If it doesn't go up in value, then it's losing money and it's a bad investment that should be sold. Positive gearing means that you have borrowed money on a property, but the rent exceeds all of the costs. Effectively, you are cash-flow positive, hence the term *positive* gearing.

There's no right or wrong when it comes to positive gearing or negative gearing. Generally speaking, it makes more sense for people on high incomes to negative gear and for those on lower incomes to positive gear.

So why don't we all positive gear our investment properties? Many properties in major cities do not have high enough rent to provide positive cash flow income after you have borrowed money to buy them, but they do have a history of positive growth — to the tune of about 8.5 per cent average over 20 years according to the Russell Investments report of 2012. Variation around the growth rates of property Australia-wide will be significant especially in recent years when some properties fell by 30 per cent and others rose by 10 per cent or more. Essentially, if you can claim a tax deduction on the cash-flow loss but the property goes up in value, then the net effect is that you are better off over the long term because you have used someone else's money — the bank's — to make you money. People often come unstuck because they buy the wrong properties in the wrong areas, and there isn't any or enough capital growth to make the investment worthwhile.

Proponents of positive cash flow property argue that they get the best of both worlds: rising property prices and positive cash flow. Some areas that have positive cash flow property, such as country or rural areas, can have lower rates of growth and sometimes finding tenants can be difficult. That's nothing a bit of good research can't fix and, with the mining boom of recent years, many country towns have had booming house prices and record low vacancy rates, so positive cash flow investors have done very well.

Let me illustrate with an example of a two-bedroom terrace in Newtown in the inner city of Sydney valued at $800000, and a house in Port Hedland, also valued at $800000, for both of which we borrow 100 per cent (interest only) of the purchase price: you can see the reason why either method of investment (negative gearing versus positive gearing) is good in table 14.10.

Table 14.10: example of positive gearing versus negative gearing

Description	Port Hedland	Newtown
Value	$800000	$800000
Interest @ 7% per year	$56000	$56000
Rent	$80000	$41600
Level of income	10%	5.2%
Annual growth rate	10%	10%
Annual growth amount	$80000	$80000
Cash flow	$24000 positive	($14400) negative

In the example you can see that Port Hedland is a far superior investment in the medium term than the inner-city investment, as its growth rate is the same but it's better off, in cash-flow terms, by $38400 per year. This is a realistic view of what's been happening in mining towns around Australia over the past few years.

Table 14.11 (overleaf) shows a much more realistic example of most country areas that are not affected by the mining boom. In this example, the city property has a growth rate of 12 per cent, while a country area such as a suburb on the south coast of New South Wales moves at just 4 per cent over a 10-year period. As you can see, the city property is a far superior investment, despite the negative cash flow of $14400 carried forward from the previous example, under the following growth conditions.

Table 14.11: example of city versus country property growth rate

Description	City	Country
Starting property value	$800 000	$800 000
Growth rate	12%	4%
Year 1	$896 000	$832 000
Year 2	$1 003 520	$865 280
Year 3	$1 123 942	$899 891
Year 4	$1 258 815	$935 887
Year 5	$1 409 873	$973 322
Year 6	$1 579 058	$1 012 255
Year 7	$1 768 545	$1 052 745
Year 8	$1 980 771	$1 094 855
Year 9	$2 218 463	$1 138 649
Year 10	$2 484 679	$1 184 195

You need to understand the risks and the cyclical nature of commodity prices and mining combined with the property dynamics (such as supply and interest rates) in certain areas and how they will change over time. For example, the mining companies adding their own housing will increase supply, which may affect demand and thus pricing in the future.

I've chosen the inner-city property market for comparison, because there is a ready supply of tenants and a shortage of housing. I am also happy to take the tax deduction each year and the growth in housing has been consistent for decades, so it's a system that works for me. I can also drive past my houses when I want to — I always say, 'Don't buy properties you can't drive past', but that's just me. You need to find the system that works for you and make sure you do your research before you commit.

Strategy 9: transition-to-retirement income stream

If you're over 55 and still working, starting a transition-to-retirement income stream (TRIS) allows you to decrease your tax and increase your super. If you are over age 55 and less than age 65, you are able to draw on your super while you are still working. You have to draw between a minimum (4 per cent of your fund balance) and a maximum (10 per cent) amount every year. Your investments in your super fund are free of capital gains tax and earnings tax while you are drawing your super, so a TRIS has some added benefits over and beyond saving you income tax.

Effectively, you have two super accounts with your provider: one transition-to-retirement pension that holds most of your investments and one accumulation account that you will be salary sacrificing into. Salary sacrificing for self-employed people simply means that you can add lump-sum concessional contributions before the end of June and claim a tax deduction. If you are employed, you have to add to your super gradually and you can't make a lump-sum concessional contribution (which will be taxed at 15 per cent in your super fund; you can, however, make lump sum non-concessional contributions, which are not taxed in your super fund).

Tip

If you are planning to make a superannuation contribution at the end of June, don't leave it until the last minute. Make sure it's in the fund well before 30 June so you don't miss the cut-off date and have to pay excess contributions tax or restrict next year's super contribution.

The example in table 14.12 (overleaf) illustrates the situation for David who, in option 1, does not have a transition-to-retirement income stream; in option 2 he has a transition-to-retirement income stream, assuming he has $350 000 in super ($250 000 taxable and $100 000 non-taxable). In this example David is 55 years old, earning $76 000 per year and his employer is paying in his 9 per cent superannuation guarantee. Taking the TRIS allows David to salary sacrifice more into his super, without reducing his disposable income, allowing him to boost it over time.

Table 14.12: the benefits of a TRIS compared with not taking a TRIS after age 55, assuming 7 per cent annual return on investments

David	Option 1: no TRIS ($)	Option 2: TRIS ($)
Income	76 000	76 000
Super balance	350 000	350 000
Income from super	0	13 867
Super contribution (including 9% SG)*	7 200	25 000
Total tax paid (incl. Medicare, super contributions tax and TRIS rebate)	17 387	13 094
Annual tax saving	0	4 293
After tax cash flow Year 1	58 613	58 613
Super at age 65	720 247	822 840
Dollar value benefit of TRIS		102 593

*The superannuation guarantee (SG) will increase to 12 per cent over tax years 2013–2019.

Graphically, the difference between doing nothing and establishing a TRIS looks like figure 14.4.

As you can see in this example, if we assume David can achieve a 7 per cent return over the next 10 years on his super and his tax savings, he will be $102 593 better off in retirement, yet his cash flow will be fairly similar so he won't feel the pain of the salary sacrifice.

In summary, a TRIS will reduce your tax and boost your super without any pain to you.

Figure 14.4: the effect on a super balance comparing doing nothing with taking out a TRIS and increasing super contributions

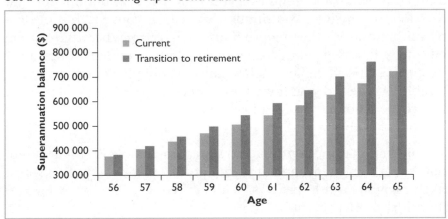

Source: © BT Financial Group.

Strategy 10: reduce your CGT by contributing to super

People often ask about strategies for reducing their capital gains tax (CGT). As CGT is simply a part of your income tax, there are ways to reduce your assessable income. One obvious way of reducing capital gains on assets held in your own name, in joint names, as tenants in common or in the name of a trust, is the 50 per cent discount rule, which applies to all assets held for more than 12 months. Companies do not receive the 50 per cent capital gains tax discount.

For example, if you buy a property for $300 000 and sell it for $400 000 fourteen months later, your capital gains tax liability will be $400 000 − $300 000 (plus any capital improvements) = $100 000. But as you have owned the property for more than 12 months, you receive a discount of 50 per cent on the capital gain (50 per cent × $100 000 = $50 000). So only $50 000 is added onto your taxable income for the financial year in which the contract was exchanged (not settlement). If the property is in joint names or equal tenants in common, the taxable amount is $25 000 each.

In the event that the property is in one name, you can contribute $25 000 to your super fund as a concessional contribution. You can therefore use a super contribution to reduce your taxable income by this amount to thus reduce your CGT payable, because you are effectively lowering your taxable income by the amount contributed to super. As I said earlier, capital gains are simply added onto your taxable income and your normal rates of tax are applied. So if you can reduce the amount that is to be taxed, you will effectively lower the amount of tax being paid.

The amount that you contribute to superannuation will still be taxed, but only at 15 per cent and not at your normal marginal tax rates (most likely ranging from 19 per cent to 45 per cent tax), so the savings can be as high as 66 per cent in tax.

For example, if you earn $80 000 per year and sell a property for a taxable gain of $50 000, as in the previous example, $50 000 would be added to your taxable income (if the property is held in a single name). So your taxable income becomes $130 000, for which you would pay approximately $36 046 income tax. You can save $5500 by using this strategy if you contribute the full $25 000 to super, as shown in table 14.13.

Table 14.13: minimising CGT through superannuation contributions

Description	$0 into super ($)	$25 000 into super ($)
Normal income	80 000	80 000
Capital gain	50 000	50 000
Additional super contribution*	0	(25 000)
Net taxable income	130 000	105 000
Tax payable†	36 046	26 796
Super contributions tax	0	3 750
Total tax paid	36 046	30 546
Tax saving	0	5 500

* Excludes 9 per cent superannuation guarantee amount for the sake of illustration.
† Excludes Medicare levy of 1.5 per cent.

Strategy 11: superannuation re-contribution strategy

A re-contribution strategy can be used to increase the tax-free portion of your super fund, which will reduce income tax for those aged under 60 (and drawing an account-based pension income stream) and reduce the taxable portion of their super, which would be taxed after their death before it's passed on to non-dependants, such as adult children.

In 2004 the ATO specifically allowed the re-contribution strategy, so it is legal. Importantly, it won't fall under the provisions of part IVA of the *Tax Act*, which suggests that it is not legal to set up a scheme to avoid tax. Part IVA is deliberately vague in its scope to deter people from inventing ways to evade tax.

This strategy involves cashing out part of your super and then re-contributing it back into the fund as a tax-free non-concessional contribution. The strategy utilises the low tax-free threshold of $175 000 (in the 2012–13 tax year and indexed annually by $5000 increments), which allows you to withdraw up to this limit from the taxable component of your super without incurring any tax. As a general rule, you must also withdraw part of your tax-free components in proportion to your current benefits.

Superannuation re-contribution case study

Steve is retiring at age 55 with $1 200 000 in his super fund, which is made up of $1 000 000 of taxable and $200 000 of non-taxable contributions. If he does nothing and commences drawing an account-based pension of $60 000 per year (5 per cent of his fund balance; the minimum he is required to take is actually 4 per cent), he would pay $1110 tax per year on his income. By using a re-contribution strategy, Steve can reduce his income tax to $0 by increasing his tax-free component and undertaking a re-contribution strategy. Steve can also reduce the amount of tax payable on his superannuation when it's passed onto his adult children.

Table 14.14 (overleaf) shows Steve's current benefit components and their original percentages.

Table 14.14: superannuation benefit components

Benefit components	Total super ($)	Original percentage in balance (%)
Taxable	1 000 000	83.33
Tax free	200 000	16.66
Total	1 200 000	100

The good news is that the first $175 000 (2012–13) of the taxable portion is tax-free on withdrawal and so if we simply deduct this amount from the taxable portion and an equivalent proportion (it works out to be 14.5 per cent = $175 000 ÷ $1 200 000) amount from the tax-free component, there will be no tax on withdrawal and therefore no cost in undertaking the strategy, as shown in table 14.15.

Table 14.15: components to withdrawal

Benefit components withdrawal	Calculation of percentages	Steve ($)
Taxable	14.58% of $1 000 000	175 000
Tax-free	14.58% of $200 000	30 000
Total withdrawal		205 000

So Steve takes out $205 000 from his fund and puts the money into his personal account. The next day, he transfers the funds back into his super fund as a non-concessional (tax-free) contribution.

Table 14.16 shows Steve's super account after re-contribution. His tax-free components have significantly increased, although there is no change in the balance of his total account.

Table 14.16: resulting benefits after re-contribution

Benefit components	Steve ($)	Percentage of account (%)
Taxable	825 000	68.75
Tax-free	375 000	31.25
Total	1 200 000	100

As you can see from this table (compared with table 14.15), his taxable portion has dropped from $1 000 000 to $825 000 and his tax-free components have increased from $200 000 to $375 000.

Steve is drawing an income of $60 000 from his super fund to live on and as he is aged 55 he will have to pay tax on the taxable portion of his pension income. Table 14.17 shows the tax effect on his income before and after re-contribution strategies. Steve is $366 better off per year than he was before undertaking the re-contribution strategy.

Table 14.17: Steve's income before and after re-contribution

Description	Before re-contribution ($)	After re-contribution ($)
Income	60 000	60 000
Proportion of tax-free income	9 600	18 750
Proportion of taxable income	50 400	41 250
Tax on income	7 926	4 953
15% rebate	7 560	(up to) 7 560
Tax payable	366	0

In addition to the tax savings, Steve can also reduce the amount of tax that his adult beneficiaries will pay on Steve's passing. In today's terms, we have reduced his taxable portion from $1 000 000, which would attract 16.5 per cent tax ($165 000) to $825 000, which would reduce his tax to $136 125, representing a saving of $28 875 for his children. I call this 'future-proofing' your super.

The non-concessional limits of $150 000 per year or $450 000 over the three-year bring-forward arrangement apply when re-contributing funds back into super. The bring-forward arrangement is automatically triggered when your non-concessional contributions exceed $150 000 in a particular year.

Strategy 12: account-based pension to eliminate all taxes entirely

An account-based pension is simply a retirement income stream established with money from superannuation; it was previously known as an allocated pension. You can start an account-based pension from your super when you meet a condition of release, though it is liable to income tax until you reach age 60, when the income stream is free of income tax. The earnings from the investments that make up an account-based pension are also tax-free and the investments are not subject to CGT on their sale. The account-based pension for the over-60s is entirely free of all taxes.

To establish an account-based pension, you must meet a condition of release: you must be over 55 and have declared retirement, or be over the age of 65, working or not (there are other conditions of release but these are the main two affecting most people). Also be aware of the rising preservation age from age 55 to age 60 (see table 7.6 for the details of preservation age).

There is no maximum amount that you can take from your allocated pension any more, but you must draw a minimum amount each year. The minimum is set by a percentage applicable to an age bracket. For example, for a person aged 55 to 64 the minimum percentage is 4 per cent; for those aged 65 to 74 the minimum is 5 per cent (and so on). However, for the past two years the government has allowed a further 25 per cent reduction on the minimum amounts. For a person aged 55 to 64 the minimum over these years has been 3 per cent (4 per cent × 75 per cent). This was designed to allow for people's money to recover after the drop in asset values following the global financial crisis (GFC).

If you have $800 000 in your super fund and you are 60 years of age and have declared retirement, you must draw 4 per cent of your account balance ($32 000) per year. In the years in which a 25 per cent discount has applied to the minimum, the new minimum would be $24 000 (3 per cent × $800 000).

On the $800 000 invested, you will pay no tax on the earnings. So if you have interest from cash, there is no tax payable. If you have rent from a property in an SMSF, there is no tax on the rent. If you have dividends from shares, you pay no tax on the dividends. Furthermore, if you have dividends that are fully franked (the company whose shares you own has paid tax on your behalf), you receive the franking credit back. For example, if you own $10 000 worth of CBA shares with a dividend of 5.5 per cent per year that is fully franked, your real return would be 7.86 per cent because of the franking credit refund you would receive from the tax office. Importantly, if you sell an asset inside an account-based pension investment in your SMSF, you will not pay CGT.

Tip

These benefits are available for all super funds, not just SMSFs. However, you can only own direct property in an SMSF. Many super funds, including industry funds, will allow you to hold cash and direct shares these days.

A great deal of consideration should be given to buying assets inside superannuation if you have an SMSF. In fact, the closer you are to retirement, the more it makes sense. For example, if you buy a property inside your SMSF, borrowing to buy it, and repay it with funds that attract only a 15 per cent tax rate (instead of your normal 19 per cent, 32.5 per cent, 37 per cent or 45 per cent tax rate), you will pay off your property faster. Further, you can then sell it in retirement, under an account-based pension structure, free of CGT.

Five sample strategies

- Pay off your non-deductible debt that attracts the highest interest rate first, and then start investing your savings in assets that increase in value rather than liabilities that drain your cash flow.

- Salary sacrifice up to the full $25 000 concessional superannuation contribution cap per year to boost your super and reduce your tax—it's better in your pocket than with the ATO.

- Set up a transition-to-retirement income stream (TRIS) to eliminate capital gains tax on sales of assets, eliminate earnings tax from your assets and reduce or eliminate tax on drawings if you are over 55 and under 64. (Income is tax-free if you are over 60).

(continued)

Five sample strategies *(cont'd)*

- If you have met a condition of release after age 55, set up an account-based pension to eliminate CGT, earnings tax and income tax once you reach 60.

- Undertake a re-contribution if you have reached a condition of release to reduce the tax your dependants will otherwise have to pay.

Five sample tactics

- Make a list of your debts and order them based on the amount of interest you pay from high to low so you know which one to pay first.

- Do a budget so you can calculate how much to salary sacrifice this year to make the most of your tax savings and to boost your super.

- Call your super fund or accountant if you are aged over 55 and ask how to set up a TRIS.

- Contact www.depreciator.com.au to get a tax depreciation schedule completed on your investment property as soon as possible. You can even backdate your tax return by asking your accountant for an amendment for up to four years! It's money for nothing!

- If you or your partner earn less than $46 920, make a $1000 non-concessional contribution to super to obtain up to $500 via the co-contribution strategy. Do it for your working (over 30 hours if under 18) kids and show them how super works, if you can afford it. Money education is a valuable investment indeed!

KEY POINTS

- These 12 strategies give you practical recommendations and examples that you may be able to implement in the immediate future.

- Each strategy is appropriate to different circumstances so do some research before undertaking any of the strategies.

- If you have any hesitation seek professional advice as these strategies may need to be carefully tailored to your individual situation.

- Make sure you always understand the downside risks of any strategy.

CHAPTER 15

COMPLETING YOUR ONE-PAGE FINANCIAL PLAN

Change your life today. Don't gamble on the future, act now, without delay.

Simone de Beauvoir, French existentialist philosopher and writer

You have probably heard the saying that if you fail to plan, you plan to fail. Well, it's absolutely true. But a bigger mistake than not having a plan is to draw up a plan and then fail to implement it. All too many executives write detailed business plans that sit on shelves gathering dust. You can have the best ideas in the world and incorporate them into a brilliant plan, but if you don't implement your plan you are wasting your time.

Think of all the new year's resolutions to eat better and exercise more that go up in smoke because, in the end, the people who make them aren't prepared to step out of their comfort zone and change their daily routine. There's a good reason why Nike chose as their slogan 'Just do it'. For example, if you're serious about getting more exercise, you need to set a goal, devise an exercise strategy and undertake some action items (tactics) to begin fulfilling your goal. Without a goal, your interest may swiftly wane and your chance of successful exercising will disappear quickly. For example, your goal may be to lose 2 kilograms, your strategy is to go running and your tactical approach may involve setting the alarm half an hour earlier, at 6.30 instead of 7 am, and running for 3 kilometres three days a week. Specifically, you need to book time on, say, Monday, Tuesday and Thursday mornings from 6.30 am to 7.00 am to start your program — and maybe you'll need a personal trainer to give you that extra motivation and ensure you follow through. Yes, it will cost more that way, but think of the benefits. You'll have more energy; you'll lose weight; you'll feel better; you'll look better in your swimsuit — and it will boost your self-confidence because you will have done something for yourself and created a sense of accomplishment. As they say, 'no pain, no gain'.

Making changes to your financial life is no different. You need to develop a practical, written plan with a definite time frame, to help you meet your needs, goals and objectives for the long term. You also need to know that you don't have to go it alone. Just as you may need a fitness coach to achieve your fitness goals, in order to reach your financial goals you'll sometimes need advice and reinforcement from a financial adviser, an accountant or some other specialist. In other words, at times you'll need to take a team approach. And when in time you reap the benefits in terms of a higher income and the freedom this gives you to achieve your lifestyle goals, your self-confidence will *really* take a leap.

This chapter provides you with two practical tools — or rather, two versions of the same tool — that will make it as easy as possible for you to implement your financial plan successfully. First, there's a simple, seven-step process that explains exactly what you need to do, from setting your goals and objectives to reviewing your net wealth and structures on a regular basis. Second, there's an easy-to-use one-page financial plan based on the seven steps.

Seven steps to successful implementation

These seven steps reflect the process used by the best professional financial advisers in Australia. In effect, they are a briefer, do-it-yourself form of that process.

- Assemble your team.
- Compile your personal information.
- Establish your (SMART) goals and your objectives.
- Decide on your strategies.
- Work out your tactics.
- Implement your plan.
- Review your progress.

Your one-page financial plan

The one-page financial plan makes it easy for you to follow the seven steps in your own life. It also provides a convenient document you can refer to regularly to monitor where you are going and how your investments have been performing. You can download or print out a copy of the one-page financial plan from www.samhenderson.com.au, or you can photocopy the following page to allow you to complete it as you work through the process outlined throughout the book and summarised here. I have included a blank plan for you to complete (see figure 15.2) and a completed example (figure 15.3, pp. 300–301) as a guide.

The graph in figure 15.1 gives you another useful way to track your net wealth. It's easy to construct a graph like this using a program such as Microsoft Excel®. It's up to you to decide whether this graphic approach is helpful for you, but it has the advantage of showing you at a glance where you are now and where you have come from. If you like the idea of a graph as well, it's a good idea to print the one-page financial plan on one side of a sheet of paper and the graph on the other, so that you have both to hand for ready reference.

Figure 15.1: example of graph designed for the back of the one-page financial plan

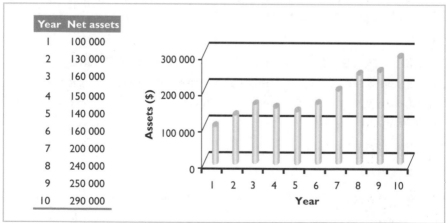

Year	Net assets
1	100 000
2	130 000
3	160 000
4	150 000
5	140 000
6	160 000
7	200 000
8	240 000
9	250 000
10	290 000

Figure 15.2: blank one-page financial plan

One-Page Financial Plan *for:* _____ Date: __ / __ / __

01 Team	02 Current Situation	03 Goals & Objectives	04 Strategies	05 Tactics	06 Implementation	07 Review of Plan
Who is going to help you?	Where are you at now?	What do you want to achieve?	What do you need to do to achieve your goals?	Your plan of action to implement your strategies	Your tactical action plan checklist	Your regular strategy review checklist
FINANCIAL ADVISER	TOTAL ASSETS $_____	GOAL 1	STRATEGY 1	TACTIC 1	Contact _____ Forms Finished? Yes ○ No ○	Review What? _____ When? _____ In Diary? Yes ○ No ○
ACCOUNTANT	TOTAL LIABILITIES $_____	GOAL 2	STRATEGY 2	TACTIC 2	Contact _____ Forms Finished? Yes ○ No ○	Review What? _____ When? _____ In Diary? Yes ○ No ○
SOLICITOR	NET WORTH $_____	GOAL 3	STRATEGY 3	TACTIC 3	Contact _____ Forms Finished? Yes ○ No ○	Review What? _____ When? _____ In Diary? Yes ○ No ○
MORTGAGE BROKER	GROSS INCOME BEFORE TAX $_____	GOAL 4	STRATEGY 4	TACTIC 4	Contact _____ Forms Finished? Yes ○ No ○	Review What? _____ When? _____ In Diary? Yes ○ No ○
INSURANCE SUPPLIER	TOTAL EXPENSES $_____	GOAL 5	STRATEGY 5	TACTIC 5	Contact _____ Forms Finished? Yes ○ No ○	Review What? _____ When? _____ In Diary? Yes ○ No ○
SHARE BROKER	NET INCOME AFTER TAX $_____	GOAL 6	STRATEGY 6	TACTIC 6	Contact _____ Forms Finished? Yes ○ No ○	Review What? _____ When? _____ In Diary? Yes ○ No ○
REAL ESTATE AGENT	SUPERANNUATION BALANCE $_____	GOAL 7	STRATEGY 7	TACTIC 7	Contact _____ Forms Finished? Yes ○ No ○	Review What _____ When? _____ In Diary? Yes ○ No ○

Insurance Strategy

Client	○ Life $_____ ○ Income Protection $_____	○ TPD $_____ ○ Trauma $_____
Partner	○ Life $_____ ○ Income Protection $_____	○ TPD $_____ ○ Trauma $_____

Estate Planning Strategy

Client	○ Wills ○ Power of Attorney	○ Guardianship ○ Binding Death Nomination
Partner	○ Wills ○ Power of Attorney	○ Guardianship ○ Binding Death Nomination

Source: Henderson Maxwell.

One-Page Financial Plan *for:* James & Ann Smith   Date: 22 | 05 | 2013

01 Team — Who is going to help you?	02 Current Situation — Where are you at now?	03 Goals & Objectives — What do you want to achieve?	04 Strategies — What do you need to do to achieve your goals?	05 Tactics — Your plan of action to implement your strategies	06 Implementation — Your tactical action plan checklist	07 Review of Plan — Your regular strategy review checklist
FINANCIAL ADVISER Sam Henderson Henderson Maxwell T: (02) 9222 1422	TOTAL ASSETS $400,000	GOAL 1 To understand where my income goes and set a budget.	STRATEGY 1 Do a budget for the past 12 months.	TACTIC 1 Download budget planner from **samhenderson.com.au** and complete it to understand cash flow.	Contact: Sam Henderson Forms Finished? Yes (✓) No ○	Review What? Budget When? December 31st In Diary? Yes (✓) No ○
ACCOUNTANT James Squire Squire Fitzgerald T: (02) 9222 1411	TOTAL LIABILITIES $ 230,000	GOAL 2 To build a share portfolio worth $100 000 within 7 years.	STRATEGY 2 Invest $800 per month into a regular share trading account investing every three months.	TACTIC 2 Open an account with E*TRADE and set up a direct debit of $800 per month from my bank account.	Contact: E*TRADE Forms Finished? Yes (✓) No ○	Review What? Shares When? July 1st In Diary? Yes (✓) No ○
SOLICITOR Ken Citizen Citizen Legal T: (02) 9234 5678	NET WORTH $ 170,000	GOAL 3 To own two investment properties within 5 years.	STRATEGY 3 Save for a deposit to buy an investment property.	TACTIC 3 Organise an $800 per month direct debit to internet savings account from my monthly pay to save for deposit.	Contact: ING Forms Finished? Yes (✓) No ○	Review What? Savings When? July 1st In Diary? Yes (✓) No ○
MORTGAGE BROKER None	GROSS INCOME BEFORE TAX $ 80,000	GOAL 4 To obtain personal insurances within 3 months.	STRATEGY 4 Obtain quotes for insurances and undertake health tests.	TACTIC 4 Obtain quotes from ING, MLC and Zurich for life, TPD, income protection and trauma insurance.	Contact: OnePath Forms Finished? Yes (✓) No ○	Review What? Life When? June 30th In Diary? Yes (✓) No ○
INSURANCE SUPPLIER OnePath	TOTAL EXPENSES $ 40,000 p.a.	GOAL 5 Set-up a SMSF.	STRATEGY 5 Establish a SMSF after June 30th.	TACTIC 5 Talk to adviser about SMSF after June 30.	Contact: Sam Henderson Forms Finished? Yes (✓) No ○	Review What? SMSF When? July 1st In Diary? Yes (✓) No ○

One-Page Financial Plan *for:* James & Ann Smith

Date: 22 | 05 | 2013

01 Team	02 Current Situation	03 Goals & Objectives	04 Strategies	05 Tactics	06 Implementation	07 Review of Plan
Who is going to help you?	Where are you at now?	What do you want to achieve?	What do you need to do to achieve your goals?	Your plan of action to implement your strategies	Your tactical action plan checklist	Your regular strategy review checklist
SHARE BROKER E*TRADE Australia T: 1300 987 654	NET INCOME AFTER TAX $ 23,539	GOAL 6 To have a will and powers of attorney within 3 months.	STRATEGY 6 Have a will and powers of attorney drawn up.	TACTIC 6 Book an appointment with Ken Citizen to obtain wills and powers of attorney.	Contact: Ken Forms Finished? Yes ✔ No ○	Review What? Estate When? July 1st In Diary? Yes ✔ No ○
REAL ESTATE AGENT None	SUPERANNUATION BALANCE $ 67,987	GOAL 7 To own my house outright within 15 years.	STRATEGY 7 Repay principal and interest on house and set loan over 15 years.	TACTIC 7 Call bank to refinance house and obtain a line of credit facility to use for future investment purposes.	Contact: Bank Forms Finished? Yes ✔ No ○	Review What? Mortgage When? July 1st In Diary? Yes ✔ No ○
	STRUCTURES Assets in personal name. No family trust, company or self managed super fund.				Contact Forms Finished? Yes ○ No ○	Review What? When? In Diary? Yes ○ No ○

Insurance Strategy

Client	✔ Life $ 500,000	✔ TPD $ 89,659
	✔ Income Protection $ 4,000 per month	✔ Trauma $ 300,000
Partner	✔ Life $ 400,000	✔ TPD $ 81,789
	✔ Income Protection $ 3,500 per month	✔ Trauma $ 250,000

Estate Planning Strategy

Client	✔ Wills	✔ Guardianship
	✔ Power of Attorney	✔ Binding Death Nomination
Partner	✔ Wills	✔ Guardianship
	✔ Power of Attorney	✔ Binding Death Nomination

Source: Henderson Maxwell.

Now let's walk through the seven-step process and see exactly what you need to do.

Step 1: assemble your team

Since it is virtually impossible to undertake all administrative and investment tasks yourself, you will need to assemble a team of professionals and contacts (see table 15.1) to help you manage your financial affairs. You will probably need at the very least a financial adviser, accountant, solicitor, mortgage broker and others, such as a share broker, SMSF administrator or real estate agent.

Good advice is worth paying for, and remember, 'Price is what you pay and value is what you get'.

Table 15.1: advisers and their contact details

Adviser	Name	Company	Contact
Financial adviser			
Accountant			
Solicitor			
Stock broker			
Real estate agent			

If you have several advisers in certain areas, you may need to add a few lines to the Team column in your one-page financial plan (or attach a separate list to your plan). For example, you may have several real estate agents if you own properties in different areas that are managed by multiple agencies. You may be able to consolidate some of your advisers — for example, if you engage a financial adviser who also has an accountancy firm — or you may decide to dispense with a particular adviser altogether if you have the relevant skills yourself or they no longer add value to your situation.

In the one-page financial plan, contacts are listed in the first column for ease of reference and to give the rest of the plan better continuity. You probably won't know exactly who you'll need until you have developed your strategies and tactics, but fill it out as best you can now.

Step 2: compile your personal information

This step is all about knowing where you are now in terms of your total assets, total liabilities and net assets. If you worked through the process set out in chapter 1, you will already have this data to hand. (If you didn't, I suggest you go back and do it now.) You then need to add your current superannuation balance, the structures you have in place for your investments, the various forms of insurance you hold and your estate-planning details, so that you have an accurate summary of your financial situation. Keep note that you do not need to monitor your structures in the one-page financial plan as we are more concerned with your overall situation. However, we do record superannuation, as it requires some special attention given the regular regulatory changes, tax effectiveness and the fact that it may one day be your largest asset.

In chapter 1, I discussed the financial planning process and, in order to ensure that you have all the information you need to accurately understand your starting point, I recommended you complete the following four items as a matter of importance:

1 personal financial questionnaire

2 budget

3 risk profile questionnaire

4 last two years' completed tax returns.

Tip

Download my Henderson Maxwell Client Questionnaire, Budget and Risk Profile Questionnaire for free, and without obligation, from my website. Just completing these forms will help you to assemble much of your personal financial information. It will take you about an hour or more and, if you are in a relationship, I highly recommend you do it together to ensure you have buy-in from both partners. It's a great starting point and you'll learn a lot about your current situation just by completing the forms.

Once you have completed the forms, fill in the missing data to summarise your information into the one-page financial plan.

Assets and liabilities

Your assets are simply the combined value of the worldly goods that you own. They may include property, shares, cash, artwork, cars, home contents or anything of material value. Your superannuation can be excluded from this calculation. Your liabilities are the combined value of your loans and debts. Your net assets are the total value of your assets minus your liabilities, or debts. See table 15.2.

Table 15.2: your current situation—assets and liabilities

Your current situation—assets and liabilities	
Assets	
1	$
2	$
3	$
4	$
5	$
Total assets	$
Liabilities	
1	
2	
3	
4	
5	
Total liabilities	$
Net assets	$
(Assets – Liabilities = Net assets)	

Income and expenses

Your income and expenses calculation is one of the most important calculations that you need to familiarise yourself with, because it's your net income that will allow you to save and invest. Your net income is simply your gross income minus your taxes and expenses. Basically, it's what's left over after you've met your financial obligations to everyone else. Your net income is also your key resource in building investments because it's essentially all you have to play with. That's why in chapter 2, I investigated ways in which you may be able to boost your income or use it better to achieve your goals.

After you have downloaded the budget spreadsheet, enter your gross income, expenses and net income in table 15.3 so you can record the figures in summary form in your one-page financial plan. Each time you review your plan, make sure you update your budget so any changes can be reflected in your one-page financial plan.

Table 15.3: your current situation — income

Your current situation — income	
Gross income	$
Expenses	$
Net income	$

Superannuation balances

As the name suggests, you need to list and quantify your superannuation balances in table 15.4 (overleaf) and record the total combined balance in the bottom line. The total combined balance will then be carried forward to your one-page financial plan in the box so named.

Tip

Before you fill out the final combined superannuation balance, make sure you go to the ATO website and undertake a superannuation search to attempt to locate any lost super that you may have floating around the superannuation ether. There is around $20 billion in lost superannuation in Australia so there is a good chance some of it may be yours. You'll just need your tax file number, name and date of birth. Go to www.superseeker.super.ato.gov.au

Now enter each of your superannuation fund balances into table 15.4 (overleaf). If you are part of a couple, just list all of your funds and note who owns which fund then tally the total balance at the bottom. If you have more than five funds, just add some lines and it's probably an indication that you need to clean up your super as a matter of importance.

Table 15.4: your current situation—superannuation

Your current situation—superannuation	
1	
2	
3	
4	
5	
Combined superannuation balances	$

Insurance strategy

List your current personal insurance policies in table 15.5. Remember, your superannuation accounts will probably have some insurance attached to them, so make sure you check them by calling your super fund or checking your superannuation fund annual statements to check your level and type of personal insurance. For example, you may have life, TPD and income protection inside your super fund. If you hold your personal insurances directly, outside of your super, then remember to add the two together to arrive at the total figure. Once you have done this, and recorded it, then you can reassess it as we discussed in chapter 10 to ensure you have the right level and type of insurance to meet your goals and objectives for you and your partner, if you have one.

Table 15.5: current insurance

Personal insurance (Partner 1)	Life and TPD	$
	Income protection	$
	Trauma	$
Personal insurance (Partner 2)	Life and TPD	$
	Income protection	$
	Trauma	$

Estate planning strategy

The area of tick-boxes under the Estate Planning Strategy heading is to ensure that you have followed my instructions in the estate planning chapter to update your wills, powers of attorney, guardianship and binding nomination of beneficiaries (sometimes called a death, or death benefit, nomination) to ensure they meet your goals and objectives in the event of death, incapacity or if you are not in a position to act for yourself (you may be overseas and need an important document signed). If you haven't had a chance to do that yet, then just address what you do have in place by ticking a box and putting a cross in the tick-boxes to indicate it needs attention and is not yet complete. See table 15.6.

Table 15.6: estate-planning details

Estate-planning documents in place (Partner 1)	Will (Yes/No)
	Power of attorney (Yes/No)
	Guardianship (Yes/No)
Estate-planning documents in place (Partner 2)	Will (Yes/No)
	Power of attorney (Yes/No)
	Guardianship (Yes/No)

Step 3: your goals and objectives

Money for its own sake is not a chief motivator for most people. There is no point in simply wanting more money (although there are a few people who do seem to want this). People have the perception that having money will make life easier and, to a certain degree that is correct, but it won't make you happy or make you a better person. As Warren Buffett once said of billionaires, 'If they were jerks before they had money, they are simply jerks with a billion dollars.'

Look back at the goals and objectives you developed in chapter 1 and write them — or new ones, if some of yours have changed as you've read through this book — in table 15.7, overleaf (five should be fine, but you may have more and I've allowed for seven). Try not to have too many goals, because it can lead to your losing focus on the important goals and objectives so try to limit the number. You can add new objectives as each goal is met. Remember that your goals and objectives will inevitably change over time, so whenever you update your one-page financial plan, you will need to update your goals as well. (Similarly, as you achieve your goals, you will develop new, more ambitious goals that will require you to formulate different strategies and tactics.)

Table 15.7: goals and objectives

Goals and objectives
1
2
3
4
5
6
7

Step 4: decide on your strategies

Your strategies and tactics will help you attain your goals and objectives, and truly instigate significant financial change and freedom in your life. Strategies are simply a list of the things that you need to do to improve your financial situation. Now that you've almost reached the end of this book, you have most likely developed some ideas about what you need to do to achieve this.

There is a whole chapter in the book on strategies and tactics (see chapter 14), and most chapters have a set of five sample strategies and tactics to assist you with each topic, so if you are stumped for ideas, you don't have to reinvent the wheel — just look at the ones suggested and decide which will suit you. You may also need some advice at some stage to help implement your strategies to ensure they are completed in their entirety.

To help you on your way, here are some further examples of strategies I've developed with my clients:

- Establish a self managed super fund.
- Establish a family trust to distribute your personal income from your business.
- Establish a regular savings plan of $200 per week and invest the balance into a share-based portfolio every three months.

- Establish a regular savings plan of $2000 per month to save for a property to the value of $400 000.

- Salary sacrifice $25 000 per year to save $2500 in tax per year and build your retirement savings by an additional $350 000 over the next 10 years.

- Make a non-concessional contribution on behalf of your partner to obtain a $500 co-contribution bonus into your partner's super fund when your do your tax returns.

- Sell your existing investment property, make a concessional contribution to superannuation of $25 000 each, if you have a partner (to reduce capital gains tax), and contribute the balance into your super fund as a non-concessional contribution to boost your retirement savings.

- Sell your current shares and withdraw your managed funds and invest your spare cash in a new portfolio of investments that are more appropriate for your risk profile and personal objectives.

- Consolidate superannuation by rolling over your existing superannuation fund accounts and establishing a self managed super fund (or rolling the balances into a chosen single fund).

- Establish a self managed super fund and, using a 30 per cent deposit from your existing superannuation balance, borrow 70 per cent of the value of a new investment property as a long-term investment strategy.

- Undertake a superannuation fund search on the ATO website and type 'super seeker' into the search engine (or go to www.superseeker.super.ato.gov.au); you'll need your tax file number (TFN), date of birth and personal name to find any lost super you may have.

- Consult a lawyer to prepare a will (including a testamentary trust), an enduring power of attorney and guardianship. Consider guardianship for the children or elderly parents.

- Ensure you and your partner have adequate life, TPD and income protection insurance.

Your strategies will change over time, and you'll obviously need to add new strategies from time to time to deal with specific issues such as retirement, redundancy, divorce, family issues, sickness, sabbaticals and other life events that will have an impact on your finances.

> ## Tip
>
> Since you don't know what you don't know, it may be worth making an appointment with a financial adviser to see if he or she can suggest any strategies that you may be unaware of. Legislation is constantly changing, and keeping up with those changes is a challenge at the best of times. If you are not looking for continuing services, consider engaging an adviser on a fee-for-service basis. Plenty of advisers will be willing to help you, but I suggest you choose an independently owned planning firm that is not aligned to a major institution. It's also a good idea to check out advisers who have won an award, so you know that they are at the top of their game.

Step 5: work out your tactics

Step 5 is all about the tasks that need to be undertaken to ensure that your strategy is implemented. Tactics are the specific, detailed and time-frame-bound tasks you need to undertake to get the job done. Some of these tasks can be outsourced to professionals, so you need to give some thought to the people you want in your team.

Strategies and tactics are often covered together in plans prepared by professional advisers. For the purpose of your personal financial plan, however, it's best to separate them to ensure that you clearly identify the individual and specific tasks that need to be undertaken to implement your strategies.

If you have a large number of individual tasks to complete, you may need to attach a separate list of tactics to your one-page financial plan.

Here are some examples of tactics required to implement strategies.

Strategy: to establish a self managed super fund
Tactics:

- Speak to an adviser or accountant to set up a new SMSF trust deed.
- Complete the forms to obtain an ABN and TFN for the fund.
- Obtain a certificate of compliance for your SMSF so you can roll over your current super balances into your fund.

- Open a bank account with a bank for your SMSF.

- Complete rollover forms, send the certificate of compliance to the existing super funds and roll over the existing super funds to the SMSF fund bank account.

An example of the strategy and tactics in operation follows.

Strategy: salary sacrifice $25 000 per year into superannuation.

Tactics:

- Contact HR department at work and obtain correct form to change salary payment arrangement.

- Provide certificate of compliance for your SMSF to HR and existing super fund to ensure salary sacrifice contributions go into my SMSF.

- Provide a dollar figure of how much you want to salary sacrifice into super.

Strategy: set up a regular savings plan of $200 per week and invest the balance every three months into a share-based trading account.

Tactics:

- Open a share-trading account with E*TRADE Australia by calling E*TRADE.

- Complete E*TRADE account application, sign and return it to them.

- Arrange a direct-debit facility from your personal account to a cash account inside your share-trading account by speaking to the bank, completing and signing the form and sending it back to them.

- Enter a reminder in your diary every three months to transfer the balance into a share portfolio inside the share-trading account.

As with the strategies section, you may need someone to help you implement at least some of your tactics in order to ensure that your strategy as a whole is properly implemented. You can then choose to manage the strategy yourself or have someone else manage it for you, depending on what's involved and how engaged you want to be in the process.

Step 6: implement your plan

It's worth remembering this: only 20 per cent of Australians own an investment property and about 33 per cent own shares. These low ownership figures indicate that opportunity stands before you and is there for the taking. If you can implement your plan effectively, consistently and conservatively, you will be ahead of the majority of Australians over time and well on your way to a more secure financial future and emancipation. Once you've implemented the first few strategies, you can put your plan into cruise control and wait for sharemarkets to rise further, dividends to grow and flow, rents to grow and house prices to rise. But implementation is the key.

Quite simply, the Implementation column of your plan is your tactical checklist. You need to list your contact points, complete forms and indicate whether your tactic has been completed to ensure implementation is thorough and your strategy can be fulfilled. Some of the tasks required will be quite simple and others more time and resource consuming.

An Implementation column has been included in your one-page financial plan as a means of checking that you have done what you said you were going to do — and, if you haven't, to establish a time frame for what needs to happen and to identify who is going to do it.

Remember, the job is not complete until every tactic has been implemented. Failing to implement even one of your tactics could potentially cost you thousands of dollars, if not tens of thousands or hundreds of thousands of dollars. It may also open the potential for greater risk if a particular strategy has not been implemented or the tactics remain outstanding. The checklist will assist in identifying what is outstanding. It's your action plan.

Print out a copy of your plan and keep it where you'll see it easily and regularly. Enter regular reminders in your diary (whether it's your desk diary or your electronic diary) to review your plan and, once you've revised it, print out a copy and put it back in the same place.

I recommend printing the one-page financial plan and putting it in a plastic sleeve and placing it somewhere where you will see it regularly, such as the fridge, white board or in your study.

Step 7: review your progress

One of the problems of owning assets is that you often find yourself thinking about what to do with them. Should I sell and buy something else? Should I invest in some shares and sell the properties? This kind of internal dialogue seems to be a constant for most investors, but if you are having this conversation with yourself, then there is a fair chance that you've made some money.

Review column

You'll have noticed the final column in your one-page financial plan headed Review. The boxes below the heading indicate that you need to record:

- what you are going to review
- when you are going to review it
- if any forms are required
- has the task been completed?

It's always a good idea to discuss your plan with your team or partner on a regular basis to help keep you on track and remind you of your financial progress and what may need to be done in the future.

If you aren't making progress, then you may need to change your plan. But don't change it too much. If you own blue-chip assets, such as top 150 shares or inner-city property, then you may simply need to allow more time for your assets to appreciate in value. Assets rarely appreciate in a linear fashion, and depending on economic conditions, different rates of return will be experienced.

Sometimes when assets go down in value and they are good-quality assets, it may be a good strategy to buy more rather than sell — the opposite of what the crowd tends to do when things get challenging. So, too, it's important to know when to exit an asset and sell it if it does not perform to your expectation. But be careful. Disposing of assets can trigger taxes and transaction costs, so make sure you understand the ramifications of making changes to your portfolio. Also remember the principle 'never sell property' unless you have to or unless you have a better use for the money; the same goes for good-quality shares.

Finally, I can't stress enough that implementing your financial plan is the key to a successful financial future. Most people don't take the time to do it, or to do it properly leaving themselves open to risk—but if you do take the time to do it, you will be well in front of the investment game.

I wish you the best of luck!

Feedback welcome

If you've found this journey helpful (or otherwise), I want to hear from you. I'd like to know how this book has helped you and if you need more information to help you fulfil your financial goals and objectives. Please go to my website at www.samhenderson.com.au and tell me what you think.

KEY POINTS

- You need to develop a practical, written plan with a definite time frame, to help you meet your needs, goals and objectives for the long term.

- You will need to follow seven steps to complete your one-page financial plan:

  - Step 1: assemble your team.

  - Step 2: compile your personal information.

  - Step 3: establish your (SMART) goals and your objectives.

  - Step 4: decide on your strategies.

  - Step 5: work out your tactics.

  - Step 6: implement your plan.

  - Step 7: review your progress.

- If you are going to draw up a plan, make sure you implement it — don't leave it on your desk to gather dust. Implement it and make a big difference to your life, starting today!

- Download your one-page financial plan from the resources page on www.samhenderson.com.au.

- Keep your one-page financial plan in a place where you can see it regularly and update it easily.

- Set up reminders in your desk or electronic diary for specific tasks that need to be done and for your regular reviews.

CHAPTER 16

YOUR NEXT STEPS: ADVICE OR DIY?

Success is a journey not a destination. The doing is usually more important than the outcome. Not everyone can be number 1.

Arthur Ashe, former world no. 1 tennis player

The process of learning only ever ceases when you choose to stop it. Depending on how involved you want to be in managing your own finances, you can go on learning forever. Some people like to manage their own assets and others like to have someone do it for them. It's a bit like fitness training: some people hire a fitness trainer to provide the motivation, focus and expertise needed to achieve their personal needs, goals and objectives, while others prefer to just go for a run around the block or hit the gym by themselves. Managing someone's finances works in exactly the same way. You can pay for advice or you can do it yourself.

I often say to my clients that they can be as involved or uninvolved as they want to be in the planning process. Some glaze over when I start talking about superannuation strategy or portfolio management theories, but they want me to arrange, manage and implement those strategies for them. But others like to choose and trade shares themselves and want to learn about the various superannuation strategies. It all depends on how much time and effort you are prepared to put into the process.

And of course you have a life to live beyond managing your portfolio of assets. So if you don't want to implement the ideas in this book yourself, then it may be best to seek advice from a professional who can help you.

The DIY approach

People who have the confidence and time to learn about financial matters often choose the DIY approach. Some people who buy this book may already be DIY investors, and I hope you have learned a few things reading this book. The internet has opened up a veritable smorgasbord of websites focused on helping people make decisions about their financial affairs. It is also, unfortunately, full of websites and information designed to fleece people of their hard-earned dollars by selling poor advice and products of questionable integrity. Therefore, caution needs to be exercised, because there are plenty of people exerting their own investment biases to get their hands on your money.

If you are taking the DIY approach, there are a multitude of ways to learn about various subjects, and many are free. Seminars, webinars (seminars on the internet), free information packs, websites, magazines and newspapers will provide valuable information. The more you read, the more you will learn, and you'll find certain providers, authors, companies and philosophies that match your own way of thinking and investing.

The most important piece of advice I can give you is to *never* sign up for anything at a seminar, because emotions will sway your decisions and spruikers are highly trained in raising your emotions and expectations. With any of your investing or educational activities, take your time, consider the facts and do your homework before you commit to any contract or agreement with a company. Always read the information about the product, such as the product disclosure statements (PDSs), including the small print. If you can't be bothered reading the PDS you shouldn't invest in the product. Ask yourself, what's in it for them? How do they make their money? What is their motivation?

You should look for philosophical and fiscal alignment with any company or fund you invest with: any company you deal with should have your best interests in mind. For example, if a Queensland property developer just sells property on the Sunshine Coast or Townsville, then their chief motivation will be to convince you that this is the best area to invest. However, you will have a choice as to where to invest and that choice is far and wide. Do your research and make sure you understand the consequences of committing to a contract of any kind. An independent legal opinion can be a valuable investment.

It always surprises me how valuable some of the free information available to you can be. The opposite is also true, but I often find that investment magazines are extremely helpful in providing education about certain strategies or topics, and they illustrate their points well with examples or case studies that the readers can directly relate to. I have been writing for *Money* magazine for many years, and I know that it is a good example. Its direct competitor *Smart Investor* is equally, good, and many of the property magazines also have extremely helpful articles and case studies. However, property magazines appear to be full of advertisements from spruikers of all types, so be cautious: attend a free seminar or webinar, but do your homework and exercise great prudence before you make any legal commitments.

I have listed some great resources that are well worth visiting, reading or watching on the web. Also, many companies and share advice newsletters offer free trial periods of their products, and it's a great way to attempt to establish value in the information and advice that they provide.

Financial news and information
- Nine MSN (www.finance.ninemsn.com.au)
- Money Manager (www.moneymanager.com.au)
- Sky News Business (www.skynews.com.au)
- Bloomberg (www.bloomberg.com)
- Reuters (www.reuters.com).

Shares
- Australian Stock Exchange (www.asx.com)
- Trading Room (www.tradingroom.com.au)
- E*TRADE (www.etrade.com.au)
- CommSec (www.comsec.com.au)
- Iress (www.iress.com.au) — for the very serious investor.

Property
- Domain (www.domain.com.au)
- Realestate (www.realestate.com.au)
- Residex (www.residex.com.au)
- RPdata (www.rpdata.com.au)
- Australian Property Monitors (www.apm.com.au).

Magazines
- *Money* magazine (www.finance.ninemsn.com.au/money-mag)
- *Smart Investor* (www.afrsmartinvestor.com.au)
- *Australian Property Investor* (www.apimagazine.com.au)
- *Your Investment Property* (www.yourinvestmentpropertymag.com.au)
- *Wealth Creator* (www.wealthcreator.com.au).

Working with professional advisers

Many professionals also provide an array of different services to help clients like you — solicitors, accountants, financial planners, stock brokers, mortgage brokers, real estate agents, insurance brokers and many more. If you do seek help make sure you clearly articulate your needs, goals and objectives to your chosen professional. Call me cynical, but even professionals can revert to the 'what's in it for them' scenario, where they may be too enthusiastic to sell you a product or service that serves them well but is not necessarily the ideal outcome for you.

Keep focused and communicate clearly when working with professionals in any field. It's no different from working with tradespeople. You need to check licensing, credentials, association memberships, as well as seek referrals and get to know and trust them before making a commitment. A good place to start for financial advice, for instance, is a website called Money Smart (www.moneysmart .gov.au) to check licensing and complaints against financial services license holders. Any financial adviser must hold an Australian Financial Services Licence (AFSL) or be an authorised representative of an AFSL holder. If your chosen professional is just an authorised representative, make sure you check the credentials of the AFSL holder as well as the individual authorised representative.

> ## Tip
>
> If you invest money in any way, you need to visit the Money Smart website (www.moneysmart.gov.au). It provides unbiased, plain-English information on a multitude of financial products and services. It also provides warnings on what to avoid and what to look out for when investing or seeking advice. It's an invaluable resource and a must-go destination for all investors.

The other word of caution is about scams. With the advancement of technology comes the ability for criminals to invent more and more elaborate means of defrauding you of your money. The website Scam Watch (www.scamwatch.gov.au) was set up by the Australian Securities and Investments Commission (ASIC) to assist consumers by educating them about scams and the latest trends in fraud. If you are investing money in any way, you need to go to this website to learn about the latest and greatest scams.

The naive and trusting need to be very vigilant. A large proportion of people who are defrauded are elderly people, and many don't find out they have been defrauded until some time after the crime was committed. Please be aware and as I always say, 'There's never a silly question when it comes to your own money', so make sure you ask lots of the right types of questions when seeking financial advice. The Money Smart website has a sample list of questions to ask when you sit down with an adviser or salesperson.

Look back at figure 1 (see p. xvi), to remind yourself about some of the areas in which a good adviser or group of advisers may be able to help you. Financial planners help you to achieve your goals and objectives; accountants may help with cash flow and tax; your super fund will help with saving for retirement in the most tax-effective way; a mortgage broker may help with property purchases and loans; solicitors, with estate planning; and insurance brokers with risk management and life insurance. There are also plenty of companies that can help with all of the services listed on the diagram. Sometimes using someone who can do all of these things is helpful, but just be careful of jack of all trades, master of none. You may be more likely to find the full array of services at larger firms that have many advisers and offer multiple services.

Need help?

My own business, Henderson Maxwell, provides comprehensive, fee-for-service financial advice to clients who are looking for a long-term relationship with a firm. Visit www.hendersonmaxwell.com.au for more information.

For more help in obtaining advice from professionals, see the following organisations:

- Financial Planning Association (www.fpa.asn.au)
- Association of Financial Advisers (www.afa.asn.au)
- Association of Independently Owned Financial Advisers (www.aiofp.net.au)
- Certified Practising Accountants (www.cpaaustralia.com.au)
- Chartered Accountants (www.charteredaccountants.com.au)
- Real Estate Institute Australia (www.reia.com.au)
- Finance Brokers Association of Australia (www.fbaa.com.au)
- National Insurance Brokers of Australia (www.niba.com.au)
- Stock Brokers Association Australia (www.stockbrokers.org.au).

Finish where you began

I want to finish this book where I began. Remember, in the introduction, I discussed the five steps — or 'shons' — to your personal financial revolution: motivation, education, organisation, application and emancipation.

If you have reached this stage in the book, you are obviously still motivated, and completing your one-page financial plan will help you get organised. The bulk of the book will assist with your education, so now it's up to you to apply what you have learned and financially emancipate yourself. You may like the idea of a financial overhaul and the benefits it may bring to you, but you need to realise that until you actually take action, nothing will change.

We are all seeking emancipation from the things that we do not like doing. We often think that money is the solution to all of those problems, so I would encourage you to write down a list of the things that frustrate you, the activities that you do not like doing or the activities that take you away from the family. Once you have that list, then write down how you think you may be able to address each problem, when you may be able to put a solution in place and how much it will cost to solve. A list like mine in table 16.1 is a good place to start.

For example, I used to get really frustrated and stressed that I had to iron my shirts on a Sunday night for the week ahead when all I wanted to do was relax from my busy weekends. My solution was to organise someone to pick up my shirts from my house and deliver them ironed every two weeks. I then had two weeks of perfectly ironed shirts, no stress and more time with the kids on the weekend.

Another big issue I see is that workers don't take their holidays. Many people have months of holiday leave accumulated and complain that they are stressed and can't get away. Open your diary and book your holidays months in advance. Then you have plenty of time to pay for them progressively and you know that you don't have to get stressed out about working too hard. It will be better for your work, your health and your mental wellbeing.

Table 16.1: my list of things I wanted to change

	Problem	Solution	Cost
1	Ironing shirts	Pick up and delivery service	$40/fortnight
2	Cleaning the house	Hire a cleaner	$50/week
3	Accumulated leave	Book holidays in advance	Money and time
4	Mowing the lawn	Hire a lawn mowing company	$50/month
5	Washing the car	Take it to a car wash	$60/month

Good luck on your journey to financial emancipation

Emancipation comes in many forms and history is full of extreme stories of emancipation from slavery, evil and the oppression of others. We are so lucky in Australia to be able to live, for the most part, free of malevolence, so the things that bother us most are not life and death situations. We therefore have the luxury to focus on the things that make us feel better and help others such as spiritual enlightenment, wellbeing and philanthropy.

Your ideals of financial emancipation will differ from what someone else wants. Some people want to leave their job and retire; some want to travel whenever they feel like it; and others simply want to provide better opportunities for themselves and their families. Undoubtedly, we all want different things, but we all want to be happy, we all need an income and we all want to be secure.

Financial emancipation, whatever that means for you, is an extremely liberating state. I hope this book has helped to motivate you, educate you, organise you, encourage you to apply yourself and ultimately help you on your many steps on the journey to financial emancipation. I hope I can help to liberate you from your job or your bank and take you to wherever it is that you'd like to go. Begin your personal financial revolution today and I wish you the best of luck on your journey!